Encyclopedia
of Australian
Wildlife

Text by Pat Slater

Steve Parish
DISCOVER & LEARN
ABOUT AUSTRALIA

www.steveparish.com.au

CONTENTS

CONTENTS

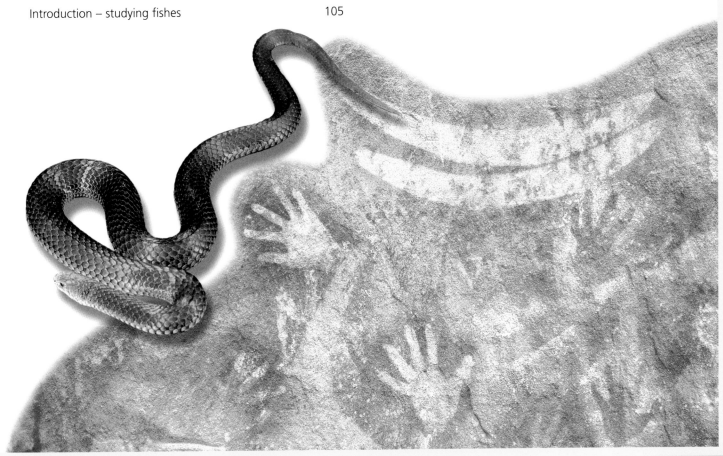

Foreword

We all dream of exploring strange places and discovering creatures no one has ever seen before. I count myself the luckiest of people because I have been able to live my dream. Since my teenage years, I have been able to roam wild places and to live there with some of the world's strangest and most fascinating wild creatures.

Some of the pictures in this Encyclopedia were taken in my very earliest photographic days when I was a teenager learning about the ocean in Jervis Bay, New South Wales. In those days, almost every dive brought me face to face with some strange marine creature, sometimes species new to science. I got myself into underwater scrapes, got out of them again and learned that adventure is waiting everywhere. Gradually I realised that nature photography was going to be my lifelong passion.

Since then I have travelled around Australia many times, seeing wild places and photographing wild creatures. Today I have a library of many thousands of photos (some of the latest taken are also in this book) and a memory crammed full of wonderful scenes involving animals from wombats to Wedge-tailed Eagles, kangaroos to Koalas, endangered turtles to venomous taipans.

The books in the Steve Parish **Discover and Learn** collection aim to share the wonderful world of Australia's wildlife with all those adventurous people of any age who enjoy animals and nature.

This Encyclopedia takes a look at some of the world's most amazing animals. Who, in their wildest dreams, would have conjured up such wondrous creatures as the Platypus, the Koala, the Superb Lyrebird, anemonefishes which live in stinging tentacles deadly to any other fish, the Thorny Devil or the Frilled Lizard? Tree-kangaroos and gliders, frogs that rear their young in their stomachs, dolphins that visit land to meet people – Australia is a land of marvellous and improbable animals.

After you have learned something about our amazing wildlife from this book and the others in our **Discover and Learn** collection, why not discover these fascinating creatures "live", in their wild homes and in parks, zoos and sanctuaries. You'll be glad you did!

Steve Parish

The animal's common name.
This may change from place to place but is accepted by most people.

The animal's scientific name.
This does not change. It allows an animal to be identified by anyone, anywhere, speaking in any language.

A picture of the animal.
The photo shows as many characteristic features as possible.

Initial capital letters are used to name a particular species. **Lower case letters** are used to refer to a group of related animals. So capitals are used for a Black-tailed Phascogale, but lower case for all phascogales.

The animal's size and weight.

HB = length of head and body combined
T = length of tail

HBT = length of head, body and tail combined

♀ female

♂ male

m = metres   mm = millimetres
g = grams   kg = kilograms
(Size range or greatest size given)

The meaning of the scientific name.
This is given if it is of interest.

A summary of characteristics.
This includes:
• where the animal is found on the mainland and Tasmania, and smaller islands (if significant);
• the habitat in which the animal may be seen;
• a general description of the animal's size, shape, outer covering, colour and other features by which it may be identified;
• facts about how the animal lives and behaves.

The symbol [G] means that a word is in the Glossary (pp. 124–5). It appears at the word's first use.

Brush-tailed Phascogale
Phascogale tapoatafa
(= pouched-weasel called by Aborigines *tapoatafa*)

This rare climbing marsupial is found in open coastal forest around Australia. It is the size of a large rat, with soft, grey body fur and a long, bushy black tail.

Phascogales can leap up to 2 m between trees. Each hind foot can turn through 180° as its owner runs up and down trunks, and under branches.

The Black-tailed Phascogale spends the day in a tree hollow. At night, it hunts insects, small mammals and roosting birds.

All male phascogales die after mating. They succumb to stress-related illnesses, or are taken by predators[G]. The pregnant females give birth to the following generation. The 3–8 young are dragged around attached to their mother's nipples for 7 weeks, then they are fed in a nest for another 13 weeks.

Length: HB ♀ 180 mm ♂ 200 mm; T ♀ 190 mm ♂ 210 mm
Weight: ♀ 160 g ♂ 230 g

| STATUS | X | E | **P** | V | S | SIZE | | RANGE | |

The animal's survival status.
The red box marks the species's current status. See key below.

Size. The animal's size is compared to some part of an adult human.
(In a very few cases the size range is so great that comparison would be meaningless. In those instances this bar is blank.)

A map. The coloured shading shows the range[G]: the areas of Australia where the animal is thought to live at present.

SURVIVAL STATUS

X =	**Presumed extinct**[G]	There is no physical evidence to prove that the species has existed in the wild for 50 or more years.
E =	**Endangered**	The species is disappearing at such a rate that, without human action being taken to save it, it will soon become extinct.
P =	**Possibly endangered**	Although the species is decreasing in number and/or the area where it is found is shrinking, considerable numbers can still be seen in the right habitat.
V =	**Vulnerable**	At present there seem to be no problems. However, if the environment is changed, or other factors come into play, the species could be at risk.
S =	**Secure**	There is no foreseeable threat to the species continuing to exist.

Conservation

It is not always easy to judge the survival status of an animal. Even when scientists agree that an animal is endangered, there may be little they can do to help its chances of survival.

Probably the best way to ensure the survival of endangered species is to set aside areas of suitable, unaltered habitat that are kept clear of introduced[G] animals, such as foxes, cats, sheep and cattle.

Survival status is not fixed.

A species may "crash" in numbers, as the Northern Quoll has "crashed" with the advance of the Cane Toad.

Or, like the Humpback Whale, a species may slowly recover from near extinction once the major threat, in this case being hunted by humans, has stopped operating.

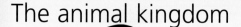

Animals & Other Life Forms

Earth has an enormous variety of life forms. These include bacteria^G, other single-celled organisms^G and multi-celled organisms such as fungi, plants and animals.

All living things are able to reproduce themselves or take a part in reproducing organisms like themselves. They may reproduce asexually^G, by budding off an animal exactly like themselves. They may reproduce sexually^G, so that their reproductive cells combine with those of another individual of the same sort to produce offspring that inherit characteristics from both parents.

No matter how different the bodies of different sorts of living things appear, at the very simplest level their basic structure is very similar. All their tissues are made up of tiny particles called molecules, which are based on the element^G carbon. The chemical processes by which organisms' bodies keep themselves running are also very much alike.

Living things probably first existed around 3800 million years ago, as primitive^G, simple, single cells drifting in the world's oceans. It took another 2400 million years for more highly developed cells to appear. These advanced single cells developed into today's single-celled plants and animals. By 670 million years ago, oxygen levels on earth had increased and multi-celled animals such as sea jellies and worms had appeared.

Food chains

Plants form the first link in almost every living food chain.

Plants contain a green substance called chlorophyll^G. This gives them the ability to use solar power to process non-living substances into sugars. These sugars provide the plants with energy and with the building blocks for new tissue.

Animals cannot process non-living substances by using the sun's power. Herbivorous^G animals eat plants and use the plants' stored food substances. Carnivores^G and scavengers^G eat other living or dead animals. Omnivores^G eat both plants and other animals.

Nectar^G is eaten by a Sugar Glider, which becomes food for an Olive Python. When the python dies, its remains form food for plants.

How Australia's wildlife has changed over the ages

The firm crust of the earth is a thin, constantly moving skin, floating on a huge ball of molten rock. Until around 55 million years ago, Australia was part of a huge landmass called Gondwana. Gradually the landmass separated, and, by 45–35 million years ago, Australia was drifting slowly northwards. It is still moving, at about the rate human fingernails grow.

"Ark Australia" carried with it many living things. As millions of years passed, the northward movement continued, the earth's climates^G altered and Australia became much drier.

Some life forms, such as the crocodile, remained almost unchanged. Others, like the Koala, adapted to changing conditions, such as the gradual replacement of rainforest with eucalypts and other plants that could survive dry seasons. The animals that could not adapt died out.

The coming of humans brought about more change. The Aborigines burned areas of country to bring on new growth. The arrival of the Dingo affected other predators^G. Since 1788, the rate of change has become much faster.

What is wildlife?

Many animals live in a large country such as Australia. Today quite a number of these animals are domestic pets or stock, living with, or in the care of, humans. Creatures that were already living in Australia before Europeans arrived in 1788 are known as "wildlife". Not many of these animals have been made into pets or turned into farm stock by humans. However, many parrots have become popular cage birds, and the Emu, Saltwater Crocodile and large kangaroos may be farmed for meat and skins.

Cockatoos are caged as pets.

The Emu may be farmed.

Naming and grouping living things

Scientists have so far discovered more than one million different sorts of living animals. Many more still wait to be discovered. Zoologists[G] are the scientists who study animals. Zoologists who sort animals into groups of creatures related to each other are called taxonomists[G].

Taxonomists use a system of grouping animals known as the Linnaean system, after the Swedish Karl Von Linne, who lived from 1707 to 1778. He was the first person to give each different sort of animal, or species, a name of its own. This scientific name is usually based on Latin or Greek, and Von Linne's name has been Latinised to "Carolus Linnaeus". In the eighteenth century, Linnaeus had to classify animals according to similarities and differences he could see in the structures of their bodies. Today, scientists can examine the genetic[G] material (DNA[G]) in an animal's cells to trace its relationships.

A two-name system

Linnaeus gave each species a two-word name. Taxonomists still use this binominal system[G].

The first word is the genus name for the group to which the animal is most closely related. It is always capitalised.

The second word is the species name for that particular animal. It always begins with a lower-case letter.

One species carries this name, no matter what the language of the person talking or writing about it. The species may have local names as well, but the scientific name is its "real" name.

The Red Kangaroo is *Macropus rufa*. This means "big-foot red". Its closest relatives are other members of the Macropus (big-foot) family, which includes wallabies and kangaroos.

An animal of one species can only produce fertile[G] offspring if it mates with another member of the same species. So a male Red Kangaroo might interbreed with a female Grey Kangaroo (*Macropus giganteus*). However, even if the joey survived to become an adult, it would be a "mule"[G], unable to have offspring.

These birds are two species.

The Laughing Kookaburra (*Dacelo gigas*) and Blue-winged Kookaburra (*D. leachi*) are two species. They do not interbreed. If they did, their chicks would not be fertile.

These birds are one species.

The Eastern Reef Egret (*Egretta sacra*) has two colour phases, grey and white. The two colour phases breed with each other. Chicks of both colours may be seen in one nest.

Grouping the groups

A **kingdom** is made up of related **phyla**.
A **phylum** is made up of related **subphyla**.
A **subphylum** is made up of related **classes**.
A **class** is made up of related **subclasses**.
A **subclass** is made up of related **orders**.
An **order** is made up of related **families**.
A **family** is made up of related **genera**.
A **genus** is made up of related **species**.
A **species** is made up of individuals that can produce fertile offspring only when they mate within their group.

How the Red Kangaroo is classified.

KINGDOM:	Animalia	Living, multi-celled things that are not plants, bacteria or fungi.
PHYLUM:	Chordata	Animals with cords along their backs.
SUBPHYLUM:	Vertebrata	Chordates with backbones made up of vertebrae.
CLASS:	Mammalia	Vertebrates with hair.
SUBCLASS:	Marsupialia	Mammals whose young are born small and undeveloped.
ORDER:	Diprotodontia	Marsupials with only one pair of front teeth.
FAMILY:	Macropodidae	Diprotodont marsupials with strong hind legs, each with a big fourth toe.
GENUS:	*Macropus*	Macropods with large grinding back teeth and a stomach divided into sections, in which grass fibre is digested by tiny organisms. Males are usually much larger than females and have powerful forearms.
SPECIES:	*rufa*	The Red Kangaroo. A very large, grass-eating macropod with red or grey fur and a naked muzzle. Males are much larger than females. Found in drier areas of Australia.

Australia – physical features & national parks

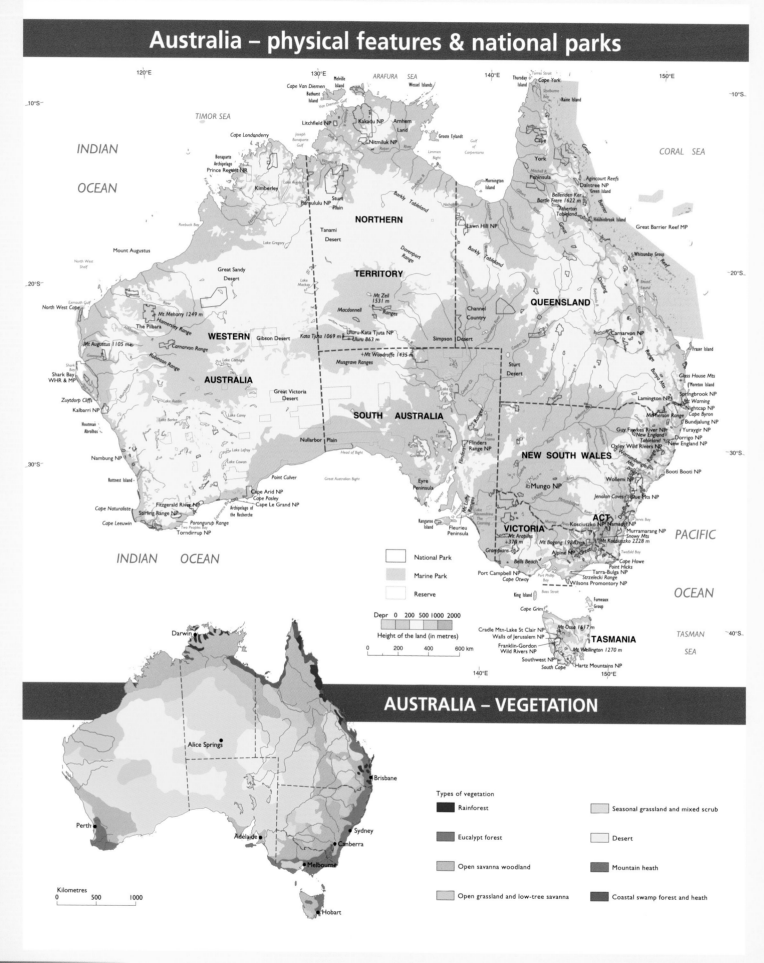

National Park

Marine Park

Reserve

Depr 0 200 500 1000 2000
Height of the land (in metres)

0   200   400   600 km

AUSTRALIA – VEGETATION

Types of vegetation

- Rainforest
- Eucalypt forest
- Open savanna woodland
- Open grassland and low-tree savanna
- Seasonal grassland and mixed scrub
- Desert
- Mountain heath
- Coastal swamp forest and heath

Kilometres
0   500   1000

Australian wildlife habitats[G]

Temperate[G] coasts: habitat for the Australian Sea-lion, Little Penguin, Bottlenose Dolphin, Silver Gull, Pied Oystercatcher, temperate sea fishes and other marine[G] life.

Tropical[G] wetlands: habitat for the Agile Wallaby, Black-necked Stork, Pied Heron, freshwater turtles, Saltwater Crocodile, Arafura File Snake, Water Python and Giant Frog, among others.

Tropical coasts: habitat for the Humpback Whale, Eastern Reef Egret, Brown Booby, Green Turtle, Golden Seasnake, coral reef fishes and other marine life.

Desert: habitat for the Red Kangaroo, Bilby, Spinifex Hopping-mouse, Dingo, Wedge-tailed Eagle, Crimson Chat, Central Netted Dragon, Thorny Devil and Water-holding Frog, among others.

Plains and waterways: habitat for the Red Kangaroo, Fat-tailed Dunnart, Emu, Brown Falcon, Major Mitchell Cockatoo, Australian Bustard, Shingleback Lizard and freshwater turtles, among others.

Rainforest: habitat for the Platypus, Lumholtz's Tree-kangaroo, Green Ringtail Possum, Satin Bowerbird, Rainbow Lorikeet, Taipan, Green Python and Green Tree-frog, among others.

Forest and bushland: habitat for the Sugar Glider, Koala, Eastern Quoll, Crimson Rosella, Eastern Yellow Robin, Eastern Water Dragon, Brown Snake and Lace Monitor, among others.

City and town: habitat for the Brush-tailed Possum, Common Ringtail Possum, Australian Magpie, Welcome Swallow, Noisy Miner, Bearded Dragon, Carpet Python and Dainty Tree-frog, etc.

Farms and grazing land: habitat for the Eastern Grey Kangaroo, Dingo, Galah, Masked Lapwing, Magpie-lark, Australian Kestrel and Eastern Bluetongue Lizard, among others.

Australia's Mammals

What is a mammal?

- A mammal is a vertebrate[G] animal. Its spinal cord[G] and brain are protected by a backbone and skull.

- A mammal is "warm-blooded" (the correct word is endothermic[G]). Its body temperature remains more or less the same no matter what the temperature of its surroundings.

- A mammal has four limbs. These may be adapted for various purposes, e.g. climbing, hopping, digging. Bats' limbs are adapted for flying. Some water-living mammals have developed flippers for swimming. Their hind limbs may be very reduced.

- A mammal's skin is usually covered by hairs. Even if the mammal is nearly naked, hair will exist somewhere on the body.

- A mammal's heart has four chambers. This keeps blood containing oxygen[G] and de-oxygenated blood containing waste products separate.

- A mammal has mammary, or milk, glands[G]. These are better developed in the female and produce milk to feed her young.

- Examples of mammals: humans, kangaroos, bats, whales.

Parts of a kangaroo

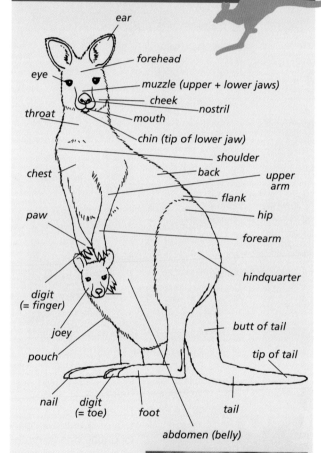

ear
forehead
eye
muzzle (upper + lower jaws)
cheek
nostril
throat
mouth
chin (tip of lower jaw)
shoulder
back
chest
upper arm
flank
paw
hip
forearm
hindquarter
digit (= finger)
joey
butt of tail
pouch
tip of tail
nail
digit (= toe)
foot
tail
abdomen (belly)

Mammal names

A mammal may be known by several names:

1. **An official common name**; e.g. Common Wombat.

2. **A scientific name**; e.g. *Vombatus ursinus*. This is used all over the world. It is written in italics, and the word order is reversed from the order used in English. The scientific name may be several centuries old. It also has a meaning (*Vombatus ursinus* means "bear-like wombat").

3. **Unofficial/ local names**; e.g. the Common Wombat is also called the Naked-nosed Wombat, the Forest Wombat.

Native and introduced mammals

An **introduced animal** has been taken from its original country and placed in another country. It may be turned loose or escape to the wild to live there as a **feral[G] animal**. Introduced animals have enormous effects on the **native[G] animals** that already live in a country.

The introduced Dingo.

The effect of the Dingo on Australia is an example of this.

The Dingo was introduced from South-East Asia around 3500 years ago. The native Thylacine and Tasmanian Devil could not compete with its ability to kill animal prey. Thylacines had disappeared from the mainland by 2000 years ago, and Tasmanian Devils by 430 years ago.

After 1788, humans introduced many sorts of animals. The sheep,

The European Fox can kill a 5-kg wallaby.

cow, pig, goat and rabbit ate the local plants that many native animals depended on for food. Europeans also over-grazed the country, causing erosion[G]. Humans destroyed native animal habitat by clearing land for pasture and towns.

European settlers also introduced cats, foxes and dogs, which killed wildlife.

All of these destructive effects are still operating on the native mammal population today.

In the past 200 years, 18 species of Australian mammals have become extinct[G]. Twenty-two species are now in danger of extinction. Eighteen more are vulnerable to extinction. Many Australian mammals can survive only where there are no introduced animals.

How mammals' bodies deal with heat and cold

A mammal is an endothermic (warm-blooded) animal. Its body processes food and oxygen to produce energy and new tissues. This process produces heat. The heat keeps the mammal's body within a limited range of temperatures. Sometimes a mammal becomes overheated or too cold. Then its body and its behaviour change to protect it.

Warming up

- **Fluffing up the hair** helps keep air warmed by the body from escaping. (Goosebumps form on the skin and pull the hairs upright.) Mammals that live in cold conditions have thick coats of hair.
- **Surface blood vessels contract**, so warm blood stays deeper within the body.
- **Eating more** produces body fat, which helps keep body heat in. Marine mammals have thick under-skin fat called blubber.
- **Shivering** helps muscles warm themselves.
- **Sheltering** from wind and rain, **huddling** with other mammals, and **basking** in sunshine all keep a mammal warm.
- **Migration**[G] **to warmer places** avoids winter cold.
- **Hibernation**[G] (winter sleep) is used by some mammals to survive cold periods when water and food are scarce.

Chilling out

- **Sleeking the hair** leaves no space for warm air next to the skin. (However, hair may keep hot sun off the body.)
- **Surface blood vessels expand**, allowing warm blood to shed heat into the air.
- **Eating less** gets rid of body fat. Body heat is lost more easily.
- **Sweating and panting** allow sweat[G] and saliva[G] to pass into the air. This has a cooling effect.
- **Sheltering** from sun and hot, dry winds.
- **Resting during the hottest time** of the day prevents the body getting overheated from activity.
- **Migration** to cooler places avoids summer heat.
- **Aestivation**[G] (summer sleep) is used by some mammals to survive hot periods when water and food are scarce.

Monotremes, marsupials and placental mammals

The mammals of the world are separated into three groups, according to the ways in which they produce young. Members of all three groups are found in Australia.

MONOTREMES

This Short-beaked Echidna is a monotreme.

Monotremes lay soft-shelled eggs. The tiny baby that hatches from a monotreme egg is naked and blind, and has undeveloped hind limbs. Using its fore limbs, it drags itself to its mother's belly. Here it suckles milk, which oozes onto the skin. One monotreme, the Short-beaked Echidna, has a pouch. The other, the Platypus, has no pouch.

MARSUPIALS

Marsupials bear their young after a very short period of development. The newborn is naked and blind, with undeveloped hind limbs. Using its fore limbs, it drags itself to its mother's belly. Here it attaches itself to a nipple[G] and completes its development. It may be sheltered by a pouch or a fold of skin. It may spend a long time with its mother after weaning[G].

These Red-necked Wallabies are marsupials.

PLACENTAL MAMMALS

These Black Flying-foxes are placental mammals.

A young placental mammal grows inside the mother's body until it is well developed. A placenta[G] links the mother's blood vessels and those of the baby, which prevents the mother's body from rejecting the baby's body as a foreign object. A newborn placental mammal can suckle milk from its mother's nipples when it is hungry.

Groups of Australian Mammals

The world's mammals are placed in one big group named Class Mammalia (Mammals).

Class Mammalia is divided into three Subclasses: Monotremes, Marsupials and Placental Mammals.

Each of these Subclasses is further divided into Orders.

Each of these Orders is further divided into Families.

This table shows how Australia's mammals fit into this system of classification. Some animals are introduced, e.g. cat.

Class: MAMMALIA (= animals that feed their young on milk)

Subclass: MONOTREMES

Order: MONOTREMES
2 Families

    Platypus
    Echidnas

How scientists classify two monotremes.

Short-beaked Echidna
(*Tachyglossus aculeatus*)

Class: Mammalia
Subclass: Prototheria (monotremes)
Order: Monotremata (monotremes)
Family: Tachyglossidae (echidnas)
Species: *Tachyglossus aculeatus*
    (= spiny fast-tongue)

Platypus
(*Ornithorhynchus anatinus*)

Class: Mammalia
Subclass: Prototheria (monotremes)
Order: Monotremata (monotremes)
Family: Ornithorhynchidae (Platypus)
Species: *Ornithorhynchus anatinus*
    (= duck-like bird-snout)

Subclass: MARSUPIALS

Order: CARNIVOROUS MARSUPIALS
3 Families

    Dasyurids
    Thylacine
    Numbat

Order: BANDICOOTS & BILBIES
2 Families

    Spiny bandicoots
    Other bandicoots & bilbies

Order: HERBIVOROUS MARSUPIALS
10 Families

    Koala (1 family)
    Wombats (1 family)
    Possums (6 families)
    Macropods (2 families)

Order: MARSUPIAL MOLES
1 Family

    Marsupial Mole

How scientists classify a marsupial.

Green Ringtail Possum
(*Pseudochirops archeri*)

Class: Mammalia
Sub-class: Marsupiala (Marsupials)
Order: Diprotodontia (one pair of incisors in the lower jaw)
Family: Pseudocheiridae (ringtail possums & Greater Glider)
Species: *Pseudochirops archeri*
    (= Archer's false-hand)

Subclass: PLACENTAL MAMMALS

Order: BATS
7 Families

    Megabats[G] (1 family)
    Microbats[G] (6 families)

Order: RODENTS
1 Family

    Rodents

Order: DUGONGS & MANATEES
1 Family

    Dugong

Order: CARNIVORES
4 Families

    Dogs
    Cats
    Eared seals & sea-lions
    Earless seals

Order: RABBITS & HARES
1 Family

    Rabbits & hares

Order: SINGLE-HOOFED ANIMALS
1 Family

    Horses & donkeys

Order: CLOVEN-HOOFED[G] ANIMALS
4 Families

    Cattle & goats
    Camels
    Deer
    Pigs

Introduction

Date: 4 March, 1996
Time: 6:30 a.m.
Place: Lot 17B, Arcadia Rd, Dural. NSW

Weather: cool and dry
Observers: Jana, Ric and Simon Evans
HB = 19 cm T = 20 cm

grey
white
black

Notes: Ric found dead female Brush-tailed Phascogale by side of road outside our house. Neck broken – killed by car? Body cold and limp. No baby in pouch. Froze it in a plastic bag. Contacted Dr Graves at Australian Museum. Sydney. Will take it to Museum.

Things to note:

Size – relate size to a well-known mammal, e.g. a rat, mouse, cat, dog or goat.

Shape – note shape of head, neck, body, tail, legs.

Colour – note the colour of parts of the body.

Identifying a mammal

It is usually easy to identify a mammal as a member of a group, e.g. a wallaby, but difficult to tell just which species it is. In the field, make notes and a drawing. Later, identify the animal from a reference book. First find the group to which the animal belongs in the index. Then turn to the text and illustrations. Eliminate some species on range and habitat, then identify the animal on shape, colour and markings.

Food – what is it eating?

Habitat – where does this mammal feed and shelter? Is this its natural place to be, or not?

Range[G] – find out if this mammal is usually present in this area.

Collect droppings[G] – if available, take droppings (in a plastic bag) to a museum for identification.

Where to see native mammals

Many Australian mammals are shy or rare. Most are active at night. Some bolder ones, such as possums and bats, may visit backyards and town parks. Koalas, kangaroos and wallabies can be seen in national parks. Seals, whales and dolphins can be seen at the coast. Wildlife parks and sanctuaries[G] are good places to see mammals. Some have nocturnal[G] houses, where night animals can be viewed.

A backyard Brushtail Possum

A Common Wombat in a sanctuary

Bottlenose Dolphin at the beach

Kangaroos in a national park

Some record-setting mammals found in Australia or around its coasts

Largest marsupial: A male Red Kangaroo may stand more than 2 m tall, measure up to 2.4 m in total length and weigh up to 85 kg.

Smallest marsupial: The Long-tailed Planigale may have head and body length of 55–65 mm, tail length of 44–60 mm, and weigh 3.9–4.5 g.

Fastest marsupial: An adult female Eastern Grey Kangaroo was recorded at 64 km/h. A male Red Kangaroo was paced for 1.6 km at 56 km/h, then died from its efforts.

Highest jumper: An Eastern Grey Kangaroo cleared a 2.44 m fence. A hunted Red Kangaroo jumped a stack of timber 3.1 m high.

Longest jumper: A hunted female Red Kangaroo made a leap of 12.8 m. An Eastern Grey Kangaroo jumped nearly 13.5 m.

Oldest marsupial: A Common Wombat died in London Zoo in 1906 at the age of 26 years 22 days.

The Numbat has a boring diet.

Fastest marine mammal: A bull[G] Killer Whale (or Orca) about 7 m long was timed swimming at 55.5 km/h.

Largest mammal: The Blue Whale may grow to 33.58 m and weigh 190 t.

Deepest diver: A bull Sperm Whale can dive to over 3000 m.

Most venomous[G] mammal: The male Platypus has spurs on its ankles. Venom from its upper-leg glands can be injected through these.

Smallest number of nipples[G]: The Short-beaked Echidna and the Platypus have no nipples at all.

Most stressed breeders: All the males of nine species of small carnivorous marsupial die after mating.

Least likely to get sunburned: The Marsupial Mole spends nearly all its life underground. It "swims" through desert sand.

Most boring diet: The Numbat eats only termites.

Least likely to need sleeping pills: The Koala's gumleaf diet is so low in energy that it sleeps 20 hours of each 24.

Most unusual home defence: A wombat attacked in its burrow uses its rump to squash the intruder against the walls or roof.

Highest marsupial lifestyle: The Mountain Pygmy-possum lives on the summit of Mt Kosciusko (2230 m), Australia's highest peak.

The Mountain Pygmy-possum lives high in the mountains.

Biggest microbat in the world: The bat-eating Ghost Bat grows to 130 mm long and weighs up to 165 g. (The world's smallest bat may be 29 mm long and weigh 1.5 g.)

Worst prospect for dentist: The Honey Possum has only 22 teeth and its molars (grinding teeth) are just tiny cones.

Monotremes are mammals whose babies hatch from eggs. A baby monotreme suckles milk from two patches on its mother's belly. A monotreme has only one opening, the cloaca, through which body wastes and reproductive products (eggs and sperm[G]) pass to the outside.

Platypus

Ornithorhynchus anatinus (= duck-like bird-snout)

This unique mammal is found in, or near, fresh water along the east coast of the mainland and in Tasmania.

It has smooth, brown fur and a flattened body. There are no visible ears and the muzzle ends in a leathery bill. The tail is broad and the feet are webbed. A male has venomous spurs on its ankles.

The Platypus is most active at dawn and dusk. A swimming Platypus makes a V-shaped bow wave. It catches small creatures under water, holds them in its cheek pouches, and surfaces to eat. The Platypus digs a burrow in the river bank.

A female Platypus lays two rubbery eggs (17 mm across) in a nest burrow. She keeps them warm between her tail and body for 2 weeks. The young drink milk from two patches on her belly for 4–5 months. A baby Platypus has teeth, but loses them at weaning.

Platypuses disappear when their habitat is altered.

Length: HBT: ♀ up to 540 mm ♂ up to 550 mm

Weight: ♀ up to 2 kg ♂ up to 2.2 kg

STATUS	X	E	P	**V**	S	SIZE	RANGE

Short-beaked Echidna

Tachyglossus aculeatus (= spiny fast-tongue)

The spine-covered echidna lives almost anywhere in Australia where there is bush.

It is a long-snouted, ground-living animal, with powerful claws and a tiny tail. A male echidna has ankle spurs, but they are not connected to venom glands.

An echidna uses its claws to break open ant and termite nests. Then it pokes in its sticky tongue, pulls out insects and eats them. Echidna droppings often contain plenty of earth.

In the mating season, "trains" of several male echidnas follow one female, hoping to mate with her. She will lay one egg, incubate[G] it for 10 days in her pouch, then suckle the young one for 12 weeks. After the baby's spines harden, it is left in a burrow.

A threatened echidna digs into the ground or wedges itself into a hollow. As it rolls into a ball, its spines stand up and become bristling armour.

Length: HB 300–450 mm

Weight: 2–7 kg

STATUS	X	E	P	V	**S**	SIZE	RANGE

Marsupials are mammals whose babies are born in an early stage of development. A baby marsupial climbs to its mother's belly and attaches itself to a nipple. Then it suckles milk until it is ready for independence. Many female marsupials have belly pouches that shelter their young.

Tasmanian Devil

Sarcophilus harrisii (= Harris's flesh-lover)

The Tasmanian Devil is Australia's largest marsupial carnivore. It was common on the mainland until around 430 years ago. However, today it is only found in Tasmania, most often in the north-east of the island.

A black, bulky, dog-sized animal, the Tasmanian Devil has white markings on its chest and rump.

A Tasmanian Devil spends daytime in a den. From dusk to dawn it hunts for dead animals, insects and small mammals to eat. It may come into the outskirts of towns to find food. A group feeding at roadkill or other food may squabble loudly, opening their mouths threateningly. The Devil is not dangerous to humans or to their domestic animals.

The 2–4 young are born in April, then carried around in their mother's rear-opening pouch. After 16 weeks they are too big to carry and are left in a den while she finds food. After 40 weeks, they can survive on their own.

Length: HB ♀ 570 mm ♂ 650 mm T ♀ 240 mm ♂ 260 mm

Weight: ♀ 7 kg ♂ 9 kg

STATUS	X	E	P	V	**S**	SIZE 	RANGE

Brush-tailed Phascogale

Phascogale tapoatafa
(= pouched-weasel called by Aborigines *tapoatafa*)

This rare climbing marsupial is found in open coastal forest around Australia. It is the size of a large rat, with soft, grey body fur and a long, bushy black tail.

Phascogales can leap up to 2 m between trees. Each hind foot can turn through 180° as its owner runs up and down trunks, and under branches.

The Black-tailed Phascogale spends the day in a tree hollow. At night, it hunts insects, small mammals and roosting birds.

All male phascogales die after mating. They succumb to stress-related illnesses, or are taken by predators. The pregnant females give birth to the following generation. The 3–8 young are dragged around attached to their mother's nipples for 7 weeks, then they are fed in a nest for another 13 weeks.

Length: HB ♀ 180 mm ♂ 200 mm; T ♀ 190 mm ♂ 210 mm

Weight: ♀ 160 g ♂ 230 g

STATUS X E **P** V S SIZE  RANGE

Yellow-footed Antechinus

Antechinus flavipes (= yellow-footed hedgehog-like* animal)

This little hunter may be seen in many habitats, including gardens, from north-eastern Queensland to south-western Western Australia. At a distance, it looks like a large mouse with big ears and a longish snout. Seen closer, it has a grey head and light rings around its eyes. It has a reddish rump, belly and sides, yellow-brown feet and a black-tipped tail.

At night, this antechinus feeds on insects, house mice and other

small animals. It may even enter houses searching for prey. It moves in quick rushes, scratches noisily through the leaf litter, and may climb bushes and trees.

In spring, male antechinuses mate (for up to 12 hours), then die. For five weeks after giving birth, the female drags around up to 10 young attached to her nipples. The babies are then left in a nest, being fed there for another 15 weeks.

Length: HB ♀ 105 mm ♂ 120 mm; T ♀ 85 mm ♂ 100 mm

Weight: ♀ 34 g ♂ 56 g

* When wet, the fur stands up in spikes.

STATUS X E P V **S** SIZE  RANGE

Kultarr

Antechinomys laniger (= woolly furred mouse-like animal)

The Kultarr lives in Australia's inland deserts, on stony and sandy plains.

This large-eared hunter is the size of a big mouse. It has long hind legs and a long, tuft-ended tail. Brown-grey above and white below, it bounds rather than hops.

During the day, the Kultarr shelters in a burrow. At night it hunts for insects, spiders and other creatures.

For 4 weeks the 6–8 young are carried on their mother's belly, protected by a fold of skin. She feeds them in a nest for another 9 weeks. When old enough, they ride on her back while she hunts.

Length: HB 85 mm T up to 130 mm

Weight: up to 30 g

STATUS X E P **V** S SIZE  RANGE

Fat-tailed Dunnart

Sminthopsis crassicaudata (= fat-tailed mouse-like animal)

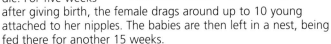

This dunnart lives in woodlands, plains and farmlands across southern Australia.

It is slightly bigger than a house mouse, with grey-brown fur, large ears and a fat tail. Its big eyes are set in dark eye-rings, its muzzle is sharply pointed, and it has long, narrow hind feet.

During the day, dunnarts shelter in holes or under logs. At night they hunt for small animals and may eat house mice. Good hunting allows fat to be stored in the tail as a winter food reserve. In cold weather, several dunnarts may share a nest.

The 5 young are carried in their mother's pouch for 5 weeks, and are then fed in a nest for another 5 weeks.

Length: HB up to 90 mm; T up to 70 mm

Weight: up to 20 g

STATUS X E P **V** S SIZE RANGE

Spotted-tailed Quoll

Dasyurus maculatus (= spotted hairy-tailed animal)

The Spotted-tailed Quoll is becoming rarer as its forest habitat disappears, and as it has to compete with the fox and feral cat for food. However, it can still be seen in isolated forest areas on the mainland east coast and in Tasmania. The size of a small dog, this quoll is the largest marsupial meat eater on the mainland. It climbs trees, and its prey ranges from insects and lizards to small wallabies. It will also eat carrion[G].

Quolls may mate for up to 8 hours. The female develops a pouch, and her 4–5 young are carried there for around 7 weeks. They are fed in a nest for another 6 weeks. The male Spotted-tailed Quoll will bring food to the female and young.

Length: HB ♀ 450 mm ♂ 760 mm; T ♀ 420 mm ♂ 550 mm

Weight: ♀ 4 kg ♂ 7 kg

STATUS	X	E	**P**	V	S	SIZE			RANGE	

Thylacine

Thylacinus cynocephalus (= dog-headed pouched-dog)

The Thylacine may still survive somewhere in Tasmania. However, the last known wild Thylacine was killed in 1933. The last captive one died in 1936.

A dog-like marsupial, it had a large head, a striped back and a striped, thick-based tail. An adult was about as big as a kelpie dog.

Thylacines once lived on the mainland. However, some 2000 years ago Dingoes took their place. Possibly only a few thousand Thylacines existed in Tasmania at any time. They chased down wallabies and smaller animals. After European settlement, they were ruthlessly killed.

The 2–3 young grew up in a rear-opening pouch. Large young were left in a den until able to hunt with their mother.

Length: HB 1–1.3 m; T 0.5–0.65 m

Weight: 15–35 kg

STATUS	**X**	E	P	V	S	SIZE		RANGE	

Numbat

Myrmecobius fasciatus (= banded ant-eater)

Once the Numbat was found across southern Australia from western New South Wales to the coast of Western Australia. Today it is endangered, surviving in a few isolated forests in south-western Western Australia.

The Numbat is red-brown in colour. Its darker rump is banded with white and it has a dark stripe across its eye. An active Numbat's long tail looks like a bottle-brush.

It is one of the few marsupials that feeds during daylight. A Numbat shelters and sleeps in a hollow fallen log. Sometimes it may dig a burrow.

Although Numbats feed on termites, they cannot tear open termite mounds. Instead, they scratch open termite runways or pull apart soft, rotting wood. Then they use their long tongues to lick up the insects.

A female Numbat has 4 young. They are born in January, carried around for 5 months, and then fed in a nest for another 5 months.

Much of the Numbat's habitat has been cleared. In the limited areas where it lives, it is under threat from bushfires and foxes. Where foxes are controlled, Numbats repopulate.

Length: HB 240 mm; T 170 mm

Weight: 460–484 g

STATUS	X	**E**	P	V	S	SIZE			RANGE	

TERMITES ON THE MENU

The Short-beaked Echidna and the Numbat join many Australian birds, reptiles, frogs and other creatures in eating termites. These blind insects are a rich food.

Termites eat wood and other plant matter. In the termites' guts are tiny organisms that break down tough plant fibres. The other animals that eat termites get the benefit of this pre-digested food and so do not need to have gut organisms of their own to make food from plant fibres.

Marsupial Mole
Notoryctes typhlops (= blind southern digger)

The Marsupial Mole is not a mole. It got its name because it looks and behaves like the unrelated true moles.

It lives in sandy deserts from central Australia to the north-west coast of Western Australia.This blind, rat-sized burrower has silky golden fur. It has no visible ears, and its nose is protected by a horny shield.

The Marsupial Mole digs tunnels, using two blade-like claws on each paw. The tunnels collapse after it passes. When it finds an insect or other small creature, the mole grips it with its claws and eats it. A female Marsupial Mole has a rear-opening pouch and two nipples.

Little is known about this creature's habits. Occasionally, usually after rain, someone will find one on the surface.

Length: HB 120–160 mm; T 26 mm

Weight: 40–70 g

STATUS	X	E	**P**	V	S	SIZE		RANGE	

Southern Brown Bandicoot
Isoodon obesulus (= equal-toothed* rather fat animal)

The Southern Brown Bandicoot is found in south-western and south-eastern Australia.

It is the size of a cat, with a pointed muzzle, humped back and thin tail. It is grey-brown above and white below. It bounds when moving fast.

During the day, a bandicoot shelters alone in a ground nest. At night it feeds on worms, insects and fungi. Cone-shaped holes show where a bandicoot has been digging for food.

Up to 6 young ones are carried in a rear-opening pouch. They are weaned[G] at around 9 weeks.

Each bandicoot needs a home range[G] of up to 7 ha to find enough food. Ranges may overlap if food is plentiful.

Bandicoots need places to hide from dogs, foxes, cats and other dangers. They disappear from an area when undergrowth is cleared. They increase where limited bushfires bring new green growth.

Length: HB ♀ 300 mm ♂ 330 mm; T ♀ 110 mm ♂ 120 mm

Weight: ♀ 700 g ♂ 850 g

* Refers to the length of the incisor teeth.

STATUS	X	E	P	**V**	S	SIZE		RANGE	

Greater Bilby
Macrotis lagotis (= hare-eared large-eared animal)

The rare and endangered Bilby was once found across the south of the continent. Today it survives only in desert areas of central Australia.

A cat-sized, burrowing marsupial with long ears, it has a long muzzle, soft, grey fur and a black, white-tipped tail.

During the day, a Bilby shelters in a burrow that may be 3 m long and 2 m deep. At night, it feeds on insects, seeds and fungi. To get food, it may dig holes up to 10 cm deep. A Bilby can survive on the water it gets from its food.

The 2 young stay in the rear-opening pouch for about 11 weeks.

The Bilby is threatened by over-grazing by stock and rabbits, by fire, and by foxes. Concerned people are breeding Bilbies in captivity. They hope some Bilbies can be released into fenced areas where their enemies are kept under control.

Length: HB ♀ 394 mm ♂ 550 mm T 240–250 mm

Weight: ♀ 1.1 kg ♂ 2.5 kg

STATUS	X	E	**P**	V	S	SIZE		RANGE	

DESERT SURVIVORS

Mammals that live in the desert must shelter from the heat. Many spend the day in burrows, where the temperature is far lower than on the surface. Some rest under bushes or trees, or amongst rocks. They all come out in the late afternoon and feed through the cooler night.

Some desert mammals have bodies that can make water from the food they eat. However, they need juicy green shoots and grass to provide enough moisture to feed young ones. Larger mammals such as kangaroos need to live near water.

Koala

Phascolarctos cinereus (= ash-coloured pouched-bear)

Koalas live in eucalypt forest in eastern Australia. They prefer trees growing on fertile soil. Southern Koalas are considerably larger than northern ones.

The Koala's body is admirably suited to life in the treetops. Its dense, grey-brown, woolly fur is waterproof. Each fore paw has two thumbs, and all digits end in strong, sharp claws. A Koala's big-bellied body has just a stub of a tail.

Koalas eat eucalypt leaves, which have low energy content. This means Koalas sleep for up to 20 hours out of every 24.

Koalas live alone, except when nursing young or mating. A male Koala claims a territory[G] that may include areas of the home range of several females. The male calls loudly to attract females that are ready to mate.

A female Koala carries 1 young in her rear-opening pouch for 6 months. The baby rides on the mother's back for a further 6 months.

The Koala is threatened by disease and bushfires. However, habitat destruction by humans is probably the greatest threat to its survival.

Length: HB ♀ 730 mm ♂ 820 mm

Weight: ♀ 11 kg ♂ 12 kg

STATUS	X	E	P	**V**	S	SIZE		RANGE

Common Wombat

Vombatus ursinus (= bear-like wombat)

The size of a large, stocky dog, the Common Wombat lives in forested ranges, from north-eastern New South Wales to south-eastern South Australia.

The Common Wombat is a ground-living burrower with grey to brown, coarse fur. Its outline is rounded and it has a large head and short ears. It has a naked nose.

Wombats are active at night and during sunny winter days. They eat native grasses, shrubs and roots. Each wombat lives alone, but the burrows it digs may connect with those of other wombats. A big burrow may be up to 20 m long, with several chambers and entrances.

A female carries 1 young in her rear-opening pouch for 6 months. It follows her for another 11 months.

This wombat is not protected in some areas of eastern Victoria.

Length: HB 0.9–1.15 m; T 25 mm

Weight: 22–39 kg

STATUS	X	E	P	V	**S**	SIZE		RANGE

Southern Hairy-nosed Wombat

Lasiorhinus latifrons (= broad-headed hairy-nose)

The rare and endangered Southern Hairy-nosed Wombat is found only in the desert bordering the Great Australian Bight in South Australia.

It is a bulky, ground-living marsupial with soft, silky brown fur. The fur on its nose is white.

This wombat rarely gets water to drink. When it rests in its burrow, its body functions slow down to save energy and water. At night, the wombat eats native grasses.

Several wombats may share a network of burrows.

A female hairy-nosed wombat carries 1 young in her rear-opening pouch for up to 9 months. It is weaned at 12 months.

Three years of good rain are needed to grow enough grass for a young one to be raised and weaned.

Length: HB 770–935 mm; T 25–60 mm

Weight: 19–32 kg

STATUS	X	E	**P**	V	S	SIZE		RANGE

Common Brushtail Possum

Trichosurus vulpecula (= little fox-like hairy-tail)

The Common Brushtail Possum has adapted well to living with humans. It is found from Queensland to Tasmania and in the far north-west and south-west of Western Australia.

It is a cat-sized, tree-living marsupial with a foxy face and long oval ears. The bushy tail has a short naked area underneath. An agile climber, this possum sits upright and holds food in its paws.

The call is a coughing or hissing.

Common Brushtails spend the day in a tree hollow, cave or ceiling. At night they eat leaves, flowers and fruit.

The male marks his territory with chin, chest and anal glands[G].

The female carries 1 joey in her pouch for 4–5 months. It stays with her for another 2 months, often riding on her back.

Length: HB 350–550 mm; T 250–400 mm

Weight: ♀ 2.4 kg ♂ 2.9 kg

STATUS	X	E	P	V	S	SIZE		RANGE	

Common Ringtail Possum

Pseudocheirus peregrinus (= wandering false-hand)

The Common Ringtail is found in forests and gardens down the east coast of Australia from Cape York Peninsula to Tasmania.

This common possum has short ears and a sleek, white-tipped, prehensile[G] tail. This tail has a naked area beneath it, and is used as a fifth limb (the "false-hand" of the animal's scientific name). The colour of the fur varies from copper to grey.

The call is soft, high and twittering.

A Common Ringtail spends the day in a ball-shaped, leaf-lined nest it builds in a hollow or in dense foliage. At night it eats leaves and flowers. This possum is one of the few animals that can digest eucalypt leaves.

Male and female stay together for the breeding season. They both care for the 2 young. These are carried in the female's pouch for 4 months, then left in the nest for another 2 months.

Length: HB 300–350 mm; T 300–350 mm

Weight: 0.7–1.1 kg

STATUS	X	E	P	V	S	SIZE		RANGE	

Green Ringtail Possum

Pseudochirops archeri (= Archer's false-hand)

Each hair in the Green Ringtail Possum's coat is banded in black, yellow and white. This makes the fur appear green.

This possum is only found in dense mountain rainforest near Townsville and Mossman, Queensland.

During the daytime, it sleeps curled into a ball on a branch. Its green fur blends with the surrounding leaves. When startled while feeding at night, it curls into sleeping position and freezes[G].

The Green Ringtail eats the leaves and fruits of rainforest figs and other trees. Like the Common Ringtail, it passes special soft droppings during the daytime. These can be eaten at night, so that extra food value is gained from them.

A female has 1 young, which rides in her pouch and then on her back.

Length: HB 280–380 mm; T 310–370 mm

Weight: 0.7–1.35 kg

STATUS	X	E	P	V	S	SIZE		RANGE	

Spotted Cuscus

Spilocuscus maculatus (= spotted spotted-cuscus)

The Spotted Cuscus is found in the rainforests of Queensland's Cape York Peninsula, north of Coen.

This cuscus is sometimes mistaken for a monkey. It has a round, bare-skinned face, large round eyes and tiny ears. Its prehensile tail is two-thirds naked underneath. The male is blotched grey and white above, while the female is simply grey.

A cuscus spends the day sleeping on a branch or on a platform it has made from leaves and twigs. At night, it climbs slowly through the treetops eating leaves, fruits and flowers. In captivity, a cuscus may also eat some animal food.

There is usually 1 young, which is carried in its mother's pouch for some time, then on her back.

Length: HB 350–580 mm; T 310–435 mm

Weight: 1.5–5 kg

STATUS	X	E	P	V	S	SIZE		RANGE	

Eastern Pygmy-possum
Cercartetus nanus (= dwarf cercartetus*)

This tiny possum is found down the eastern coast of Australia, from southern Queensland to south-eastern South Australia, and in Tasmania. It lives in rainforest, eucalypt forest and scrubby heaths.

It is a mouse-sized possum, fawn above and white below. Its tail is prehensile[G].

These pygmy-possums spend the day in their nests. At night they eat pollen[G], fruits and insects. They gather nectar with their brush-tipped tongues.

In very cold weather, Eastern Pygmy-possums stay in their nests in tree hollows. All their body systems slow down and they live on fat stored at the base of the tail.

A female pygmy-possum carries 4 young in her pouch for 4 weeks. She then feeds them in a nest for 5 weeks.

Length: HB 70–110 mm; T 75–105 mm

Weight: 15–43 g

* Possibly means "tail-in-air".

STATUS X E P V **S**   **SIZE**   **RANGE**

Sugar Glider
Petaurus breviceps (= short-headed rope-dancer)

The Sugar Glider is found in coastal forests and patches of woodland from the Kimberley, Western Australia, across the north, then down to south-eastern South Australia and Tasmania. It sometimes lives in nest boxes in gardens.

It looks very much like Leadbeater's Possum. However, it has a gliding membrane[G] stretching from the fifth finger to the first toe on each side of its body.

Sugar Gliders live in tree hollows, in colonies consisting of up to 7 adults and their young. A group recognises its members by scent. At night, the gliders feed on tree sap, nectar, pollen[G] and insects. In cold weather, the group huddles for warmth and may become torpid[G].

A female carries 2 young in her pouch for 2–3 months. They leave the nest aged 4–5 months. At 7–10 months, young Sugar Gliders leave their group to find a new range. Many do not survive this perilous journey.

Length: HB 160–210 mm; T 165–210 mm

Weight: ♀ 135 g
♂ 160 g

STATUS X E P V **S**   **SIZE**   **RANGE**

Leadbeater's Possum
Gymnobelideus leadbeateri (= Leadbeater's naked* glider)

This endangered possum is found only in the wet mountain forests of Victoria's central highlands. The species was not sighted from 1909 to 1961. It nests in hollows found only in trees over 120 years old. However, 75% of its habitat is in timber-production forests, and only 3% is in nature reserves.

These possums are grey to brown above with a dark stripe from the face down the back. The long tail broadens at the tip.

Leadbeater's Possum lives in colonies[G] of up to 8, consisting of a breeding pair and their offspring. They nest together in a tree hollow and identify each other by scent. These possums will combine to defend a group member attacked by a predator.

Leadbeater's Possum feeds on insects and tree sap.

A female carries 1–2 young in her pouch for over 3 months. They leave the nest at 4 months.

Length: HB 150–170 mm; T 145–180 mm

Weight: 100 (spring)–166 (autumn) g

* Refers to lack of gliding membranes.

STATUS X **E** P V S   **SIZE**   **RANGE**

Greater Glider
Petauroides volans (= flying glider-like animal)

This is the largest gliding possum. It lives in eucalypt forests on Australia's east coast and coastal ranges.

The Greater Glider is grey to brown above and whitish below. It has a long, furry tail, which is not prehensile. Its muzzle is short and its ears are large.

The gliding membrane stretches to its elbow, not to its wrist. When gliding, it brings its paws up under its chin.

During the day, a Greater Glider rests in a tree hollow. It comes out at night and glides to one of its feeding places. Like the Koala, it eats almost nothing except eucalypt leaves.

One young is carried in its mother's pouch for 3–4 months. Then it is carried on her back or left in a nest for another 5 months.

This glider needs old forests with big tree hollows.

Length: HB 350–450 mm; T 450–600 mm

Weight: 0.9–1.7 kg

STATUS X E P **V** S   **SIZE**   **RANGE**

FURRY SWOOPMASTERS

Squirrel Glider

Gliders do not fly by beating their limbs up and down. They glide (volplane) by extending their membranes, landing on a tree, then scampering up its trunk to gain height for another glide. A Greater Glider can glide for 100 m and change direction up to 90° while in the air. The Feathertail Glider uses its unique tail as a rudder, a brake and an anchor. The feathery fringes increase its surface area. The Yellow-bellied Glider has sharp, backward-curving claws and can run along the underside of a branch.

Feathertail Glider

Acrobates pygmaeus (= pygmy acrobat)

This tiny marsupial is the world's smallest gliding mammal. It is found in tall forests and woodlands in eastern Australia.

The Feathertail Glider is mouse-sized, with grey fur on its back and a white belly. Its long, prehensile tail has a fringe of hair on either side. The gliding membranes stretch between elbow and knee.

Groups of up to 20 of these tiny gliders nest together in tree hollows. At night, they feed on nectar, which they lick up with brush-tipped tongues. They also eat pollen and insects.

The 3–4 young are carried in their mother's pouch for 9 weeks, then fed in the nest for 5 weeks. A female may carry embryos[G] that remain at an early stage of development, only developing fully and being born once larger young ones have been weaned or lost.

Feathertails will build their bark and leaf nests in tree hollows, old ringtail possum nests and garden nest boxes.

Length: HB 65–80 mm; T 70–80 mm

Weight: 10–14 g

| STATUS | X | E | P | **V** | S | SIZE | | RANGE |

Striped Possum

Dactylopsila trivirgata (= three-striped naked-finger)

The Striped Possum lives in rainforest north of Townsville, Queensland. Often its noisy passage through the treetops is heard before it is seen.

The size of a small, slender cat, this possum has black and white stripes along its head, body and tail. Its toes and fingers, particularly the fourth finger, are long. It has a strong, sweet odour, rather like newly hardened fibreglass.

A Striped Possum sleeps in a nest in a tree hollow during the day. At night, it runs along branches and leaps boldly between trees. Using its sharp teeth, it pulls away bark. Then it pokes grubs or other insects out of holes in the wood with its tongue, or hooks them out with its long fourth finger.

Fighting or mating Striped Possums are very noisy. The female has 2 young.

Length: HB 250–270 mm; T 310–340 mm

Weight: 250–530 g

| STATUS | X | E | P | **V** | S | SIZE | | RANGE |

Honey-possum

Tarsipes rostratus (= long-nosed tarsier*-foot)

The mouse-sized Honey-possum is found only in the coastal heathlands of south-western Western Australia.

It has a long snout and eyes set on top of its head. Its fingers and toes have broad tips and nails, not claws. The tail is long and prehensile. It is grey-brown above, with a darker stripe down its back. A Honey-possum has the fewest teeth of any marsupial.

During the day, a Honey-possum sleeps in an old bird nest or hollow grasstree stem. At night, it eats nectar and pollen, feeding with its long, brush-tipped tongue. It carries pollen from one flower to another. In cold weather, this tiny possum becomes torpid.

The 2–3 young are carried in their mother's pouch for 2 months. Then they are fed in a nest for 2 weeks.

Length: HB 40–94 mm
T 45–110 mm

Weight: 7–12 g

* Tarsiers, like humans and honey-possums, have nails rather than claws.

| STATUS | X | E | P | V | **S** | SIZE | | RANGE |

Musky Rat-kangaroo

Hypsiprymnodon moschatus
(= musky animal with teeth like a potoroo)

The Musky Rat-kangaroo is the smallest of the kangaroo group. However, like a possum, it has a big toe, while other kangaroo relatives have lost theirs.

This little marsupial lives in the rainforest of north Queensland. It needs large areas of forest for survival.

It has a compact^G body and a long, scaly tail, and moves in bounds.

A Musky Rat-kangaroo feeds in the morning and late afternoon. It eats seeds, nuts, fungi and insects – its digestive system cannot process grass. Sometimes it hides seeds in the leaf litter, and then eats them later.

At night a Musky Rat-kangaroo sleeps in a nest. The leaves for this are carried in the builder's coiled tail.

Two joeys are born (other allies of the kangaroo have one). They are carried in the pouch for 5 months, then fed in a nest.

Length: HB 270 mm; T 160 mm
Weight: ♀ 510 g ♂ 530 g

STATUS	X	E	P	**V**	S	SIZE		RANGE

Long-nosed Potoroo

Potorous tridactylus (= three-toed* potoroo)

This little hopping marsupial was described near Sydney by Governor Phillip in 1789. Since then, its numbers and range have dwindled as its habitat has been cleared.

It lives in the coastal south-east of Australia, in forests and heaths with sandy soil and thick groundcover. It had not been seen in Western Australia for over 100 years until rediscovered at Two Peoples Bay in 1994.

It is a fat-cat-sized marsupial with grasping paws and short feet. It has grey-brown fur, and bare skin stretches from its nose up its long snout.

This potoroo digs up fungi, roots, insects and spiders to eat.

One joey is carried in the pouch for 4 months.

Length: HB ♀ 340 mm ♂ 380 mm; T 250 mm
Weight: ♀ 1.3 kg ♂ 1.6 kg

* Actually, it has four, the second and third being joined together.

STATUS	X	E	P	**V**	S	SIZE			RANGE

WHY ARE THEY VANISHING?

Over the past 200 years, 18 species of native mammals have become extinct. Twenty-two more species are now listed as being in danger of extinction. At least 18 more will become endangered if conditions do not change.

Clearing of habitat and overgrazing by introduced mammals (including the rabbit) are major reasons for the disappearance of native mammals. Many native mammals had become adapted to the seasonal slow burning of habitat by the Aborigines. They could not adjust quickly to loss of the green plants that followed these burns, or to the new, hot bushfires.

The introduced cat and fox are major predators of native mammals. The cat can kill animals up to 2 kg in weight. The fox can kill animals ranging up to 5 kg in weight.

Brush-tailed Bettong

Bettongia penicillata (= brush-tailed bettong)

The rare and endangered Brush-tailed Bettong was once widespread. Today the "Woylie" (its Aboriginal name) is found only in three tiny areas of forest in south-west Western Australia.

The Woylie is a yellowish grey, cat-sized marsupial with a black crest on its tail. It hops with its head held low and its tail held straight out behind.

Daylight is spent in a nest. The grass or bark for nest building is carried in the builder's tail. At dusk and before dawn, a Brush-tailed Bettong searches for underground fungi, bulbs, seeds and insects to eat.

A joey is carried in its mother's pouch for around 3 months. It then follows its mother around and shares her nest.

This bettong needs dense undergrowth for survival. The fox is a major predator.

Length: HB 300–380 mm; T 290–360 mm
Weight: 1.1–1.6 kg

STATUS	X	**E**	P	V	S	SIZE			RANGE

Rufous Hare-wallaby
Lagorchestes hirsutus (= hairy dancing-hare)

The Rufous Hare-wallaby is also known as the Mala. It was once common throughout dry central and western Australia. It now survives only on Bernier and Dorre Islands off the coast of Western Australia.

This cat-sized, red-brown or grey-brown wallaby has a blackish brown tail.

It lives on sandy country with low shrubs and spinifex grass. During the day it shelters in a hollow it has scraped under a clump of spinifex or a shrub. Startled from its nest, it zigzags away at speed.

Rufous Hare-wallabies will eat spinifex, but prefer juicier grasses. They benefited from the Aboriginal practice of burning small areas.

Feral cats have hampered efforts to reintroduce these little wallabies into the wild.

Length: HB 310–390 mm; T 240–300 mm

Weight: 1.25–1.96 kg

STATUS X E **P** V S   SIZE   RANGE

Quokka
Setonix brachyurus (= bristle-footed short-tail)

Once the Quokka was common in the wetter areas of mainland south-western Western Australia. Now it is rarely seen except in the extreme south-west. The biggest population is on Rottnest Island, off the coast near Perth.

The Quokka is a cat-sized ally of the wallabies, with short ears and a very short, stiff tail. It has bristly hairs on its toes.

This was the second Australian marsupial to be noted by a European. In 1696, Dutch captain Willem de Vlamingh thought it was a big rat.

The Quokka eats leaves rather than grass.

The single joey stays in the pouch for about 5 months and is weaned 2 months later. A female may be pregnant with an embryo that does not develop further until after her joey is weaned.

Length: HB 470–49 mm

T 270–290 mm

Weight: 2.9–3.6 kg

STATUS X E P **V** S   SIZE    RANGE

Red-legged Pademelon
Thylogale stigmatica (= pouched-weasel with tattoos*)

The Red-legged Pademelon is found in coastal eastern Australia, from Cape York to Sydney. It lives in dense eucalypt forest and in rainforest.

This small, stocky wallaby has a short, stiff tail. Grey-brown above and cream below, it has reddish cheeks, arms and hind legs. Like all pademelons, it rests with its tail forward under its body.

During the day, it feeds in the forest on fallen leaves and fruits. At night, it hops along runways to search just outside the forest for grass.

A female carries her single joey in her pouch for about 28 weeks. It is weaned about 9 weeks later.

Length: HB ♀ 460 mm ♂ 490 mm; T ♀ 360 mm ♂ 440 mm

Weight: ♀ 4 kg ♂ 5 kg

* This refers to faint dotted markings on neck and hip.

STATUS X E P V **S**   SIZE    RANGE

Red-necked Wallaby
Macropus rufogriseus (= red-grey great-foot)

This medium-sized wallaby is found in the eucalypt forests of south-eastern Australia. In Tasmania, it is known as Bennett's Wallaby.

It has a reddish grey head and back and a reddish brown neck. Its muzzle, paws and largest toe are black, and it has a white stripe on its upper lip.

Red-necked Wallabies spend the day in the forest. In the evening they come onto the forest edges to eat grass and leaves. When disturbed, a feeding group splits up into single animals. In Queensland and Tasmania, this wallaby may be hunted during declared open seasons.

A Red-necked Wallaby joey is carried in its mother's pouch for 40 weeks. Then it is suckled for up to 28 weeks.

Length: HB ♀ 770 mm ♂ 820 mm; T ♀ 720 mm ♂ 800 mm

Weight: ♀ 14 kg ♂ 19 kg

STATUS X E P V **S**   SIZE   RANGE

Whiptail Wallaby
Macropus parryi (= Parry's great-foot)

This common marsupial is sometimes called the Pretty-faced Wallaby. It is found in coastal eastern Australia from Cooktown, Queensland, to northern New South Wales.

Of medium size, it has a long, slender tail. It is grey or brownish grey above, and white below. The base of its ears, its forehead and a stripe from the neck down to the shoulder are dark brown. It has a white stripe on the upper lip and hip.

Whiptails live in groups of up to 50. They signal danger by thumping the ground with their hind feet. A female carries her joey in her pouch for 37 weeks. It then suckles for another 37 weeks (see photo). When the joey leaves the pouch, a reserve embryo already present in the female begins to develop.

Length: HB ♀ 755 mm ♂ 920 mm; T 940 mm
Weight: 26 kg

STATUS **X E P V S** SIZE RANGE

Agile Wallaby
Macropus agilis (= agile great-foot)

The large Agile Wallaby is common in grasslands across northern and north-eastern Australia.

It is brown above and whitish below, with a light stripe on the thigh, a dark stripe up the forehead and a pale stripe on the cheek. Males are much larger than females.

This wallaby hops with its body almost upright and its tail held straight out behind it. Agile Wallabies live in groups of up to 10. Where good grass is available, they may gather in large mobs. They are wary and easily alarmed.

A joey stays in the pouch for 7–8 months, then follows its mother until it is 12 months old. A reserve embryo develops when the pouch has been vacated.

Length: HB ♀ 650 mm ♂ 800 mm; T ♀ 640 mm ♂ 770 mm
Weight: ♀ 11 kg ♂ 19 kg

STATUS **X E P V S** SIZE RANGE

Yellow-footed Rock-wallaby
Petrogale xanthopus (= yellow-footed rock-weasel)

This rare and colourful wallaby lives in dry, rocky country. It is found only in the Flinders Ranges, South Australia, and in the Adavale Basin, Queensland.

Yellow-footed Rock-wallabies were once hunted for their skins. Today they have to compete with feral goats and rabbits for food. Drought may kill off 60% of the wallabies in an area.

This rock-wallaby is grey-fawn above and white below, with a white stripe on the cheek, side and hip. Its ears, arms, hind legs and feet are orange-yellow. Its tail is ringed with orange and dark brown.

These rock-wallabies live in colonies of up to 100. They eat grass and leaves. A joey stays in the pouch for 6–7 months.

Length: HB 480–650 mm; T 570–700 mm
Weight: 6–11 kg

STATUS **X E P V S** SIZE  RANGE

Bridled Nailtail Wallaby
Onychogalea fraenata (= bridled nailed-weasel)

The Bridled Nailtail was once common in inland eastern Australia. Today it is found only in one area near Dingo in central Queensland.

A nailtail wallaby has a small, horny spur at the end of its tail. No-one knows what this is used for. It also has long, strong claws on its fore feet. These are used to dig hollows under a bushes, which are used as daytime nests.

The Bridled Nailtail has a white "bridle" from the back of the head down each side of the body to behind the forearm. Instead of fleeing, a startled Bridled Nailtail freezes.

This wallaby eats grass and leaves at night. It uses its fore feet to rake aside dry matter in its search for green shoots.

Bridled Nailtails are usually seen on their own, though a female may have a large joey following her.

Length: HB 430–700 mm; T 360–540 mm
Weight: 6–11 kg

STATUS **X E P V S** SIZE RANGE

Common Wallaroo (Euro)
Macropus robustus (= strong great-foot)

This large kangaroo is usually found in rocky, hilly country. It lives in the drier areas of Australia.

Its coarse fur is dark grey or brown above and paler below. The area between its nostrils and its lip is naked.

This tough animal is called different names in eastern and western Australia. The shaggy, dark-grey Eastern Wallaroo lives on the coastal and inland slopes of the Great Dividing Range. The shorter-haired, reddish Euro takes its place across to the west coast.

A wallaroo shelters under rock ledges during the heat of the day. At night it eats grasses and shrubs. The joey stays in the pouch for between 32 and 34 weeks.

Length: HB ♀ 1.6 m ♂ 2 m; T ♀ 750 mm ♂ 900 mm
Weight: ♀ 25 kg ♂ 47 kg

STATUS X E P V **S** SIZE RANGE

Eastern Grey Kangaroo
Macropus giganteus (= gigantic great-foot)

Grey kangaroos live in scrubland, woodland and forest. The Eastern Grey is found from the inland plains to the east coast of the mainland and in north-eastern Tasmania. It is a large grey or grey-brown kangaroo with paler underparts. Unlike other kangaroos, it has hair on its muzzle between the nostrils and the upper lip.

Grey kangaroos live in mobs. They rest in the shade during the day. From late afternoon to early morning, they graze.

Males are larger than females. Dominant[G] males mate with the most females.

The female carries a joey in the pouch for 11 months, and then suckles it for another 9 months. A reserve embryo may develop when the pouch is vacant.

Length: HB ♀ 800 mm ♂ 1.2 m; T ♀ 840 mm ♂ 110 mm
Weight: ♀ 32 kg ♂ 66 kg

STATUS X E P V **S** SIZE RANGE

Lumholtz's Tree-kangaroo
Dendrolagus lumholtzi (= Lumholtz's tree-hare)

Tree-kangaroos live in far north Queensland's mountain rainforests.

Lumholtz's Tree-kangaroo is a medium-sized, climbing kangaroo. It is blackish brown, with lighter fur on its lower back. Its long tail is used for balance, not for holding branches. The four strong limbs end in grasping paws, broad feet and sharp claws.

A tree-kangaroo lives alone. It spends the day asleep in a treetop. At night, it eats leaves and fruit, holding them in its front paws.

The joey stays in its mother's pouch for around 33 weeks.

Length: HB ♀ 600 mm ♂ 650 mm; T 700 mm
Weight: 6–7.5 kg

STATUS X E P **V** S SIZE  RANGE

Red Kangaroo
Macropus rufus (= red great-foot)

The Red Kangaroo is the largest living marsupial. It lives on the plains and in the open woodlands of inland Australia.

The male is red, with a muscular upper body. The smaller female is blue-grey or reddish above, and whitish below. Both have black and white patches at the sides of the muzzle, and a white stripe from mouth to ear. The area between the nostrils and lip is naked.

Red Kangaroos rest in cool places during the heat of the day and feed at night. In drought, the rate of breeding slows and pouch young may die. After rain, when green feed is available, breeding is successful.

A mob of Red Kangaroos is led by a dominant male.

Length: ♀ 1.1 m ♂ 1.4 m; T ♀ 0.9 m ♂ 1 m
Weight: ♀ 35 kg ♂ 85 kg

STATUS X E P V **S** SIZE RANGE

A placental mammal's baby remains inside its mother's body until well developed. During this time, it is maintained by an organ called a placenta[G]. After birth, the baby is cared for by its mother. It feeds on milk suckled from her nipples, and is kept warm by her body, or by its own hair or fur.

Spectacled Flying-fox
Pteropus conspicillatus (= spectacled wing-foot)

The Spectacled Flying-fox is found in or near rainforest in north-eastern Queensland.

It is a big bat with a black body and wings. There is yellowish fur around its eyes and down its muzzle, and it has a neck ruff of yellow hair.

These bats fly out after dusk to feed. The seeds from the fruit eaten pass out with the droppings. This helps to spread rainforest trees.

One young is born at a time. It is carried by its mother on her nightly feeding flights until it is about 5 months old.

Length: HB 220–240 mm

Weight: ♀ 650 g

♂ 850 g

STATUS X E P **V** S   SIZE   RANGE

Ghost Bat
Macroderma gigas (= giant large-skin)

Groups of the endangered Ghost Bat survive in scattered locations across northern Australia. They roost in caves and mine shafts. When these are disturbed, the bats disappear.

This rare bat has large eyes. Its big ears are joined at their bases. It has a simple noseleaf[G].

At night, a Ghost Bat goes hunting. It can find prey by sending out sound waves and "reading" the objects from which they echo back. This is called echolocation.

Ghost Bats eat small animals, including other bats. The prey is carried to a perch to be devoured.

One young is born between September and November.

Length: HB 100–130 mm

Weight: 140–165 g

STATUS X E **P** V S   SIZE    RANGE

Bush Rat
Rattus fuscipes (= dusky-footed rat)

The Bush Rat lives in coastal forests, woodland and scrub where there is dense undergrowth. It is found in south-west, south-east and north-east Australia.

It is a rodent, and like all rodents has chisel-edged[G] front teeth. It has pink, rounded ears, and its tail is shorter than its head and body combined. (The introduced Black Rat has a tail longer than its head and body combined.)

The Bush Rat eats grass-stems, leaves, fungi and insects. It does not live around human dwellings.

Females are much smaller than males. There are 5 young in a litter. They are independent of their mother at 4–5 weeks. Only the last season's young survive winter to breed in springtime.

In the alpine country of south-eastern Australia, these rats survive winter in runways under the snow.

Length: HB 110–210 mm; T 100–190 mm

Weight: 40–225 g

STATUS X E P V **S**   SIZE   RANGE

Spinifex Hopping-mouse
Notomys alexis (= Alexandria Downs southern mouse)

Spinifex Hopping-mice live amongst spinifex on sand dunes and sandy flats in arid north-western and central Australia.

This rat-sized desert-dweller uses all four limbs when moving slowly. When going fast, it hops like a tiny kangaroo. However, it is a rodent, not a marsupial. It has large ears, long hind feet and a very long, brush-tipped tail. There is a pouch under its throat.

Its silky hair is pale brown above and white below.

Hopping-mice shelter from the heat in below-ground nest chambers connected by shafts to the surface. At night they emerge to eat seeds, roots and insects. The 3–4 young are left in the nest while their mother looks for food. Either a female or a male may retrieve a young one that has wandered from the nest.

Rare in drought, this hopping-mouse breeds up after rainfall.

Length: HB 95–110 mm; T 130–150 mm

Weight: 27–45 g

STATUS X E **P** V S   SIZE   RANGE

LIVING IN THE OCEAN

Mammals that live in the sea need special body features to keep them warm. Many, such as whales and dolphins, have thick layers of fat under their skins. Some, such as fur-seals and sea-lions, have dense hair coats.

Marine[G] mammals need streamlined[G] bodies so they can slide through the water as they swim and dive. Their nostrils are often on top of their heads so they can take in air quickly. When they submerge, their nostrils close automatically.

Often the front limbs of a marine mammal have become flippers. The hind limbs may be enclosed in the body and the tail provides power for swimming.

Some marine mammals rid their bodies of excess salt by "crying" extra-salty tears.

Australian Sea-lion

Bottlenose Dolphin
Tursiops truncatus (= short-faced dolphin)

Bottlenose Dolphins frequent coastal waters around the mainland and Tasmania. They can be seen riding the bow waves of boats, or swimming in the shallows near beaches.

These dolphins are large, streamlined[G] marine mammals. They have beaky snouts, rounded foreheads and backward-pointing dorsal[G] fins. Grey above, they have paler grey sides and are off-white below.

Usually Bottlenose Dolphins swim in small groups. They eat fish, squid and other marine animals. They locate prey and other objects by sending out sounds and "reading" the echoes (echolocation).

A dolphin may dive for up to 4 minutes. When it surfaces, it shows its forehead but not its beak.

A baby dolphin is born tail-first and weighs about 25 kg. It doubles its birth weight in 2 months. It suckles for up to 18 months even though it begins to eat fish at 4 months.

Length: 1.9–3.9 m
Weight: 150–650 kg

STATUS	X	E	P	V	**S**	SIZE	RANGE

Dingo
Canis lupus dingo (= dog-wolf)

Dingos or partbred Dingos may be seen all over mainland Australia, though not in Tasmania.

This kelpie-sized wild dog is usually yellowish ginger, but can be black and tan, or even white. Usually it has white markings on chest, tail-tip and paws. The ears are pricked and the tail is bushy.

These hunters live in packs that may remain together or meet at intervals. Once a year, the dominant male and female of the pack may breed. The other pack members help rear the pups.

Dingos take whatever prey is common at the time, from insects to large mammals such as kangaroos.

The Dingo probably developed from the Indian Wolf around 6000 years ago. It was brought to Australia less than 4000 years ago by seafarers. The pure Dingo is increasingly crossbreeding with the domestic dog.

Length: HB 0.9–1.2 m; T 260–380 mm
Weight: 9.6–24 kg

STATUS	X	E	P	V	**S**	SIZE	RANGE

Dugong
Dugong dugon (= dugong)

The Dugong lives in shallow, calm, warm, subtropical and tropical coastal waters. It is found from Shark Bay, Western Australia, around the northern coastline to Moreton Bay, Queensland.

It is the only marine plant-eating mammal. Large and blunt-muzzled, it has flippers and horizontal[G] tail flukes[G]. It is grey to brown above, paler below.

Dense bones keep a Dugong on the sea bottom while it uses its broad upper lip to gather seagrasses into its mouth.

Dugongs feed in herds. A female does not breed until she is 9 years old. Her calf rides just above her back. It stays with its mother for up to 2 years.

The species is vulnerable because its habitat is being altered. It may be hunted, caught in nets or hurt by powerboat propellors.

Length: HBT ♀ 3.3 m ♂ 3.15 m
Weight: 420 kg

STATUS	X	E	P	**V**	S	SIZE	RANGE

Australia's Birds

What is a bird?

- Birds are vertebrate animals, whose central nervous systems[G] and brains are protected by backbones and skulls.

- Birds are "warm-blooded" (endothermic). Their body temperature remains more or less the same no matter what the temperature of their surroundings.

- Birds have four limbs, the front pair developed into wings. Most birds use these wings to fly, but some birds have developed flipper-like wings for swimming. Flightless birds have reduced wings.

- Birds' skin is covered by feathers. These have developed from scales, and birds' legs and feet are still protected by scales. A bird's plumage[G] includes all its feathers.

- Birds' bones tend to be hollow and many bones are fused[G]. Flying birds have large, keeled[G] breastbones, to which the wing muscles are attached.

- Birds' jaws are covered by bony bills, also called beaks.

- Female birds lay hard-shelled eggs in which the young develop.

- Birds communicate with each other by actions known as displays[G]. These involve songs, actions and the use of plumage.

The very first birds

The far ancestors[G] of birds were small, hollow-boned dinosaurs. Fossils show how these reptiles gradually changed into birds.

The most famous of these fossil creatures, Archaeopteryx (below left), lived around 140 million years ago. It had wings and legs like those of a bird, but a long tail, a reptilian snout and pointed teeth.

The Neornithes, the first of the modern groups of birds, appeared around 100 million years ago. Many of the groups of birds that existed during the "age of dinosaurs" survived the disappearance of dinosaurs around 65 million years ago.

Fossil feathers 125–110 million years old have been discovered near Melbourne, Victoria. Fossils of a penguin 1.4 m tall, which lived 45 million years ago, were found near Adelaide, South Australia.

Parts of a bird's body and plumage

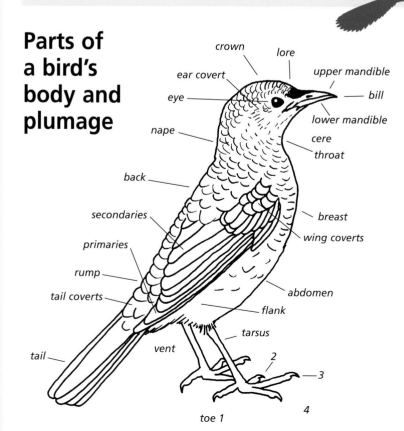

crown
lore
ear covert
upper mandible
eye
bill
lower mandible
nape
cere
throat
back
breast
secondaries
wing coverts
primaries
rump
abdomen
tail coverts
flank
tarsus
vent
tail
2
3
toe 1
4

Bird names

A bird may be known by several names:

1. **An official common name:** e.g. Rainbow Bee-eater.

2. **A scientific name:** e.g. *Merops ornatus*. This name is written in italics and the word order is reversed from the order in English.

3. **Unofficial local names:** e.g. "golden swallow", "gold-digger". In Indonesia, this bird's common name is "Kirik-kirik-australi", but its scientific name is the same, *Merops ornatus*.

Made to ride on air

The body of a bird has many features that make flying possible.

- The **feathers** provide surfaces that give lift and direction. They keep the bird's body warm as it flies through cold air.

- The **skeleton** has many hollow bones. These are made stronger by internal struts^G of bone. Some bones are fused for extra strength.

- The **breastbone** has a deep keel. This gives an attachment for the strong muscles that power the wings. (Flightless birds such as Emus and casssowaries lack this keel.)

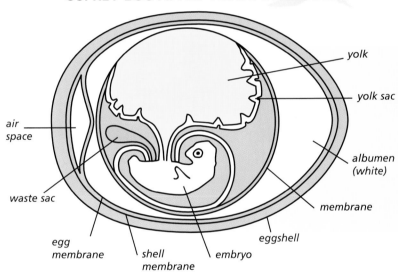

Red-tailed Tropicbird

- A **bird's lungs** remove around 25% more oxygen from each breath than any mammal lungs holding the same amount of air.

- **Air sacs** extend from a bird's lungs. These sacs may extend into some of the bird's larger bones, including the skull.

- A **bird's body** makes use of food and oxygen in a way that produces high levels of energy and heat.

Some types of feathers

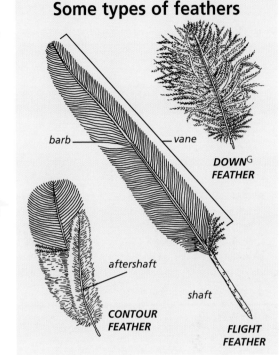

barb — vane

DOWN^G FEATHER

aftershaft

CONTOUR FEATHER

shaft

FLIGHT FEATHER

OSPREY EGG AFTER 4 DAYS INCUBATION^G

yolk

yolk sac

air space

albumen (white)

waste sac

membrane

egg membrane

shell membrane

embryo

eggshell

THE MIRACLE OF THE EGG

After a female bird has mated with a male, she lays a fertilised^G egg protected by a hard shell. If kept at a constant temperature for a suitable length of time, this egg will hatch into a baby bird. Some baby birds can look after themselves soon after hatching. Others must be protected, fed and warmed by their parents.

Feet

A bird's feet are used to perch, walk or hop, get and hold food, and preen and scratch. The foot usually has four toes (one may be small or absent). The toes may be webbed or have fleshy lobes^G. Each toe ends in a nail or claw.

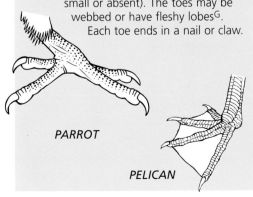

PARROT

PELICAN

The plumage of birds

A bird's feathers help it fly, protect its skin and help keep its body temperature constant at about 40°C.

The colour of its feathers may help a bird blend with its surroundings. Colour and shape of the feathers, and how they are raised and lowered, allows a bird to identify itself and give messages to other birds.

Feathers are very important to a bird and it looks after them carefully. A bird will often preen feathers by sliding them through its beak. This zips up the tiny barbs on wing and tail feathers. It also arranges all the feathers in order.

A bird may waterproof its feathers with oil from a gland on its rump. Some birds spread powder throughout their plumage. The powder comes from powderdown, special fraying feathers.

Most birds moult^G worn feathers each year while new feathers grow from underneath.

Australian King-Parrot

Groups of Australian Birds

The world's birds have been placed in 29 orders. One order, the Passerines (perching or songbirds) includes more species than all the other 28 orders put together. Australia's 750+ species of birds belong to 20 of the 29 orders. About half of Australia's species are non-passerines and half are passerines. The major groupings of Australian birds are shown below.

The 19 orders of Australian birds that are Non-passerines

OSTRICH-LIKE BIRDS
emus, cassowaries

FOWL-LIKE BIRDS
mound-builders, quail

WATERFOWL
ducks, geese, magpie geese, teal, shovelers, pygmy-geese, whistling ducks, shelducks

GREBES

PENGUINS

TUBE-NOSED SEABIRDS
giant-petrels, petrels, prions, shear-waters, diving-petrels, albatrosses, storm-petrels

WATERBIRDS WITH FOUR TOES WEBBED
tropicbirds, gannets and boobies, darters, cormorants and shags, pelican, frigatebirds

STORK-LIKE WATERBIRDS
herons, egrets, night herons, bitterns, ibises, spoonbills, storks

BIRDS OF PREY
bazas, kites, buzzards, sea-eagles, harriers, goshawks, sparrowhawks, eagles, ospreys, falcons

GROUND-LIVING BIRDS
cranes, crakes, rails, bush-hens, swamphens, moorhens, native-hens, coots, bustards

BUTTON-QUAILS

WADERS, SKUAS, GULLS & TERNS
plains-wanderer, snipe, godwits, curlews, sandpipers, redshanks, tattlers, turnstones, dowitchers, knots, stints, dunlin, phalaropes, painted snipes, jacanas, stone curlews, oystercatchers, stilts, plovers, pratincoles, skuas, gulls, terns

PIGEONS & DOVES

PARROTS
cockatoos, parrots, lorikeets, fig-parrots, rosellas, budgerigars

CUCKOOS
cuckoos, bronze-cuckoos, coucals

OWLS
hawk-owls, barn owls, boobooks

NIGHTJARS
frogmouths, nightjars, owlet-nightjars

SWIFTS
swifts, swiftlets

KINGFISHERS
kingfishers, kookaburras, bee-eaters, rollers

The Order of Passerines

Passerine birds have three forward-pointing toes and one non-reversible toe that points backwards. These toes allow passerines to perch securely on branches, and one name for this group is "perching birds". Passerines are also called "songbirds". They have well-developed voice boxes and use song to claim areas and to attract and court mates. Passerine chicks are hatched naked and helpless. Usually both parents, and sometimes other family members, feed and care for them.

pittas
lyrebirds
scrub-birds
treecreepers
pardalotes and their allies
honeyeaters
flycatchers
logrunners and chowchillas
fairy-wrens
babblers
quail-thrushes

sittellas
thickheads
monarchs
cuckoo-shrikes
orioles
crow-shrikes
birds of paradise
crows
mud-nest builders
bowerbirds
larks
pipits

finches
sunbirds
flowerpeckers
swallows
old world warblers
white-eyes
thrushes
starlings

Going birdwatching

To be sure of seeing a particular bird, you need to go where it can find food, water, safety, a mate and a place to nest.

Because most birds can fly, they often turn up in unlikely places, perhaps escaping drought or bushfires.

It's good to go birding with an expert, but it's fun to identify new birds for yourself.

Soon you will be able to recognise a bird by its "jizz" – you know immediately that only ONE sort of bird looks and behaves like that one.

Good places to look for birds

Town or city: parks; on buildings; harbour or riverside; home gardens; road verges; vacant blocks.

Bush and open forest: near water; in gullies; hollow trees; flowering trees; thick bushes.

Farmland: near water; irrigation; grain silos; crops; homesteads.

Desert: near water; in gorges; bushes and trees; plains.

Seaside: heathland; dunes; beach; ocean; estuaries[G]; mudflats.

Rainforest: near water; on forest floor; flowering trees; forest edges.

To study birds more closely:
zoo; wildlife park; museum; library; internet.

When to look for birds

The best time to see birds and to hear them singing is from before dawn to early morning, followed by late afternoon to dusk as a second choice. Fewest birds will be seen in the middle of the day, or in rainy or windy weather.

Comparative sizes of some Australian birds

Splendid Fairy-wren = Emu

Tiny (bill + body length 120–140 mm) Splendid Fairy-wren

Small (190–210 mm) Willy Wagtail

Small–medium (250–290 mm) Noisy Miner

Medium (380–440 mm) Australian Magpie

Large (690–760 mm) White Ibis

Very large (1.1–1.4 m) Black Swan

Huge (height 1.5–2 m) Emu

Watching birds is a never-ending adventure. First learn your local birds, then travel to new places and add new birds to your lifetime list. There are new discoveries to be made about even the most common birds. Write down your discoveries and draw or photograph the birds' behaviour.

Wear comfortable clothes and footwear and a hat. Take sunscreen, insect repellent, binoculars, notebook and a field guide to all of Australia's 750+ birds.

Find a place near birds, stay still, and watch quietly. In the bush, use your ears as well as your eyes.

In the open, stalk a bird by moving in zigzags towards it.

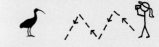

Jot down your discoveries in the field; write them up properly at home.

Check these important clues when identifying a bird:

Size – compare size to a bird you know.

Shape – of body, neck, bill, legs.

Colour – feathers, beak, cere, eyes, legs.

Behaviour – what is the bird doing?

Habitat – where is the bird feeding, nesting, etc.?

Range – could this bird be in this area?

Field notes will help you remember what you see.

Date: 4/1/96
Time: 4:30–5:30pm Place: Waterhole in State Forest, Moggill, Qld.
Weather: hot, cloudy, no wind
Observers: Sara and Brett Mitchell

Birds seen: Eastern Yellow Robin, Australian King-Parrot, Bar-shouldered Dove, Crested Pigeon, Noisy Miner, Variegated Fairywren, Tawny Frogmouth.

New bird:
Pale-headed Rosella

Emu

Dromaius novaehollandiae (= fast-footed Australian)

This huge, flightless bird is on the Australian Coat of Arms. It may be seen all over mainland Australia, except in the rainforest.

Emus must drink regularly and are usually found within walking distance of water.

They have shaggy grey-brown feathers, long necks and long legs. The bare skin on neck and face is pale blue. The female is larger than the male. She neither broods^G the eggs nor cares for the chicks.

Emus make far-carrying, booming, drumming calls.

These fast-running birds live in small mobs and eat green plants, seeds and insects. A male Emu incubates between 5 and 15 dark green eggs in a scrape on the ground for about 55 days. He cares for the striped chicks for up to 6 months.

When European settlers arrived, there were three island species of emu. These are now extinct. Today, Emus may be farmed for leather, meat and oil.

Height: 1.5–2 m
Weight: 35–50 kg

STATUS	X	E	P	V	S	SIZE	RANGE

Southern Cassowary

Casuarius casuarius (= horned head)

The Southern Cassowary lives in tropical rainforest in north-eastern Queensland. It is classed as endangered.

This huge, stocky, flightless bird has glossy black feathers. Its head bears a horny helmet and its neck and face are covered by bright blue skin. Red wattles hang from the neck.

A cassowary's inner toe has a long sharp nail. This is used as a defensive weapon.

Females are larger and more brightly coloured than males. They take no part in brooding eggs or caring for chicks.

Cassowary calls include hissing and booming.

This rare bird is generally seen alone or with chicks. It feeds on fallen fruits.

The male cassowary incubates 3 to 4 pea-green eggs on the ground for about 55 days. He then cares for the striped chicks.

Height: 1.5–1.9 m
Weight: ♀ 58 kg ♂ 34 kg

STATUS	X	E	P	V	S	SIZE	RANGE

Malleefowl

Leipoa ocellata (= eye-marked egg-leaver)

The rare and endangered Malleefowl lives in dry areas of southern Australia. These were originally covered with small eucalypt trees known as mallee.

It is a large, ground-living bird with mainly grey and fawn plumage. Its wings are marked with eye-like spots.

Malleefowl eat green leaves, seeds and insects.

Malleefowl mate for life. The male scrapes together sand to form a huge mound. Over a period, the female lays from 5 to 33 eggs in a nest of leaves in the mound. The leaves decay and warm the eggs. Each day, the male tests the temperature of the mound with the inside of his mouth. He adds sand to keep in warmth and scratches sand away to cool the eggs. A chick takes about 49 days to hatch. It does not need further parental care.

Land clearing, overgrazing by sheep and rabbits, and predation by foxes have all contributed to the decline of the Malleefowl.

Length: 600 mm
Weight: 1.5–2.5 kg

STATUS	X	E	P	V	S	SIZE	RANGE

Australian Brush-turkey

Alectura lathami (= Latham's cock-tailed bird)

This mound-builder lives in coastal rainforest from Cape York south to Gosford in New South Wales.

It is a large, mainly black, strong-legged, ground-living bird with an upright, fan-like tail. Both sexes have a nearly naked red head. The male has a bright yellow wattle that can be blown out when he is excited. The female's wattle is smaller and paler.

The male makes booming calls at his mound.

Brush-turkeys spend most of the day on the ground and roost in trees. They eat fruit, seed and insects. A male brush-turkey scratches together a nest mound of plant litter and soil. Females visit a mound to lay eggs, then are driven away. The male adds or removes material to keep the mound at 33°C.

Eggs take about 50 days to hatch, then the chicks look after themselves.

Clearing of forests has sent brush-turkeys into the outer suburbs. Their mound-building is not always welcome in gardens.

Length:
600–750 mm
Wingspan: 850 mm

STATUS	X	E	P	V	S	SIZE	RANGE

Black Swan
Cygnus atratus (= black swan)

The Black Swan, the bird emblem of Western Australia, may be seen anywhere in Australia. It may fly long distances, is always on or near water, and usually lives in flocks.

This is a very large, black swan with white wing-tips and a red bill. It may make loud bugling calls or croon softly.

Black Swans feed on waterweed and other plants growing near water. Swans nest after rain – a pair builds a nest of reeds and grasses on the ground or in shallow water. From 4 to 10 greenish eggs are incubated for up to 45 days. The cygnets stay with their parents for between 5 and 6 months.

While moulting, swans are flightless. They gather in large flocks on water.

Length: 1.1–1.4 m

Wingspan: 1.6–2 m

STATUS   X   E   P   V   **S**   SIZE   RANGE

Grey Teal
Anas gracilis (= slender duck)

The Grey Teal is probably Australia's most widespread duck. Flocks of them may arrive anywhere, even desert waterholes, after good rains fall.

This teal is small and slender for a duck. It has a steeply rising forehead and is mainly grey in colour.

Grey Teal often live in big flocks. They eat the seeds and shoots of water plants, and small water creatures.

If the rains have been heavy enough, pairs of teal nest in tree hollows or other suitable places. Each female lines her nest with down pulled from her breast. The male stays near while she broods, then helps care for the ducklings.

After breeding, Grey Teal moult heavily. They are flightless for around 16 days.

Length:
410–480 mm

Wingspan: 600–670 mm

STATUS   X   E   P   V   **S**   SIZE   RANGE

Australasian Grebe
Tachybaptus novaehollandiae (= Australian fast-diver)

The Australasian Grebe can be seen on freshwater wetlands, farm dams and park lakes in towns.

This small, grey-brown waterbird has a short bill, a dumpy body and a very short tail. When breeding, it has a yellow patch on each side of the head. The legs are set well back and the toes are lobed.

Grebes dive for fish and other water animals. If startled, they crash-dive and may stay under water for up to 20 seconds.

The nest is a small, floating platform of waterweed. Both parents incubate for 23 days. When either one leaves the eggs, it covers them with weed.

The chicks stay with their parents for 8 weeks. Adults may carry chicks on their backs.

Grebes often eat feathers, possibly to stop fishbones damaging their stomachs.

Length: 230–250 mm

Wingspan: 390 mm

STATUS   X   E   P   V   **S**   SIZE   RANGE

Little Penguin
Eudyptula minor (= small good-diver)

The world's smallest penguin lives in the sea off Australia's southern coast. It is the only penguin to breed in Australia.

The Little Penguin has sleek plumage, blue-grey above and white below.

Its calls include yaps, grunts and brays.

Little Penguins eat fish and other marine animals.

They nest on islands or coastal beaches, in burrows in sand or under rocks. Two white eggs are brooded by each parent in turn for a total of 36 days. The parents come to shore to feed their chicks at dusk, then return to the sea at dawn.

The chicks go to sea about 56 days after hatching. The adults stay on land to moult in their nest burrows.

Little Penguin colonies are threatened by beach habitat disturbance.

Length: 400–450 mm (stands 330 mm tall)

Weight: about 1 kg

STATUS   X   E   P   **V**   S   SIZE   RANGE

SEABIRDS

Birds that get their food from the ocean need to be able to fly or swim well. Many seabirds have webbed feet. Some have long, narrow wings and can glide for hours just above the waves. Others, such as albatrosses, may not come to land for many months. Seabirds can drink salt water. The water is used by the bird's body, while the salt drips out its nostrils in a very salty liquid.

Penguins, albatrosses, shearwaters, petrels, pelicans, boobies, tropicbirds, frigatebirds, cormorants, gulls and terns all find food on or in the ocean. They usually eat fish. Boobies and terns catch fish by plunge-diving. Penguins and cormorants chase fish under water. Frigatebirds chase other seabirds and peck them to make them drop their catch.

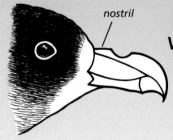

nostril

BILL OF GREAT-WINGED PETREL

Darter

Anhinga melanogaster (= black-bellied darter)

The Darter may be seen anywhere there is still, deep, fresh water. It may also be seen on or near salt water.

It is a large waterbird with a thin, kinked neck and a long tail. It is often seen sitting upright on a branch, wings outstretched. The male (right) is glossy black. The female is grey-brown above and whitish below. Young Darters are very pale in colour.

The call is a rattling, clicking noise and sometimes a hiss.

Darters swim with only their "snaky" necks and slender heads above the surface. They sink without a splash when alarmed. They spear fish under water, surfacing to shake them off their bills and swallow them.

A pair builds a large stick nest in a tree over water. Male and female incubate the 4 pale green eggs for 28 days. Both feed the young, who fledge in about 50 days.

Length: 860–940 mm **Wingspan:** 1.2 m
Weight: 1–2.6 kg

STATUS	X	E	P	V	S	SIZE		RANGE

Australian Pelican

Pelecanus conspicillatus (= spectacled pelican)

The Australian Pelican may be seen anywhere in Australia where there are water and fish. Flocks of pelicans fly high and far in search of fishing grounds.

This very large, black and white waterbird has short legs and a huge pink bill. All four of its toes are webbed.

The call is a soft grunt, or a creaking groan.

Pelicans feed on fish scooped up in their bills and throat pouches.

After heavy rain, pelicans nest in large flocks on islands in inland lakes. Two eggs are laid on the ground, brooded by both parents in turn for 32–35 days. At 25 days chicks join group "nurseries" called creches. They can fly at 3 months.

Length: 1.6–1.8 m **Wingspan:** 2.3–2.5 m
Weight: 4–6.8 kg

STATUS	X	E	P	V	S	SIZE		RANGE

Cattle Egret

Ardea ibis (= heron-ibis)

Cattle Egrets are usually seen with grazing animals, on coastal plains and wetlands.

They are medium-sized, stocky, short-necked, white herons. Their bills and feet are pale yellow. When breeding, the feathers of the neck and back are orange-buff and the bill is red.

Cattle Egrets eat insects, frogs and other small animals.

They roost over water and nest in large colonies with other waterbirds. A male chooses a nest site in a tree, then attracts a female by raising special courtship plumes[G] and waving sticks. The 3–6 pale blue eggs are incubated for 22–26 days by both parents.

This egret probably arrived in northern Australia about 1940. Since then, it has spread to all States. It does not breed in Victoria or Tasmania.

Length: 480–530 mm

STATUS	X	E	R	V	S	SIZE		RANGE

Sulphur-crested Cockatoo
Cacatua galerita (= cockatoo with a crest)

Cockatoos are large parrots with crests on their heads. The Sulphur-crested is found in forests and open country in northern and eastern Australia.

It is a medium to large cockatoo with a narrow yellow crest that it raises and fans when excited. Its plumage is mainly white with a yellow wash under the wings. The call is a harsh screeching.

Sulphur-crested Cockatoos gather in flocks when not breeding. They feed on the ground in the cooler part of the day on seeds, bulbs, roots and insect larvae. When sitting around, these sociable, playful birds may strip bark from trees.

These cockatoos nest in hollows in large, old trees, usually near water. The 2 or 3 white eggs are incubated for 30 days.

Length: 450–500 mm

STATUS	X	E	P	V	S	SIZE	RANGE

Crimson Rosella
Platycercus elegans (= flat-tailed, elegant bird)

The Crimson Rosella lives in forest edges and wood-land in eastern and south-eastern coastal Australia, from Cairns to South Australia.

It is a medium-sized parrot with a red head, rump and underparts. The back is mottled red and black. The cheek patches, outer-wing feather and tail are blue. In eastern South Australia, some birds have yellow feathers replacing the red found further east. The call is a bell-like chiming and a chattering.

These rosellas wander the forest edges looking for seeds and fruit. They feed in trees and on the ground.

Rosellas pair for life. A courting bird spreads and wags its tail. The female incubates 4–5 white eggs in a tree hollow for 19–21 days. Both parents feed the chicks.

Length: 320–360 mm

STATUS	X	E	P	V	S	SIZE	RANGE

Yellow-tailed Black-Cockatoo
Calyptorhynchus funereus (= funereal cover-beak)

These very large cockatoos are found in coastal areas and ranges from Rockhampton, Queensland, to Tasmania, and west to South Australia.

The tail makes up roughly half a bird's length. The male has black feathers edged with yellow, a small yellow cheek patch and a brown eye surrounded by pink skin. The female has a grey eye surrounded by grey skin, and a larger, brighter cheek patch.

These cockatoos eat pine, banksia and hakea seeds. From Rockhampton to Gippsland, they also eat wood-boring insect larvae.

A pair nests in a tree hollow high above the ground. The female incubates the 2 eggs for 6 weeks, while the male feeds her. Only 1 chick survives, and is fed by both parents. It does not become independent until the next nesting season.

Length: 500–600 mm

STATUS	X	E	P	V	S	SIZE	RANGE

Rainbow Lorikeet
Trichoglossus haematodus (= hair-tongued blood-red bird)

Rainbow Lorikeets live in the coastal lowlands of northern and eastern Australia. An introduced group lives in Western Australia, in Perth.

This is a medium-sized lorikeet with a red bill, blue head, green underparts, red-gold breastband and blue belly. Its call is a metallic screech, often given while in flight.

Swift, noisy flocks search for flowering trees. Lorikeets mop up nectar with their "brush-tipped" tongues. They also eat fruit, seed and insects.

Large groups roost together, chattering and screeching before settling to sleep.

A pair mates for life. The female is fed by the male while she incubates 2 white eggs in a tree hollow. Both parents feed the young.

Length: 300–320 mm

STATUS	X	E	P	V	S	SIZE	RANGE

Tawny Frogmouth

Podargus strigoides (= trap-footed owl-like bird)

The Tawny Frogmouth may be seen anywhere in Australia. It is often in a pair or family group.

It is a medium-sized, night-active bird, with mottled and streaked grey, brown, black and white plumage. It has a wide bill, weak legs and small feet. During the day it sleeps on a branch or in a fork. When alarmed, it points its beak skyward and freezes. The call, given at night, is a soft, repeated *oom-oom-oom*.

Frogmouths hunt after dark, perching, then flying down to snap up insects, frogs and other small animals.

Male and female mate for life. They build a flimsy stick nest in a tree fork, incubate 1–3 white eggs for 28–32 days, then feed the young.

Insecticides eaten with prey may be stored in a frogmouth's body fat. When this fat is used in cold weather, the frogmouth may die.

Length: 350–530 mm

STATUS	X	E	P	V	S	SIZE		RANGE

BIRDS OF THE NIGHT

Frogmouths, nightjars and owlet-nightjars are related to each other. Owls are in another family of birds altogether. All are night hunters.

Nightbirds roost and sleep during the daytime. Their plumage colours blend with their surroundings. If disturbed, they freeze, for other birds will mob them if they are detected.

Frogmouths, nightjars and owlet-nightjars have wide gapes^G, sharp-edged beaks and weak feet. They catch their prey in their beaks and use their feet only for perching and grooming themselves.

Owls have narrow, hooked beaks and strong toes ending in sharp talons. They seize their prey in their talons, killing it either with their feet or their beaks. Barn Owls can locate prey using hearing alone.

All these nightbirds have soft, flexible^G feathers that make no noise as they fly.

Barking Owl

Barn Owl

Tyto alba (= white owl)

The Barn Owl may be found all over Australia, especially in open woodland and on plains. It may live around farms and in caves.

It is a medium-sized, pale-coloured owl, with a heart-shaped, white facial disc. The eyes are dark. The bill and long, bare legs are pale. The bird has white underparts, with grey-gold upper parts, and black and white spots on the wings.

The call is a rasping hiss, like cloth ripping.

Barn Owls roost during the day in hollows, foliage or caves. Pellets of food remains accumulate under roosts.

They hunt mice and other small mammals after dark, locating prey by sound and keen night vision. Numbers build up in mouse plagues, but afterwards many owls die.

The nest is in a tree hollow or cave. The larger female incubates the 3–7 white eggs for 33–35 days. The male helps feed the chicks.

Length: 300–400 mm

STATUS	X	E	P	V	S	SIZE		RANGE

Southern Boobook

Ninox novaeseelandiae (= New Zealand night-bird)

This small, dark-coloured owl is found all over Australia. It may live in city suburbs, catching moths at outdoor lights and visiting bird baths. It is most often located by its call, a repeated *boo-book*, the first note higher than the second.

The Boobook has a circular disc around each yellow-green eye, a dark bill and shortish, feathered legs. The upper parts are brown with white spots. The underparts are streaked white, and the wings are barred.

Boobooks hunt for small roosting birds, insects and small mammals. They are most active in the hours just after sunset and just before sunrise.

A courting pair sits side by side preening^G each other. The nest is in a tree hollow. The female incubates 2–4 white eggs for about 30 days while being fed by the male. Both parents feed the young.

In the daytime, birds will mob a roosting Boobook.

Length: 250–350 mm

STATUS	X	E	P	V	S	SIZE		RANGE

Shining Bronze-Cuckoo
Chrysococcyx lucidus (= shining golden-cuckoo)

The Shining Bronze-Cuckoo can be seen in high-rainfall coastal areas from Cape York to South Australia, and in the south-west of Western Australia.

It is a small, plump bird with loose-looking feathers and a fine bill. It has a shining green-bronze back and striped underparts. The wings are slender and pointed.

The male calls in a repeated high, rising whistle, like someone calling a dog.

Cuckoos eat insects, including hairy caterpillars, which most birds will not touch.

Shining Bronze-Cuckoos winter in the islands north of Australia and arrive in Australia in August. They breed by January, then most of them migrate^G north again.

A male attracts a female by calling. After mating, the female places an egg in a host nest. She may lay up to 16 eggs in one season. Each cuckoo chick hatches in 17 days, shoves out the hosts' eggs or chicks, then is raised by the hosts.

Length: 170–180 mm

STATUS	X	E	P	V	S	SIZE	RANGE

Sacred Kingfisher
Todiramphus sanctus (= sacred tody-bill*)

In spring and summer, this kingfisher can be found all over Australia, except for the driest parts. It spends March to October in the islands to Australia's north.

It is a small kingfisher with a black mask, a buff spot in front of the eye and a white collar. The upper parts are blue-green, and it has a blue edge to each wing and a blue tail. The underparts are pale buff.

The call is a repeated, sharp *kik-kik-kik*.

Sacred Kingfishers perch on wires or branches, watching for insects, frogs or reptiles. They may catch tadpoles or small fish in shallow water.

A pair digs a tunnel in a termite nest, tree limb or earth bank. They take turns to incubate 3–6 white eggs for 16–17 days. Both feed the chicks.

Length: 190–230 mm

* Todies are West Indian birds that have long bills.

STATUS	X	E	P	V	S	SIZE	RANGE

Laughing Kookaburra
Dacelo novaeguineae (= New Guinea kingfisher)

This medium-sized bird (but large kingfisher) lives in woodland and open forest in north-eastern, eastern and south-eastern Australia. It has been introduced to south-western Western Australia.

It has a dark mask, dark eye and brown upper parts, and a white collar and underparts. There is pale blue on the wing, and the brown tail is barred black. In flight, it shows a white band across the wing.

The call is a chuckling and a loud "laughing", often made by a group. Laughing Kookaburras perch on wires or branches, watching for insects, frogs and reptiles.

They nest in tree hollows or holes in termite mounds. From 1 to 4 white eggs are incubated for 24 days by the male and helpers. Unmated young birds, up to 4 years of age, help their parents to incubate and feed the chicks.

Length: 400–450 mm

STATUS	X	E	P	V	S	SIZE	RANGE

Rainbow Bee-eater
Merops ornatus (= ornate bee-eater)

The Rainbow Bee-eater lives in open country with trees and bushes to perch on, and sand or earth banks for nesting in. It may be seen anywhere in mainland Australia.

It is a dainty, slender-winged, green-gold bird with a fine down-curving bill. It has a black mask, a black throat, gold on the head and under the wings, and two long central tail feathers.

The call is a repeated *prrrp-prrrp*, often given in flight.

Bee-eaters sit on wires or branches, darting out to take flying dragonflies, wasps or other insects. They may roost in large groups.

These birds dig a 1 m tunnel into flat, sandy ground or an earth bank. A mated pair may be helped by young, unmated birds. The 4–5 white eggs are incubated for 21–25 days. The young leave the nest at 1 month.

Rainbow Bee-eaters breed in Australia. Most spend winter in islands to the north.

Length: 210–240 mm

STATUS	X	E	P	V	S	SIZE	RANGE

A LAND OF SINGING BIRDS

Birds sing by forcing air past membranes that stretch across their voice boxes. The pitch[G] of each note is controlled by muscles that tighten or relax the membranes. Passerine birds have many muscles in their voice boxes and make some of the world's most beautiful sounds. Australian passerines, such as the lyrebirds, butcherbirds, Australian Magpie, whistlers and shrike-thrushes, are renowned for their songs.

Australia has a number of passerines found nowhere else in the world. They include lyrebirds, pardalotes and chats.

Lyrebirds are possibly the world's most remarkable mimics. They imitate not only the songs of other birds, but also a wide range of sounds.

Pardalotes live in eucalypts, eating lerps[G] and other pests of these trees.

Chats are desert nomads (wanderers), which arrive in an area after rain. They breed in small colonies, then disperse widely again as the desert dries out.

Superb Lyrebird
Menura novaehollandiae (= mighty-tailed Australian bird)

This lyrebird lives in the coastal wet forests of south-eastern mainland Australia and Tasmania. It is vanishing as its forest habitat is logged and disturbed.

The Superb Lyrebird is a large brown ground-bird. The male's long, filmy tail is thrown over the back in displays. The female has a shorter, plainer tail. Lyrebirds eat small creatures scratched from the forest floor.

A male lyrebird is a fine songster and mimic. He claims territory by singing and dancing on earthen display mounds. Females come to the mounds to mate. A female lyrebird builds a domed nest of sticks. She incubates 1 blotched egg for up to 50 days, then cares for the young by herself.

Length: ♂ 0.8–1 m
(of which tail is 500–600 mm)

STATUS	X	E	**P**	V	S	SIZE	RANGE

Spotted Pardalote
Pardalotus punctatus (= spotted spotted-bird)

This tiny bird lives in wet forests in eastern, south-eastern and south-western Australia. It is seldom seen, but its high *sleep-baby* call is often heard.

It is a short-tailed, stubby-beaked bird that feeds in the treetops. Its black crown, wings and tail are spotted with white. Back and rump are yellow to red and the undertail is yellow.

Pardalotes move quickly through the leaves of eucalypts, feeding on lerps and other insects. Flocks may fly to warmer feeding grounds in winter.

A pair digs a nest tunnel in an earth bank, wall or mound of garden soil. In a nest-chamber lined with bark and grass, male and female take turns to incubate 3–6 white eggs for 14 days. Both parents feed the chicks.

Pardalotes are found only in Australia. The Forty-spotted Pardalote, found only in south-eastern Tasmania, is an endangered species.

Length: 90–100 mm

STATUS	X	E	P	V	**S**	SIZE	RANGE

Crimson Chat
Ephthianura tricolor (= three-coloured decreasing-tail)

Chats are tiny birds that live in the drier parts of Australia. Large numbers of chats may turn up in an area after heavy rain. They breed while the good conditions last. Then they move on in search of food. They may not return to a place for years, until more rains fall.

The male Crimson Chat has a crimson crown, breast and rump, and a white bib. The back and tail are brownish. The female is less brightly coloured than the male.

The call is a high, often repeated *tseee*.

Crimson Chats walk with their heads nodding. They feed mainly on ground-living insects and will also eat nectar.

A pair of chats builds a shallow cup nest of grass in a low bush. After the 3 spotted white eggs hatch, both parents feed the chicks.

Length: 100–120 mm

STATUS	X	E	P	V	**S**	SIZE	RANGE

Noisy Miner

Manorina melanocephala (= black-headed thin-nose)

The Noisy Miner normally lives in woodlands in eastern and south-eastern Australia. It has become a common bird in gardens and parks.

A small, loud-voiced, aggressive honeyeater, it has a short bill, a white forehead, black crown, grey upper parts and white underparts. The bill, bare skin behind the eye and the legs are yellow.

The call is a loud *zwit*. The flight call is *teu-teu-teu*. Miners signal each other by calling, by posing, and by raising or lowering their head feathers to hide or flash the yellow skin near their eyes.

Noisy Miners feed on nectar, fruit and insects.

They live in groups consisting of up to 30 birds. A group defends its territory by shrieking and mobbing, and will drive same-size birds of all types away.

The nest is a cup of bark and grass in the outer foliage of a tree. The dominant female of a group builds the nest and lays 3–4 speckled eggs in it. Other group members incubate the eggs for 15–16 days, then feed the chicks.

Length: 250–290 mm

STATUS	X	E	P	V	S	SIZE	RANGE

Eastern Spinebill

Acanthorhynchus tenuirostris (= narrow-beaked spine-bill)

The Eastern Spinebill is a tiny honeyeater that lives in forests, heaths and gardens in eastern Australia and Tasmania.

This colourful honeyeater has a long, slender bill. The male has a black head and a black, curved stripe on each side of his breast. His bib, nape and abdomen are cinnamon. The female is generally duller in appearance.

Spinebills may hover in front of flowers while feeding.

The call is a short, sharp piping or a softer *chee-chee-chee*.

A pair of spinebills makes a neat cup of bark, grass and hair, bound together with cobweb, in a low bush or tree. The 1–3 pinkish or bluish eggs are spotted and blotched.

Length: 130–160 mm

STATUS	X	E	P	V	S	SIZE	RANGE

BIRDS AND FLOWERS

Honeyeaters, lorikeets, chats and sunbirds get some or all of their food from flowers. They may eat insects that gather around the flowers, or they may feed on the nectar and pollen the flowers contain.

*Some groups of Australian wildflowers have developed so that birds can easily get these rewards. While a bird is feeding, it becomes dusted with pollen. This pollen is carried to the next flower visited, and may fertilise*G *it.*

Different sorts of honeyeater have bills of different lengths. Each bill is just right for probing into a particular type of native flower.

A honeyeater's long tongue has upcurved sides and four brushes at the tip. When the tongue tip is loaded with nectar, the bird pulls it in and pushes it against the roof of its mouth. Nectar is squeezed down the grooves at the base of the tongue and down the bird's throat.

Eastern Yellow Robin

Eopsaltria australis (= southern dawn-harper)

The Eastern Yellow Robin is found in forests and woodlands with bushy undergrowth in eastern Australia.

It is a small, plump bird with yellow underparts and rump. The chin is white and the upper parts are grey. A white wingbar shows when the bird flies.

The call is a loud whistle, *tewp-tewp*; a soft piping is often given before dawn.

Eastern Yellow Robins hunt insects by perching, watching, then pouncing. They may cling sideways to tree trunks.

A mated pair holds a territory. The female builds a cup nest of bark and grass bound by cobwebs, decorated outside with lichens, in a tree fork. The male feeds her while she incubates 2–3 spotted eggs for 15–16 days. Both parents, plus helpers from previous broods, feed the young.

Length: 140–150 mm

STATUS	X	E	P	V	S	SIZE	RANGE

Golden Whistler
Pachycephala pectoralis (= breasted thick-head)

The Golden Whistler's call rings through the forests of southern and eastern Australia and south-western Western Australia.

It is a small, large-headed bird that sits upright and moves slowly when feeding. The male has a black head and collar, and a white throat. His nape and breast are gold and his upper parts are green. The female is grey-brown, with a white throat.

The call is a rich *wh-wh-wh-you wit*, with a whipcrack ending.

Whistlers are seen alone or in pairs, moving through the leaves, eating insects. Male and female both sing and defend the territory. They build a cup nest of stems and leaves bound with with cobwebs, in a fork. They take turns to incubate the 2 spotted eggs for 14–17 days. Both feed the young.

A loud noise may start whistlers singing. In winter, mountain and southern birds may move to warmer areas.

Length: 160–170 mm

STATUS				X E		P

Willy Wagtail
Rhipidura leucophrys (= white-browed fan-tail)

The Willy Wagtail can be seen anywhere in mainland Australia and in northern Tasmania.

This well-known small bird has black upper parts and throat, and white underparts and eyebrows. A dominant bird will flash its white eyebrows at another bird. The long tail is often fanned and wagged from side to side.

The song, *sweet-pretty-creature*, is often heard on moonlight nights. The aggressive call is a rattling noise.

Willy Wagtails catch insects in flight. They hop around taking prey on open ground.

Male and female build a cup nest of bark and grass, bound together with cobwebs, on a branch. They incubate the 2–4 spotted eggs for 14 days, then both feed the chicks.

Length: 190–210 mm

STATUS	X	E	P	V	S	SIZE		RANGE

Australian Magpie
Gymnorhina tibicen (= flute-playing naked-nose)

The Australian Magpie lives in open country with trees, all over Australia. It is common in towns and cities.

It is a medium-sized, strong-legged bird with a black head and underparts, a white nape and white on the wing. Over most of eastern and northern Australia, both sexes have black backs. In Victoria, Tasmania and the south-west of Western Australia, the male has a white back, the female an ashy-grey back.

The song is loud and sweet.

A group of up to 24 birds defends a territory. They feed on the ground on small creatures. A dominant male mates with several females. A female builds a nest of sticks in a tall tree, lays 3–5 blotched eggs, incubates them for 20 days and feeds the young. Once out of the nest, young may be fed by others in the group. Young birds are later driven from the group and form roving flocks. Nests supported by a dominant male have the best chance of succeeding.

(If a magpie defending a nest becomes aggressive, wear a hat, or take another route that bypasses the nest.)

Length: 380–440 mm

STATUS	X	E	P	V	S	SIZE		RANGE

BLACK AND WHITE

Australia's black and white birds include the Pied and Grey Butcherbirds, Magpie-lark, Australian Magpie, Willy Wagtail, ravens, crows and currawongs. These pied[G] birds are noted for their tolerance of humans. They live in the hearts of towns and cities and may nest close to houses.

Pied birds are aggressive in defending their territories. They use their loud songs to claim ownership of their particular area.

Often they live in family groups. Special calls signal alarm or summon other group members to harass a snake, cat or bird of prey.

Pied Butcherbird

Satin Bowerbird

Ptilonorhynchus violaceus (= blue feather-bill)

The Satin Bowerbird is found in the mountain and coastal forests of eastern Australia.

The male is a medium-sized, blue-black bird with mauve eyes. The female and young male have green upper parts and creamy underparts with dark markings on breast and belly. Males do not get full blue plumage until they are 6 or 7 years old.

Males build avenues of sticks in forest clearings. They decorate these bowers with blue objects and paint them with plant juices and saliva[G]. Each male sings, mimics and dances at his bower. A female will inspect several bowers. She mates with the male with the finest bower, then builds a twig nest in a tree. She incubates 1–3 spotted and blotched eggs for 21–22 days, then raises the young by herself.

These bowerbirds flock in autumn and winter, seeking fruit and seeds. In spring, males return to their bowers.

Length: 270–330 mm

STATUS	X	E	P	V	S	SIZE		RANGE

BIRDS IN BOWERS

Bowerbirds are fruit-eating songbirds that are usually found in the rainforests of Australia and New Guinea.

Males mate with more than one female and do not take any part in nest-building, incubation or rearing the young. They build platforms and avenues on the ground, then paint them with plant juice and saliva, using a twig as a brush. They decorate their bowers with mosses, flowers, shells, bones and other objects, then sing and dance around them to attract females. Mating often takes place in the bower.

A young male spends some years in female-like plumage. During this time he practises building bowers and hangs around the bowers of older birds.

Bowerbirds may steal sticks and decorations from each other. Females seem to choose as mates the males with the best bowers and most attractive displays. Males give their own calls and also mimic other birds' songs as well as other noises.

Great Bowerbird

Black-faced Woodswallow

Artamus cinereus (= ash-coloured butcher)

Woodswallows are unusual passerines. They soar like small birds of prey and have powderdown feathers like herons and egrets.

The Black-faced Woodswallow may be seen anywhere in Australia except for the wetter south. It is a small, long-winged grey bird with a black face and a blue, black-tipped beak.

Woodswallows perch on wires or branches. They may soar and catch flying insects in the air. Sometimes they eat nectar. In cold weather, a group of birds may huddle on a branch, or roost together in a tree hollow. Members of the group may preen each other.

A pair builds an untidy twig nest in a bush, a stump or a weathered fence post. The 3–4 eggs are white or bluish with darker blotches. Both parents rear the young. Sometimes they are helped by other woodswallows.

Length: 180–190 mm

STATUS	X	E	P	V	S	SIZE		RANGE

Zebra Finch

Taeniopygia guttata (= spotted banded-rump)

The Zebra Finch is one of the world's best-known cage birds.

Wild Zebra Finches are found all over Australia except for Cape York Peninsula, the extreme south-west of Western Australia and south-eastern Tasmania. They live where there is grass seed to eat, bushes to nest in and water to drink.

The Zebra Finch is a tiny, red-billed bird with black and white on its face and chestnut cheek patches. It has grey upper parts, a black and white rump, and red flanks with white spots on them.

The call is a nasal *tang*.

These finches can survive dry conditions. They breed after rain has fallen when seed is plentiful. The male fetches grass, while the female builds a hollow ball of grass with a side tunnel entrance. Both birds incubate the 4–5 white eggs for 12–14 days, then feed the young.

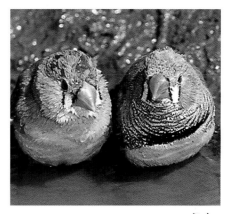

Length: 100 mm

STATUS	X	E	P	V	S	SIZE		RANGE	

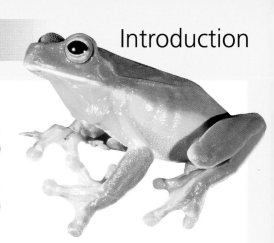

Australia's Frogs & Reptiles

What is a frog?

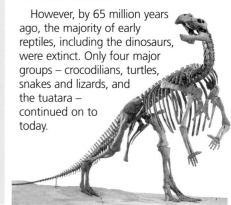

Australian Bullfrog

- Frogs are vertebrate animals, whose central spinal cords and brains are protected by backbones and skulls.

- Frogs are "cold-blooded" (ectothermic[G]). Their body temperatures are influenced by the temperature of their surroundings.

- Adult frogs have four limbs.

- A frog's skin is moist and contains glands. It may act as a breathing organ.

- Frogs shed eggs and sperm[G] in damp places or in water. Fertilised eggs hatch into tadpoles. These have tails, gills[G] and no limbs. They eat plants.

- As tadpoles mature, they lose their tails and gills, grow limbs, and develop lungs. They become air-breathing, land-living, tailless adults that eat small animals.

- Frogs are called amphibians[G], meaning "animals with two ways of living". They are the only group of amphibians native to Australia. The Cane Toad is introduced.

Common ancestors

Frogs and reptiles share common ancestors. These were the early amphibians that crawled from the seas towards the end of the Devonian Period of Earth's history (around 370 million years ago).

A group of these amphibians developed into reptiles, which became the dominant animal group on earth. These reptiles included the dinosaurs, which grew to huge sizes. There were also small dinosaurs[G].

However, by 65 million years ago, the majority of early reptiles, including the dinosaurs, were extinct. Only four major groups – crocodilians, turtles, snakes and lizards, and the tuatara – continued on to today.

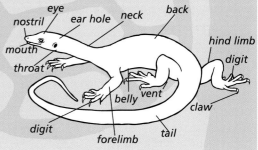

What is a reptile?

- Reptiles are vertebrate animals whose spinal cords and brains are protected by backbones and skulls.

- Reptiles are "cold-blooded" (ectothermic). Their body temperatures are influenced by the temperature of their surroundings.

- Some reptiles have four limbs. Some have two. Some have none, or only the remnants of hind limbs.

- A reptile's dry skin is covered by scales.

- Reptiles live in many habitats on land and in the ocean. They are most common in warmer climates.

- The sperm produced by a male reptile fertilises a female's eggs inside her body. The eggs are enclosed in shells and are usually laid on land. Some species retain the eggs inside the body until they have hatched.

- There are four groups of reptiles alive today. The three groups found in Australia are turtles, crocodilians, and lizards and snakes. The Tuatara survives in New Zealand.

Differences between frogs and reptiles

A FROG

Egg emerges from the mother's body in jelly.

Egg laid in moisture or water.

Egg fertilised outside the mother's body.

Tadpole (different from an adult frog) hatches from the egg.

Tadpole undergoes great changes in order to become an adult.

Adult frog has moist, glandular skin.

Frog has no tail. It always has four limbs, although in some species they are small.

Frog breathes through lungs, skin and inside of mouth.

Frogs eat insects and other animals.

Frog diagram labels: digit (finger), nostril, iris, pupil, gland, tympanum (eardrum), web, vocal sac, skin fold, groin, disc, digit (toe), vent, back of thigh

A REPTILE

Egg has tough shell that dries quickly.

Egg laid in warm, dry place.

Egg fertilised inside the mother's body.

Smaller version of adult hatches from egg.

Young reptile undergoes only minor changes as it becomes adult. Main change is growing larger.

Adult has dry skin covered with scales.

Reptile has a tail and may have 4, 2 or no visible limbs.

Reptile usually breathes through lungs or, rarely, skin.

Reptiles usually eat animals, but a few eat plants.

Reptile diagram labels: eye, neck, back, nostril, ear hole, hind limb, mouth, digit, throat, belly, vent, claw, digit, forelimb, tail

Finding frogs and reptiles

WHERE to see them

Frogs live in damp places. During the day they hide in burrows, under bark, or amongst reeds or leaves. At night, they sit in the open and search for food.

Snakes live where there is prey. They hide in burrows, amongst rubbish, under leaves, and under rocks and wood. In cold weather, they shelter under old pieces of corrugated iron.

Wildlife parks and zoos often have good reptile displays. There are people who breed and release frogs. Field trips to see rare frogs in the wild, as well as crocodiles, marine turtles, seasnakes and other reptiles, can be planned.

WHEN to see them

Frogs are most active at night, especially in rainy weather.

They are most common in damp places.

If three people shine torches from different angles at a calling frog, the frog will be where the beams meet.

Most reptiles are active during the day. Spot them basking in the sun in the early morning or late afternoon.

Some reptiles (e.g. crocodiles, geckos and various snakes) are active on warm nights. Look for them with a torch when they could be out hunting prey.

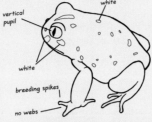

Date: 24 May, 2000
Time: 8:30 p.m.
Place: 77 Grevillea Rd.
Upper Swan. W.A.

Weather: Warm and humid: rain 5–6 p.m.
Observer: Chris Weigall

vertical pupil

white

white

breeding spikes

no webs

Length HB = 6.4 cm
Notes: Call koop-koop or coo-coo. Found frog on sandy soil near swampy area in horse paddock. Underside of first finger of hand had black spikes. Breeding male?
WESTERN SPOTTED FROG
Heleioporus albopunctatus

Remember: Frog calls are important aids to identification. Make a note of them.

Making field notes

It may be difficult to identify a frog or reptile in the field. If it is protected by law, it cannot be taken home for checking against guide books.

A field sketch can give information which, if needed, can later be checked with experts.

Some exciting frog and reptile discoveries have resulted from studying fresh roadkill. However, when looking at roadkill it is wise to avoid becoming one!

Identifying frogs and reptiles

There are many good books and field guides about groups of Australian animals.

When trying to identify an animal, it is usually easy to narrow down the possibilities from the maps and photos in a book. To identify an animal further, many books offer "keys".

A key is a list of paired descriptions, numbered in sequence from 1 onwards. It is used as follows:

Compare the animal to the first pair of descriptions (1). One or the other description will apply to the animal. On the right-hand side of that description will be either the animal's name or a number.

If the answer is a number, go to that number and read the pair of descriptions. Choose the one that fits the animal.

The matching description will lead to either the animal's name or another number (in which case repeat the process).

Eventually you will find the animal's name.

A key to identify the first five frog species in this book:

1	Tips of digits with large discs	2
	Tips of digits with small discs	**Striped Rocket-frog**
2	Colour of back green	3
	Colour of back not green	4
3	Colour of iris orange-red	**Red-eyed Tree-frog**
	Colour of iris gold	**Green Tree-frog**
4	Colour of back grey to red-brown, groin yellow	**Naked (Red) Tree-frog**
	Colour of back brown, groin and thigh red	**Blue Mountains Tree-frog**

BEWARE, take care!

Very few wild mammals or birds can be caught or handled. Frogs and reptiles are easier to lay hands on, especially if the weather is cold.

However, these animals have in-built defences and should be left alone. Injury or death can be the penalty of touching the wrong creature.

Some frogs and all Cane Toads have skin glands that produce poison[G]. If this reaches mouth, eyes or an open skin wound, the results could be serious. Frogs and toads should be handled with care. Always wash your hands after touching an amphibian.

Crocodiles are very dangerous animals. Even a small one can give a nasty bite and a large one can kill a human. Swimming where there are Saltwater Crocodiles is not a good idea.

Northern Banjo Frog: Holding a frog may harm the frog. It may also be harmful to the holder.

There are no venomous lizards in Australia. Some lizards, particularly monitors (goannas) can bite hard. Since they eat carrion, a bite may become infected.

About 20 species of Australian snakes produce venom that can kill a human. Because of this, no snake should be touched or handled.

If snakebite occurs, an elastic bandage should be wrapped firmly around the bitten limb. The victim should remain quiet. Reach medical help as soon as possible.

Bushwalkers should wear boots, socks and long trousers. Leave snakes alone.

Some wildlife parks have displays in which reptiles may be seen close up.

Being a frog

Staying damp

A frog's naked skin has no protective scales, feathers or fur. It has many glands that produce liquids of various kinds. Oxygen can pass into a frog's blood vessels through its skin. Waste substances also pass out through the skin.

Frogs' survival depends on their skin staying moist. They have developed ways of life that make this possible.

Ornate Burrowing Frogs mating. Fertilised eggs & jelly form frog spawn^G.

• Frog blood contains a chemical that slows down the process of water escaping through the skin.

• Frogs live in damp places.

• They expose their bodies to water as often as possible.

• They shelter from heat during the warmer, drier day.

• They feed and are active during the cooler, moister night.

• During hot, dry conditions some frogs dig burrows. They go into summer sleep (aestivation^G).

• Desert frogs have very brief egg and tadpole stages.

Defence and offence

The liquid that oozes from a frog's skin glands onto the skin surface helps keep the frog's body moist. This liquid also carries a number of substances:

Mucus^G is a thin slime that hardens as it dries. It helps prevent a frog's skin drying out.

Mucus also makes a frog's body slippery, so an attacker cannot get a good grip on it.

Some chemicals produced by frogs' skin glands may act as antibiotics. They protect the frogs from harmful bacteria.

Other chemicals may act as fungicides. They prevent harmful fungi growing on the frogs' skins.

Some frogs have large glands on their necks, backs, shoulders or legs. These glands produce creamy liquid that may be nasty-tasting or poisonous.

A frog with these defensive glands may have warning flashes of red, orange or yellow, and black on its skin. An attacker that bites the frog may be poisoned.

The Cane Toad can squirt the poisonous liquid from its neck or shoulder glands at an attacker. Its range is up to 1 m.

The skin glands on this Moaning Frog's back are oozing poisonous liquid.

The swellings on this Green Tree-frog's neck are full of liquid.

A FROG'S LIFE CYCLE

(a)
(b)
(c)
(d)
(e)
(f)

(a) Adult frogs mate
(b) Eggs hatch
(c) Tadpoles grow
(d) Hind legs develop
(e) Front leg emerges

(f) Other front leg emerges. Then the tail is absorbed, the lungs develop and finally the frog leaves the water

The *DEADLY* Cane Toad

Frogs are the only group of amphibians found naturally in Australia. Toads are not native to the continent. The Cane Toad is native to the northern parts of South America and Central America. In days when insect-killing chemicals were not available, this toad was introduced into around 15 countries to eat insect pests. In 1935, it was introduced to the Cairns area of north-eastern Queensland to eat beetles that damaged sugar cane. However, it did not control the beetles and it ate any small creature it could catch. Its eggs, tadpole and adult are all poisonous. Many native animals, as well as domestic pets, have died after mouthing or eating Cane Toads.

Cane Toad

Groups of Australian frogs

Scientists place the world's amphibians into one big group named Class Amphibia (Amphibians).

Class Amphibia is divided into three groups called Orders. The only Order found naturally in Australia is the Order Anura.

Worldwide, the Order Anura contains more than 2000 species of frogs and toads.

The following table shows how Australia's frogs and the introduced Cane Toad fit into this system of classification.

Family: BUFONIDAE (toads)

The differences between frogs and toads are small. Toads have warty skins. However, some Australian frogs have rough skins. The Cane Toad can be told from rough-skinned frogs by its horizontal pupils, large size and shoulder glands. Unlike the frogs, it will eat food that does not move.

Only one species, the introduced Cane Toad, lives in Australia.

Cane Toad

Class: AMPHIBIA
(= animals with two ways of living)
Order: ANURA
(= tailless amphibians)

Family: HYLIDAE (tree-frogs and their allies)

Tree-frogs and their allies are grouped together because some of their bone and muscle features are similar.

The family includes tree-frogs, which climb by using round, sticking discs at the ends of their fingers and toes. It also includes water-holding, burrowing frogs which have hard, shovel-like edges on their feet. These are used for digging.

A CLIMBING TREE-FROG: The Red-eyed Tree-frog has discs at the ends of all its digits.

Family: MYOBATRACHIDAE (southern frogs)

Many members of the southern frog group give some sort of parental care to their eggs or their tadpoles. Once, Australia was joined to South America and Antarctica. The continents drifted apart and, over millions of years, their frogs developed differently. Australia's southern frogs still have close relatives in other parts of the Southern Hemisphere.

A SOUTHERN FROG: The Corroboree Frog lives in moss beds high in the Australian Alps.

Family: MICROHYLIDAE (narrow-mouthed frogs)

These tiny frogs live in northern Australia. The largest Australian species is about 46 mm long; the smallest is 13 mm long. They can live away from water, but still need moisture to breed in. Each female lays a small number of large eggs under a log or stone. Then one parent, usually the male, stays with the eggs. The tadpoles develop into adults inside their eggs.

A MICROHYLID FROG: The tadpoles of Fry's Chirper become frogs while still in the eggs.

Family: RANIDAE ("true frogs")

These are called "true" frogs because they were the frogs first known to scientists in the Northern Hemisphere. Only one species, the Australian Bullfrog, is found in Australia, in rainforest creeks and swamps in northern Queensland. Males of all other Australian frogs have only one vocal sac. The bullfrog has two vocal sacs, one on each side of its throat.

A "TRUE" FROG: The Australian Bullfrog is found on Cape York Peninsula.

Fascinating facts about Australian frogs

One-third of Australia's known frog species burrow to escape hot, dry conditions.

Most frogs can lighten or darken their skin colour. They do this by spacing out or clumping together tiny grains of black colouring matter in the skin.

About one-quarter of Australia's known frog species lay their eggs out of water.

Male frogs attract females by calling. A female frog will respond only to calls made by males of her own species.

Some male frogs develop spikes or pads on their hands during the mating season. These help them grasp the females' slippery bodies.

New species of Australian frogs are still being discovered.

A tadpole's limbs all develop at the same time. However, the front legs emerge from its body after the hind legs do.

The male Marsupial Frog has hip-pocket pouches near his hind legs. In these, he carries eggs until they hatch.

The Rockhole Frog of northern Australia hops across water without breaking the surface film.

One Green Tree-frog lived in captivity for 23 years.

At least 3 species of Australian frogs have not been seen since the 1980s. They are possibly extinct. They include the two gastric-brooding frogs.

At least 10 species of Australian frogs are officially listed as endangered. At least 19 more are vulnerable.

Green Tree-frog
Litoria caerulea (= blue* beach-frog)

This large (cricket-ball-sized) tree-frog is found across the northern half of Australia. It lives in cool, damp places.

It has smooth, green to brown skin, sometimes spotted white on back and sides. Its underside is white, and the back of its thigh is yellow to maroon. The pupil of its eye is horizontal; the iris is pale yellow to gold. There are large glands on the back of the head. The digits end in large discs and the fingers are $^1/_3$ webbed. The toes are $^3/_4$ webbed. The call is a repeated *crawk...crawk*.

This tree-frog spends daytime in a moist place. At night it hunts small creatures. After rain falls (November to February), 200–2000 eggs are laid. The mottled brown or green tadpoles grow to between 45 and 100 mm, and take about 6 weeks to become frogs. The Green Tree-frog becomes very used to humans. If removed from a refuge, it tends to return.

Length: ♀ 60–110 mm ♂ 65–80 mm

* Named after an alcohol-preserved frog that had turned blue.

STATUS	X	E	P	V	**S**	SIZE	RANGE

Red-eyed Tree-frog
Litoria chloris (= green beach-frog)

The Red-eyed Tree-frog lives in wet forests along the northern New South Wales coast and the Queensland coast as far north as Proserpine. It is found in leafy foliage, high in trees.

It is a medium (tennis-ball-sized) tree-frog with a smooth, bright green back. The grainy underside is white to bright yellow. The back of the thigh is purple or brown.

The pupil of the eye is horizontal and the iris is gold in the centre, orange or red at the edge. The digits end in large discs, the fingers are $^3/_4$ webbed, and the toes $^7/_8$ webbed.

The call is a repeated, long, moaning *aaa-rk...aaa-rk*, followed by a soft trill.

After heavy rain, usually from October to February, males call from lower branches. Large groups gather around flooded areas to breed.

The eggs are laid singly or in clumps in shallow water. The pale brown tadpoles grow to 74 mm in length.

Length: ♀ 55–70 mm ♂ 55–65 mm

STATUS	X	E	P	V	**S**	SIZE	RANGE

Dainty Green Tree-frog
Litoria gracilenta (= delicate beach-frog)

The Dainty Green Tree-frog occurs along the Queensland and northern New South Wales coast. It lives on reeds and floating plants in streams and swamps. It may also be found in gardens and banana plantations.

It is a small (ping-pong-ball-sized), slender tree-frog, with a leaf-green dorsal surface and a yellow ventral^G surface. The upper arm and top of the thigh are yellow, while the back of the thigh is purple-brown. The tympanum is grainy and the iris of the eye bright orange. The fingers and toes are fully webbed and the discs are large.

The call is a long, drawn-out *waaaa*.

Breeding takes place in November. The eggs are attached to grass stems in ponds, and the dark brown tadpoles grow to 34 mm long. They become frogs about 14 weeks after hatching.

Length: ♀ 30–45 mm ♂ 30–40 mm

STATUS	X	E	P	**V**	S	SIZE	RANGE

Blue Mountains Tree-frog
Litoria citropa (= lemon-coloured beach-frog)

This medium-sized tree-frog lives in flowing streams in rocky, forested areas. It is found from the Great Dividing Range to the coast in New South Wales and eastern Victoria.

The smooth skin on the dorsal surface is light to dark brown flecked or mottled with black. There is green on the side of the head, on the flank and on the limbs. A black line runs from the nostril through the eye, over the tympanum to the groin. The side, groin, inner and outer thigh are orange-red.

The pupil is horizontal, the iris is gold. The digits have large discs. The fingers lack webbing, while the toes are half-webbed.

The call is a scream, followed by a soft trill.

Males call in September and October. They are usually located near fast-flowing water. The eggs may be found on rocks, or in pools in streams. The tadpole is dark brown marked with gold, and it may grow to 35 mm.

Length: ♀ 55–60 mm ♂ 45–55 mm

STATUS	X	E	P	V	**S**	SIZE	RANGE

Rocket-frog
Litoria nasuta (= large-nosed beach-frog)

The Striped Rocket-frog is a mighty leaper that lives in coastal waterways and swamps. It is found from Newcastle, New South Wales, up the east coast and across the north coast.

It is a medium-sized, streamlined frog with a long snout, long arms and very long, powerful legs. The centre of its back is pale brown, bordered by darker brown areas marked with still darker bumps. Skin folds run down the back. There are black and white stripes from the nose along the sides to the flanks. The underside is white and grainy. The back of the thigh is yellow with dark brown stripes.

The tympanum has a white border. The digits have small discs and there are no webs between the fingers.

The call is *wick–wick–wickbut... but...but.*

The Rocket-frog lives on the ground and hunts at night. It breeds between November and February. Groups of 50–100 eggs float on the surface of the water. The tadpoles are mottled with brown above and may grow to 56 mm.

Length: ♀ 35–55 mm ♂ 30–45 mm

STATUS	X	E	P	V	S	SIZE		RANGE

Water-holding Frog
Cyclorana platycephala (= flat-headed round-frog)

This frog was used as a water source by Aboriginal people. It lives in the arid inland of Australia near waterholes and swamps that fill after rain.

It is a medium-sized, round-bodied, short-legged frog. The dull grey, brown or green back may have a pale stripe down the centre and darker patches. The head is flattened, and the tympanum is much larger than the eye.

The small eye has a horizontal pupil and gold iris. The fingers are unwebbed, the toes fully webbed. There is a shovel-shaped ridge on the inner side of the foot.

The call is a repeated, lengthy *maw-w...maw-w-w...*

In dry conditions, this frog digs a burrow at the foot of a bush or tree and aestivates. Its bladder serves as a storage tank for water. Shed skin forms a water-saving cocoon (see picture above). After rain falls, the frog surfaces, sheds the cocoon, feeds and breeds.

Length: ♀ 50–75 mm ♂ 40–65 mm

STATUS	X	E	P	V	S	SIZE		RANGE

Northern Snapping (Giant) Frog
Cyclorana australis (= southern round-frog)

This large frog lives in open forest and grassland across northern Australia from the Kimberley to the western side of Cape York Peninsula.

It is a large, burrowing frog with a big, flattish head and very large eyes. The bumpy skin of its back may be pale brown, grey or green with dark markings or green patches. It has a broad, dark stripe from the tip of the nose to the flank. One skin fold runs down each side of the backbone, another on each side to the flank. The pupil is horizontal, the iris gold. The fingers are unwebbed, while the toes have small webs. There is a shovel-shaped ridge on the inner side of the foot.

The call is a short, repeated *unk...unk...unk...*

This frog will eat any creature small enough to swallow, including other frogs. It is often seen during the Wet season, sometimes basking[G] in hot sunshine beside water. During the Dry, it remains in its burrow. It breeds between December and February, laying up to 7000 eggs in temporary water. The creamy gold tadpoles grow to 70 mm and swim in large groups.

Length: ♀ 70–105 mm ♂ 70–80 mm

STATUS	X	E	P	V	S	SIZE		RANGE

WAITING FOR RAIN TO FALL

Many Australian frogs burrow into the ground to avoid hot, dry conditions. These burrowing frogs have broad heads, round bodies and short, strong limbs. Most of Australia's burrowing frogs dig down with their hind feet. These frogs often have hard, shovel-like ridges on their feet. Only two Australian species, the Sandhill and Turtle Frogs, burrow head first.

Some frogs wait out long spells of dry weather under ground. A cocoon of shed, dead skin stops their bodies losing too much moisture. Water stored in their bladders is taken back into their body tissues as it is needed. When it rains, these frogs wake up and dig to the surface. They drag their cocoons off their bodies and eat them. Then they look for food and find a mate.

Ornate Burrowing Frog

Northern Banjo Frog

Limnodynastes terraereginae (= Queensland lord-of-the-marshes)

This large, burrowing frog lives near water, in woodlands and forests in coastal eastern Australia.

The bumpy skin of the back is brown or black, with darker markings and a paler central stripe. The underside is cream. The sides are yellow with black markings and the groin is yellow and scarlet. A yellow gland runs from beneath the eye back to the shoulder and the male displays a yellow throat sac. The pupil of the eye is horizontal and the iris gold. The digits have no discs. The toes have small webs.

The call is a repeated *plonk...plonk...*, like plucking a banjo.

The Northern Banjo Frog hides during the day. From October to May, after rain falls, males call from near water.

As a female lays eggs, she paddles with her fingers. Air bubbles pass under her body, mingle with the eggs and jelly and form a floating foam nest. The tadpoles reach 65 mm, and have dark bodies and mottled tails.

Length: ♀ 55–80 mm ♂ 60–75 mm

| STATUS | X | E | P | V | S | SIZE | RANGE |

Moaning Frog

Heleioporus eyrei (= Eyre's* marsh-dweller)

The Moaning Frog lives in the high rainfall areas of the south-west corner of Western Australia, and is found on Rottnest Island. It prefers swampy coastal areas where the soil is sandy.

This medium-sized, fat, burrowing frog has a broad, rounded head. Its back is brown or dark grey, marked with patches of dull yellow or pale grey.

The call is a long, rising moan.

Male Moaning Frogs call from the mouths of their burrows, which are dug into flat, sandy land.

After a female finds a male, she lays from 80 to 500 eggs in a frothy mass in his burrow. The male fertilises them. Hatching takes place after the burrow is flooded by rain.

The tadpole is mottled with black and gold and has a red or gold stripe down its back.

Length: ♀ 45–65 mm ♂ 45-65 mm

* Named after the nineteenth century explorer Edward John Eyre.

| STATUS | X | E | P | V | S | SIZE | RANGE |

Desert Spadefoot Frog

Notaden nichollsi (= Nicholls's back-gland*)

The Desert Spadefoot lives in desert and grassland. It is found from north-western Western Australia across to south-western Queensland, and south to northern South Australia.

It is a small, fat, short-legged frog with a short head and bumpy skin. The back is green-grey to brown, spotted with yellow and red bumps. The underside is pale.

The eye has a horizontal pupil. The fingers are unwebbed, while the toes are slightly webbed.

This little frog runs rather than hops.

The call is a loud *woop...woop...woop...*

During drought, this frog aestivates at the end of a shaft sunk up to 2 m into the ground. After rain, it surfaces and feeds on ants and termites.

Males call while floating in water. Up to 1000 eggs are laid in a chain in flooded vegetation. The pale brown tadpoles grow to 45 mm. They become frogs in only 16 days.

Length: ♀ 45–65 mm ♂ 40–60 mm

* Notaden frogs have skin glands that sweat a distasteful, possibly poisonous, substance.

| STATUS | X | E | P | V | S | SIZE | RANGE |

Tusked Frog

Adelotus brevis (= short unseen-frog)

The Tusked Frog lives in forest and open country from central eastern Queensland to southern New South Wales. It is found on the coastal plain and in the Great Dividing Range.

It is a small, large-headed, flattened frog. Its back is rough with bumps and ridges, and is grey or brown, patterned darker. Its throat is grey with white flecks. The male's smooth black belly is covered with white spots, while the female's belly is blotched. There are bright red patches in the groin and on the back of the leg.

The male is larger than the female (unusual in frogs). The male's head is wider than (and may be the same size as) the body. The tusks are used in fights between males.

The call is *kuruk*, repeated several times a minute.

The pale cream eggs are laid in a foam nest, usually away from direct light. The male remains with the nest until the tadpoles hatch.

Length: ♀ 30–35 mm ♂ 35–40 mm

| STATUS | X | E | P | V | S | SIZE | RANGE |

Southern Gastric-brooding Frog
Rheobatrachus silus (= pug-nosed stream-frog)

Until 1981, this frog was found at heights above 300 m in rocky, rainforest streams in the Conondale and Blackall Ranges of south-east Queensland. It has not been seen since then.

It is a medium-sized, water-dwelling, short-snouted frog with slimy skin and large, powerful hind legs. Its bumpy back varies from brown to greenish with darker patches. The underside is white, with patches of yellow.

The large eyes, which have vertical[G] pupils, are set on top of the head. The fingers are unwebbed; the toes are fully webbed.

The call is a rising note.

A female gastric-brooding frog swallows up to 25 fertilised eggs, which develop to adult frogs in her stomach. She does not eat for 6 weeks until the froglets emerge from her mouth.

Gastric-brooding frogs sometimes float on their backs. Unlike

other frogs, they cannot flick their tongues out of their mouths. They probably feed by gulping small creatures from the water.

Length: ♀ 45–55 mm
♂ 35–40 mm

STATUS	X	E	**P**	V	S	SIZE		RANGE

PARENTAL CARE

Many of the southern frog group have special ways of helping their young survive. Some lay many eggs in bubble rafts, which float just under the surface of the water until the eggs hatch. The male may stay with the bubble nest until the tadpoles emerge. Some sorts of southern frogs lay only a few eggs. A parent may care for the eggs while the tadpoles within gradually turn into frogs. The male Marsupial Frog stays with the eggs until the tadpoles hatch. Then he carries them around in hip pouches until they emerge as tiny frogs. The female Northern and Southern Gastric-brooding Frogs swallow their eggs. These hatch into tadpoles, which develop into frogs inside their mothers' stomachs. The tiny froglets climb out of their mothers' mouths. The picture shows a Corroboree Frog with its eggs. The tadpoles can be seen in the eggs.

Australian Bullfrog
Rana daemeli (= Damel's frog)

The Australian Bullfrog lives on Cape York Peninsula, north Queensland, and in eastern Arnhem Land, Northern Territory. It is found amongst waterside vegetation.

It is a large, long frog with a narrow, triangular head. Its back is smooth and bronze-coloured, with a skin fold from behind the eye to the back of the hind leg. There is a dark stripe from the nostril past the large tympanum, and a pale stripe along the upper lip. The underside is white, speckled brown. The digits have small discs, the fingers are unwebbed and the toes are fully webbed.

The call is a repeated *yap...yap...* or a duck-like *quack...quack...* The calling male's vocal sac bulges on both sides of its throat.

The Bullfrog jumps into water when disturbed and is a powerful swimmer. It lays several thousand eggs, which float on the surface. The gold and black tadpoles grow to 60 mm.

This is Australia's only representative of a group common in other parts of the world.

Length: ♀ 55–80 mm ♂ 45–60 mm

STATUS	X	E	P	V	**S**	SIZE		RANGE

Cane Toad
Bufo marinus (= marine toad)

This introduced pest now lives in various habitats from Coffs Harbour, New South Wales, north and then west along Queensland's coast to the Northern Territory's central coast. The Cane Toad can live and reproduce in a variety of habitats.

It is a large to enormous toad with a large, short, rounded head. The skin of the back is very warty and dry, coloured pale brown and covered with darker blotches. A large, swollen gland forms a lump behind each side of the head. The underside is creamy and grainy, with dark blotches.

The eyelid is warty, the pupil is horizontal and the iris golden. The fingers are stubby and lack webbing. The toes are webbed at their bases.

The call is a purring *pop-pop-pop*.

Cane Toads are active at night. They will eat food that does not move and anything that does. The glands behind the head produce poison that can kill most animals.

A female may lay 35 000 eggs in a season, in long chains in water. The poisonous tadpoles are all-black.

Length: ♀ 90–250 mm ♂ 75–110 mm

STATUS	X	E	P	**V**	**S**	SIZE		RANGE

Australia's reptiles

There are three major groups of reptiles found in Australia.
They are: crocodilians[1], turtles[2], and snakes and lizards.

Crocodilians

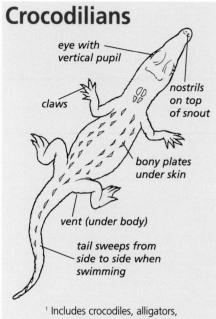

eye with vertical pupil

nostrils on top of snout

claws

bony plates under skin

vent (under body)

tail sweeps from side to side when swimming

[1] Includes crocodiles, alligators, gharials. Australia has only crocodiles.

Turtles

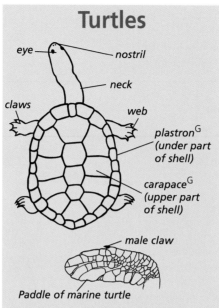

eye

nostril

neck

claws

web

plastron[G] (under part of shell)

carapace[G] (upper part of shell)

male claw

Paddle of marine turtle

[2] Includes turtles, terrapins and tortoises. Australia has only turtles.

How many reptiles?

Worldwide, there are about 6400 living species of reptiles. Snakes and lizards make up nearly 95% of these. Australia has about 700 species of reptiles (new ones are still being added to the list). There are more species in the warmer north than in the cooler south.

Hot and cold sleep

Very few reptiles have bodies that can produce their own heat. Most species take the temperature of their surroundings. The smaller the reptile, the faster it heats up or cools down. Most reptiles bask in the sun to warm themselves. To cool down, they shelter from the sun.

Dark skin takes in heat more quickly than pale skin. Many reptiles can change their skin colours to become darker or paler for this purpose. Sometimes the weather is too hot or too cold for a reptile to survive while remaining active. At these times, it goes into a kind of sleep where all its body functions slow down. During this time, its body uses water and fat stored in its tissues. "Summer sleep" is called aestivation. "Winter sleep" is called hibernation[G].

Snakes and lizards

Lizards and snakes belong to the same major group of reptiles. They have many similarities. The table below shows some of their differences.

 **ALL SNAKES**	 **MOST LIZARDS**	 **A FEW LIZARDS**
lack limbs (pythons have traces)	have limbs	have reduced or no limbs, or hind-limb flaps
lack ear openings	have ear openings or tympanums	have scaly depressions instead of ear openings
have long, slender, forked tongues	have fleshy tongues that may be notched	have long, slender forked tongues (monitors)
lack eyelids	have movable lower eyelids	have immovable lower eyelids (legless lizards, geckos and some skinks)
cannot shed tail	can shed tail and regrow part or all of it	cannot shed tail (monitors, dragons, some large skinks)
have length from snout to vent much greater than from vent to tail-tip	have length from snout to vent less than vent to tail-tip	are longer from snout to vent than from vent to tail-tip (some large skinks)
have single or enlarged belly scales (except file snakes and blind snakes)	have small underbody scales that are nearly equal in size to body scales	have large underbody scales arranged in pairs (some legless lizards)

Breath and blood

When breathing in, a reptile expands its ribs. This draws air into its lungs. Oxygen passes from the air into the reptile's blood, while waste gases pass from the blood into the air. Then the reptile's ribs contract and it breathes the air out. A few water-living reptiles can take oxygen from the water and pass out waste gases through their skins. One freshwater turtle can breathe through the lower end of its gut.

Turtles, snakes and lizards have hearts with three separate chambers. In the single lower chamber, oxygenated blood from the lungs may mix with blood that has given up its oxygen and is carrying waste gases coming from the body. Crocodiles, like birds and mammals, have four-chambered hearts. These do not allow oxygenated and de-oxygenated blood to mix.

If a reptile is warm enough, it can move fast. However, its body cannot keep up the effort for long. Reptiles can become very stressed and die if forced to move fast, or to struggle, for more than very short periods of time.

Groups of Australia's reptiles

Worldwide, there are more than 6400 species of living reptiles. Australia has around 700 species.

Scientists place reptiles into the Class Reptilia. This contains four Orders. Australia has members of three of these Orders (the fourth is the tuataras, found in New Zealand). Australia's reptiles are grouped as shown below:

Class: REPTILIA (= reptiles)

Order: CROCODILIA
(crocodiles and alligators[1])

A crocodile is a four-legged, water-living reptile. Its head and back are protected by raised scales and bony plates that are embedded in the skin.

Eyes, ears and nostrils are on the top of the head.

The front feet are unwebbed. Webs join three toes on each hind foot.

A crocodile's 66 cone-shaped teeth are replaced if lost. A flap of skin at the back of the mouth stops water entering the throat when the crocodile opens its mouth under water.

Crocodiles and alligators are the only reptiles with four-chambered hearts.

Two species of crocodile live in northern Australia.

[1] When an alligator's mouth is closed, all its teeth are hidden. A crocodile's lower canine[G] teeth can still be seen. Gharials have very long, slender snouts.

Order: TESTUDINES
(turtles, tortoises, terrapins[2])

A turtle is a four-legged, water-living reptile. Its body is protected by a shell attached to its ribs and backbone.

A turtle's head and limbs poke through gaps between the shell halves.

Most freshwater turtles have webbed feet. Only the Pig-nosed Turtle has flippers. All marine turtles have flippers.

Nearly all of Australia's freshwater turtles bend their necks from side to side. The Pig-nosed Turtle and all marine turtles bend their necks up and down.

Turtles have horny cutting edges to their jaws instead of teeth.

Australia has more than 23 species of freshwater turtles. Six of the world's 7 species of marine turtles can be found around Australia's coast.

[2] Tortoises and terrapins are not found in Australia. Their stumpy legs end in unwebbed feet.

Order: SQUAMATA
(lizards and snakes)

Lizards and snakes have skin covered with scales. Their bodies are protected by a thin, horny, outside layer of skin that is shed from time to time.

A lizard or a snake has teeth on both upper and lower jaws. Some snakes have hollow teeth called fangs, which serve to inject venom.

Australia has five families of lizards. None of these is venomous.

Seven of the world's 12 families of snakes are found in Australia.

There are 15 species of non-venomous pythons, 30 species of non-venomous blind snakes and two species of non-venomous file snakes. There are 11 species of rear-fanged snakes (some are venomous but are not harmful to humans). There are 75 species of front-fanged snakes (around 20 are potentially deadly to humans). Over 30 species of potentially deadly seasnakes are found in the oceans around Australia.

Nose-tip to tail-tip, the Saltwater Crocodile may measure up to 7 m.

The Eastern Snake-necked Turtle may have a shell up to 250 mm in length.

The head, body and tail of the Thorny Devil may measure 90 mm.

The five families of Australian lizards

GECKOS (about 100 species): Night active. Soft-skinned. Each limb has five digits ending in a pad, a claw or both. Eyes have vertical pupils. Lower eyelids are transparent, fused to upper lids. Tails may be shed and regrow.

LEGLESS LIZARDS (over 30 species): Snake-like. Night active. Overlapping scales, may be glossy. No fore limbs, flaps for hind limbs. Eyes have vertical pupils. Eyelids fused and transparent. Part of the tail may be shed.

DRAGONS (over 60 species): Day active. Rough-skinned. Head and upper-body scales end in points and may form crests. Limbs well developed. Eyes have round pupils and movable eyelids. Tails cannot be shed.

MONITORS (about 25 species): Day active. Rasping skins. Small scales do not overlap. Limbs well developed, end in strong claws. Tongue is long and forked. Eye has a round pupil. Long, strong tail cannot be shed.

SKINKS (over 300 species): Usually day active. Most have smooth overlapping scales. Limbs may be well developed, or reduced or absent. Some have movable eyelids, others have lower transparent eyelid fused to upper. May shed tail.

Freshwater Crocodile

Crocodylus johnstoni (= Johnstone's crocodile)

The Freshwater Crocodile is found in permanent fresh water (billabongs, swamps, rivers) in northern and north-eastern Australia.

It is a comparatively slender crocodile, whose upper surface is grey to green-brown with darker markings. The snout is long, slender and smooth. The teeth are slender and needle-sharp.

This crocodile is sometimes seen at night, walking overland between bodies of water. It is not harmful to humans; however, it will bite if touched.

Freshwater Crocodiles bask on banks, but spend most of their time in the water. From sunset, they hunt insects, fish, frogs, birds and reptiles in the water. A female lays 12–20 eggs in a nest in a sandbank towards the end of the Dry season (October –November). A nearby female, which may not be the mother, digs out the nest when the young hatch. She may carry the young to the water in her mouth.

Length: HBT up to 3 m

STATUS	X	E	P	V	**S**	SIZE		RANGE

Saltwater (Estuarine) Crocodile

Crocodylus porosus (= pore-skinned crocodile)

The Saltwater Crocodile lives across northern Australia in estuaries, swamps, rivers, floodplains and the sea.

It is a small to enormous crocodile whose upper surface is brown, grey or nearly black with dark markings. Its snout is short in comparison to its width, and has a grainy, bumpy surface.

These crocodiles bask or shelter beside the water during the day. They hunt animals, including cattle and humans, in or near the water at night.

A large male "Saltie" holds a territory. A female mates early in the Wet Season (December–January), then lays up to 60 hard-shelled eggs in a nest of vegetation on a river bank. She later cares for the hatchlings.

Length: HBT up to 7 m

STATUS	X	E	P	V	**S**	SIZE		RANGE

A KEY TO THE FAMILIES OF AUSTRALIAN TURTLES:

1 Limbs like paddles, without joints
   or clawed, webbed feet...2

   Limbs have joints and webbed,
   clawed feet ....**freshwater turtles**
   (about 22 species, examples pp. 58, 59)

Pig-nosed Turtle

2 Nostrils set at end
   of a fleshy snout...**Pig-nosed Turtle**
   (1 species, not described in this book, photo above)

   Nostrils set level with surface of nose.........................3

3 Paddle-like limbs have claws ....**sea turtles**
   (6 species, example p. 59)

   Paddle-like limbs have no claws .....**Leatherback Turtle**
   (1 species, not described in this book, photo below)

Leatherback Turtle

Eastern Snake-necked Turtle

Chelodina longicollis (= long-necked little tortoise)

This long-necked freshwater turtle is found in coastal and inland wetlands and rivers. It ranges from eastern Queensland to south-eastern South Australia.

It has a dinner-plate-sized carapace (upper shell). Its head plus neck measurement is as long as, or longer than, its shell length. The carapace is brown or black, with black seams between its plates. The head is flattened, the eyes look sideways and the nostrils are on the tip of the snout. The front feet are webbed, with 4 clawed digits.

This turtle basks on sandbanks or submerged logs. When submerged, it pushes its nostrils out of the water to breathe. It feeds on animals found in the water. In summer, it may wander to find water, or burrow into mud and aestivate.

A female lays 12 or more brittle-shelled eggs in a hole in an earth bank in early summer. The hatchlings emerge up to 5 months later, after rain has fallen.

Length: Carapace to 250 mm

STATUS	X	E	P	V	**S**	SIZE		RANGE

Western Swamp Turtle
Pseudemydura umbrina (= shaded false *Emydura**)

The endangered Western Swamp Turtle is found only in one small swamp at Ellenbrook, north of Perth, Western Australia.

It is saucer-sized, with a brown carapace that is almost square in outline. The plastron (lower shell) is pale, with dark seams between the plates. The broad, flat head and neck are much shorter than the shell. The front feet are webbed.

This turtle lives in an area of summer drought and winter rain. It spends 6–9 months of each year aestivating underground. It only becomes active when its habitat is flooded with water above 14°C in temperature. This is Australia's rarest reptile, whose habitat needs preservation.

A hatchling needs to grow for 2 seasons before aestivating successfully. It may not breed until over 15 years of age.

Length: Carapace to 150 mm

* *Emydura* is another genus of short-necked turtles.

STATUS	X	**E**	P	V	S	SIZE	RANGE

Loggerhead Turtle
Caretta caretta (= tortoise-shell turtle)

The Loggerhead lives in tropical and warm temperate waters around northern Australia. It is one of the 5 species of sea turtle that nest regularly along the Queensland coast. The main South Pacific nest site is on Wreck Island in the Capricorn Bunker Group. There is a mainland nest site at Mon Repos, near Bundaberg.

It is a large to enormous sea turtle with a dark reddish brown carapace, speckled darker. An adult has a massive head and powerful jaws. The flippers are small compared to the flippers of other sea turtles.

Loggerheads eat molluscs, crabs, sea urchins and sea jellies.

A female mates in the sea, then lays up to 125 eggs in a pit dug above high tide mark. After 60–80 days, the hatchlings dig from the nest at night and make their way to the sea.

Length: Carapace to 1.5 m

STATUS	X	E	**P**	V	S	SIZE	RANGE

A KEY TO THE FAMILIES OF AUSTRALIAN LIZARDS:

1 Eyes either with movable lids or without movable lids
   Has limbs (which may be small) **2**
   Has no limbs; there may be a scaly flap instead........**5**

2 Eyes with or without movable lids.
   Pupil is not a vertical slit in daylight.
   Scales on head and neck are overlapping............**3**

Three-lined Knob-tail Gecko

Eyes without movable lids.
   Pupil is a vertical slit in daylight.
   Scales on head and neck lie side by side ....**geckos**
      (over 100 Australian species, examples pp. 59, 60)

3 Scales on the top of the head are tiny and irregular **4**
   Scales on the top of the head are large, regular
   and shield-like..**skinks**
      (over 300 Australian species, examples p. 60)

4 Tongue is long, slender, deeply forked, often flickered
   in and out when owner is alert....................**monitors**
      (over 25 Australian species, examples p. 61)

Tongue is broad and flat with a small notch in front.
   Appears when owner eats and drinks............**dragons**
      (over 60 Australian species, examples p. 61)

5 Eyes are without movable eyelids...............**legless lizards**
      (over 30 Australian species, examples p. 62)

Eyes have eyelids...**some skinks**

Variegated Dtella
Gehyra variegata (= variegated *Gehyra**)

The Variegated Dtella ranges from coastal Western Australia (except for the south-western corner and Kimberley) across the interior of Australia.

It is a medium-sized, soft-skinned gecko with a flattened body and a depression at the base of the tail. Its upper surface is grey or grey-brown with many darker markings. This gecko may change colour from darker during the day to paler at night.

The lidless eye has a vertical pupil. The ends of the digits are expanded into large pads; all but the innermost end in claws. The tail may be shed and regrown.

These geckos spend the day under loose bark, in a tree hollow, under a rock flake, or in a crack in a building. Several may share a shelter. At night they roam rocks, walls and tree trunks, hunting insects and spiders.

A female lays 1 egg, often in a nest with other females' eggs.

Length: HB 55 mm; T 70 mm

* The meaning of *Gehyra* is unknown.

STATUS	X	E	P	V	**S**	SIZE	RANGE

Three-lined Knob-tail Gecko
Nephrurus levis (= smooth kidney-tail)

This large gecko is found in dry, sandy country, open woodland and grassland. It ranges from the central coast of Western Australia across the arid interior.

The Three-lined Knob-tail is a big-headed gecko with a short, fat tail ending in a small knob. Its upper surface is purple-brown, with lines of raised white dots. Yellowish bars cross the head, neck and shoulder. The digits end in claws.

This desert gecko shelters in a burrow during the day and in cold weather. The shelter may be a tunnel it has dug in the side of another animal's burrow. At night, it hunts insects, spiders, scorpions and other geckos. It can still run when cold slows down other lizards.

When this gecko is frightened or aggressive, it twitches and vibrates its knobbed tail. The tail is not easily shed.

Length: HB 90 mm; T 55 mm

STATUS	X	E	P	V	**S**	SIZE		RANGE

AUSTRALIA'S SMALL GAME

In many countries of the world, the major predators are mammals, such as lions, tigers, wolves and bears. In Australia, the most numerous predators are reptiles. They eat insects, including termites and ants, other invertebrates, fish, frogs, birds and small mammals. Some eat other reptiles. Monitor lizards will also eat carrion.

The floodplains of northern Australia support a greater weight of predators than would be found in a similar area of Africa's famous Serengeti Plains. However, instead of lions, hyenas and leopards, the Australian predators are snakes, lizards, freshwater turtles and crocodiles.

Large numbers of Water Pythons live in northern wetlands.

The Yellow-spotted Monitor feeds on live prey or carrion.

Shingleback (Lizard)
Trachydosaurus rugosus (= wrinkled, rough lizard)

The Shingleback ranges across the southern half of Australia, except for the eastern and south-eastern coastal areas.

It is a large, long-bodied, short-tailed skink with a very big head. Its upper surface is covered with enlarged, rough, pine-cone-like scales. The upper surface is pale to dark reddish or yellowish brown, with paler markings. The short tail, which is used to store fat, has a rounded, blunt end.

Shinglebacks defend themselves by opening their mouths to show their blue tongues. They move slowly across the ground during the day, eating insects, snails, vegetation and carrion. They shelter under timber or ground litter in cold weather.

A pair may stay together for long periods. They mate in spring, and 2 or 3 large young are born in summer.

Length: HB 310 mm; T 80 mm

STATUS	X	E	P	V	**S**	SIZE		RANGE

Common Bluetongue
Tiliqua scincoides (= *Scincus*-like *tiliqua**)

The Common Bluetongue ranges from south-eastern South Australia through Victoria, north to the Top End of the Northern Territory and the Kimberley. This lizard is one of the world's largest skinks.

It is a large, long-bodied skink with smooth scales. Its upper surface is pale grey to brown. It has 6–9 darker bands across its back and 6–8 across its pointed tail. Its underside is smooth and pale. The blue tongue is poked out when the owner is looking for food. It is also used as a defensive warning.

Bluetongues shelter under timber or litter in colder weather. During the day and on warm evenings, they feed on insects, snails, vegetation and carrion.

The female may produce up to 25 live young at a birth.

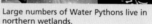

Length:
HB 370 mm; T 190 mm

* After a genus of skinks.

STATUS	X	E	P	**V**	S	SIZE		RANGE

Gould's Monitor

Varanus gouldii (= Gould's monitor*)

Gould's Monitor (or Goanna) can be seen all over Australia, except in high rainfall forests.

It is a very large, ground-living monitor, whose upper surface varies from yellow to nearly black, with lighter and darker markings. Its eyes have round pupils and well-developed eyelids. Its forked tongue flicks to carry scents to an organ in the roof of its mouth. The limbs are powerful, with strong, clawed digits.

This monitor shelters in a burrow, hunts smaller animals and may eat carrion. During the breeding season, males may fight. A female buries up to 11 eggs in a nest dug into earth in spring or summer. The hatchlings emerge the following spring.

Length: HB 0.7 m T 1 m

* Monitors were thought to watch for crocodiles and warn of their presence.

STATUS	X	E	P	V	**S**	SIZE			RANGE	

Lace Monitor

Varanus varius (= several-coloured monitor)

This large monitor can be seen in the forests, woodlands and coastal plains of eastern Australia. It also lives along the Murray-Darling River system, and in the Flinders Ranges.

The upper surface is dark blue, with scattered white or yellow scales forming spots and blotches. There are black bars across its snout, chin and throat. The tail is banded with yellow.

Lace Monitors eat nestling birds, as well as other tree-dwelling and ground animals and carrion. They may visit picnic grounds, hoping for scraps, but will not hurt humans.

A female lays up to 12 eggs in a hole dug in the ground or into a termite mound. She may return the following season to lay again. When digging out the nest, she may free hatchlings from the previous season.

Length: HB 0.8 m; T 1.3 m

STATUS	X	E	P	V	**S**	SIZE			RANGE	

Frilled Lizard

Chlamydosaurus kingii (= King's cloaked lizard)

The Frilled Lizard is Australia's reptile emblem. It is found in woodlands from the Kimberley of Western Australia across the top of the Northern Territory to Cape York Peninsula and eastern Queensland.

It is a large dragon with a frill of skin around its head and neck. The upper surface is grey to orange-brown, with darker markings. The frill may be yellow to black, flashing orange or red when opened. The male has a black belly. The eye has a round pupil and movable lids. The limbs are well developed and the digits are clawed.

These lizards perch on tree trunks and branches, their colour and broken outline acting as camouflage[G]. On the ground, they may run on their hind limbs. They eat insects and other creatures.

A female lays 8–14 eggs.

Length: HB 280 mm; T 670 mm

STATUS	X	E	P	**V**	S	SIZE			RANGE	

Thorny Devil

Moloch horridus (= bristly devil)

The Thorny Devil lives in dry country from the central coast of Western Australia to western Queensland.

A medium-sized dragon with a flattened body and bumpy, spiky skin, it has a tiny head. There is a large, two-spined hump on the neck. When threatened, the lizard bends its head so the hump becomes a false head. This dragon can slowly change its colour and pattern to match the ground.

The Thorny Devil moves around slowly during daytime, feeding on small ants (up to 5000 in a meal). It drinks from water falling on its skin, which makes its way through a series of skin grooves to the devil's mouth.

A female lays up to 10 eggs in a nest at the end of a long tunnel. The young breed after 3 years, and may live to 20 years.

Length: HB 100 mm; T 90 mm

STATUS	X	E	P	**V**	S	SIZE			RANGE	

Common Scaly-foot
Pygopus lepidopodus (= scaly-footed rump-foot)

This large legless lizard ranges across southern Australia from south-eastern Queensland to Shark Bay, Western Australia.

It has a rounded snout and its tail is more than twice the length of its head and body. The back scales have keels, or ridges. The upper surface is grey to tan, striped, spotted or blotched with darker, pale-edged markings. There are dark bars on its lips and the sides of its neck. The see-through lower eyelid covers the eye, and the pupil is vertical. There are no front limbs, and only scaly flaps instead of hind limbs.

This scaly-foot hunts spiders and insects on the ground during daytime. It rolls with them to kill them, then laps up the body fluids. It faces danger by raising its head and flattening its neck like a snake. The tail is easily broken off.

A female lays 2 eggs under a rock or log with the eggs of other females.

Length: HB 280 mm T 580 mm

STATUS	X	E	P	V	**S**	SIZE		RANGE

Burton's Snake-lizard
Lialis burtonis (= Burton's snake-lizard)

Burton's snake-lizard is found in most Australian habitats except for rainforest, extreme deserts and high mountains.

It is a large legless lizard whose long, wedge-shaped head has a sharply pointed snout. The scales on the head are small and do not form a pattern. The colour and markings are very variable and the scales of the upper surface have a metallic sheen. The underside is coloured and patterned. The eyes have vertical pupils, and the lower eyelid is fixed and see-through. There are no front limbs, and the hind limbs are small, triangular flaps.

These lizards usually hunt in the early morning and evening. They wait in hiding for other lizards to pass by, then catch and eat them.

The larger female lays 1, 2 or 3 eggs in a nest with other females' eggs.

Length: HB 290 mm; T 330 mm

STATUS	X	E	P	V	**S**	SIZE		RANGE	

A KEY TO THE FAMILIES OF AUSTRALIAN SNAKES:

1. Tail cylinder-shaped, not flattened...2

   Tail flattened and paddle-shaped..............................**seasnakes**
   (over 30 Australian species, example p. 65)

2. Scales on belly more or less equal in size
   to scales on back and sides...3

   One row of scales on belly. Each scale at least
   three times as wide as a scale on back or sides....................4

3. Eyes well developed. Body scales rough and keeled.
   More than 80 scales around middle of body........**file snakes**
   (2 Australian species, example p. 63)

   Eyes dark spots beneath scales. Body scales smooth.
   Fewer than 40 scales around middle of body....**blind snakes**
   (over 40 Australian species, example p. 62)

4. Fewer than 30 scales around middle of body 5

   More than 30 scales around middle of body...................**pythons**
   (15 Australian species, examples p. 63)

5. Two scales cover vent..**colubrid**[G] **snakes**
   (11 Australian species, examples p. 63)

   Single scale covers vent..**elapid**[G] **snakes**
   (75 Australian species, examples pp. 64–65)

Blackish Blind Snake
Rhamphotyphlops nigrescens (= blackish beaked-blind-eye)

The largest of Australia's blind snakes lives on, or in, the ground in eastern Australia's forests, woodlands and plains, from southern Queensland to Victoria.

It is a worm-like snake with shiny scales. These are the same size all around the body. The eyes are small spots and the small mouth is behind and below the snout. The upper surface is purplish to blackish, and the very short tail ends in a spine.

The head and neck produce an oily substance that helps the snake slide through soil.

This blind snake comes to the surface of the ground only on warm nights, usually after rain. At other times, it shelters under rocks, in soil under leaf litter, or in termite mounds. Sometimes it is found with others of its kind. It eats the eggs, larvae and pupae[G] of ants, as well as worms and leeches.

The female lays 5–20 eggs in mid to late summer.

When threatened, this snake may curl up with its head hidden and lift up its tail. Blind snakes are non-venomous and harmless to humans.

Length: HBT 750 mm

STATUS	X	E	P	V	**S**	SIZE		RANGE	

Black-headed Python
Aspidites melanocephalus (= black-headed shield-bearer)

This large python inhabits plains and ranges across the northern half of Australia.

It has a small, glossy black head and neck. Its snout is round and its lips lack the heat-sensing pits present in most other pythons. The upper surface of the body and tail is light tan to brown, with many darker crossbands. The eye has a vertical pupil.

This is a ground-living python that shelters in cracks in the soil, and in burrows, fallen trees, termite mounds and caves. During cool weather, the black head is pushed into morning sunlight, which warms it rapidly. At night, this python hunts for ground-living birds, mammals and reptiles, including other snakes. It lacks venom and kills its prey by crushing it in its body coils.

A female lays 5–9 eggs, coils round them and may warm them by shivering.

Length: HB 2.7 m; T 0.4 m

| STATUS | X | E | P | V | S | SIZE | | RANGE | |

Diamond (Carpet) Python
Morelia spilota (= spotted Morelia)

This python has two different colour forms, called the Diamond and the Carpet Pythons. The two forms cover Australia, except for southern Victoria, arid central Australia and the north-west.

The Diamond Python has a green-black upper surface, with cream or yellow spots forming a diamond pattern (see right). The Carpet Python has a pale to dark brown upper surface, with paler blotches, each with a dark border forming a "carpet" pattern (see below).

This python often hunts and shelters in trees, but may hunt on the ground and shelter in the burrows of other animals. It tracks birds and small mammals by their body heat, using heat-sensitive pits on its lips. Non-venomous, it is harmless to humans.

A female lays up to 50 eggs, then coils around them until they hatch.

Length: HB 3.5 m T 0.5 m

| STATUS | X | E | P | V | S | SIZE | | RANGE | |

Arafura File Snake
Acrochordus arafurae (= Arafura pointed-scale)*

This file snake lives in coastal wetlands in northern Australia.

It is a large, water-living snake with a small head and loose skin. The upper surface is grey to dark brown, marked with pale blotches. The scales are small and keeled, resembling the teeth of a file. The tail is prehensile.

This snake can move on land, but seldom leaves the water. It spends the day in shaded water and hunts at night. It anchors itself by its tail, then ambushes passing fish. It lacks venom, so holds its prey with the help of its rough scales and long, curved teeth. It can breathe through its skin as well as through its lungs.

Several males court a female, who later produces up to 27 young.

File snakes are harmless to humans. They are a traditional food of the Aboriginal people of northern Australia.

Length: HBT 1.6 m

* The Arafura Sea bounds the northern coast of Australia.

| STATUS | X | E | P | V | S | SIZE | | RANGE | |

Green Tree Snake
Dendrelaphis punctulata (= fine-spotted tree-snake)

The beautiful Green Tree Snake has no venom and is harmless to humans. It is found in gardens, forests, heaths and woodlands in northern and eastern coastal Australia.

It is a slender, tree-living snake with large eyes. It varies greatly in colour, its upper surface ranging from pale green to grey-blue to nearly black. The skin between the scales is pale blue. The underside may be yellow, lime green or pale blue. Keeled belly scales give it a good grip on branches, helped by the long, whip-like, prehensile tail. When threatened, a Green Tree Snake lifts the head and flattens the neck sideways, showing blue skin between the scales.

Green Tree Snakes live in trees and other vegetation. They shelter in tree hollows, under rocks, in caves and sometimes in buildings. They hunt during the day and evening, taking frogs and lizards.

Length: HBT 1.7 m

| STATUS | X | E | P | V | S | SIZE | RANGE | |

DEADLY AUSTRALIANS

Many Australian snakes are not dangerous to humans. However, around 75 species are front-fanged, or elapid snakes. These have a sharp, hollow tooth called a fang at each front corner of the upper jaw. Each fang is connected to a venom gland. When the snake bites, venom is forced down the fang into the wound.

Around 20 species of Australia's elapid snakes produce venom that can kill a human. Most hide or slide away when disturbed, but all will bite if harassed. A good rule is to leave any snake alone. When bushwalking, wear long trousers and sturdy boots; make a reasonable amount of noise when you move and snakes will stay out of your way.

Antivenoms^G, which combat the effects of snake venoms, are available at hospitals. A bitten person should be taken to medical help as soon as possible. The bitten part should be wrapped firmly in an elastic bandage to prevent venom entering the victim's general bloodstream.

In the mating season, male elapid snakes may twine around each other in a non-deadly form of fighting called ritual^G combat. If they do bite, they are not affected by the venom of their own species.

Northern Death Adder

Acanthophis praelongus (= very long spine-snake*)

This death adder lives in loose soil or under leaf litter. It is found in woodland or grassland across northern Australia.

It is a ground-living snake with a large head, a narrow neck and a strong body. The head scales are rough and form brow-ridges over the eyes. The upper surface is dark brown to reddish brown, with paler crossbands. The pupil is vertical in daylight. The tail tapers sharply and the end bears a spine.

Death adders shelter under ground litter during the day. Camouflaged by their colour and stillness, they lie in wait for lizards, frogs, birds and mammals. The end of the tail may be held near the head and act as a lure^G to bring prey close.

A death adder's fangs are long and its venom is powerful and potentially fatal to humans. If alarmed, it warns by flattening its body and flicking its fore body from side to side.

Length: HBT 700 mm

* Refers to spine at end of tail.

STATUS	X	E	P	V	**S**	SIZE	RANGE

Yellow-faced Whipsnake

Demansia psammophis (= Van Diemen's sand-snake)

The Yellow-faced Whipsnake is found in many habitats over most of Australia. It does not live in the tropical north.

It is a slender-bodied, thin-necked, fast-moving snake. Its upper surface varies in colour from light grey to reddish, each scale edged darker. The under-surface is grey to cream. Each large eye has a dark rim. It forms the head of a "comma" whose tail is a dark marking, bordered yellow. This slants back towards the angle of the mouth.

This whipsnake feeds on small lizards, frogs and reptile eggs. It is venomous, though reluctant to bite. Only a very large Yellow-faced Whipsnake is likely to harm a human, but, if someone is bitten, medical advice should be sought.

A female lays up to 9 eggs, sometimes in a nest with other females' eggs. Up to 20 adults shelter together in cold winter weather.

Length: HBT 1.1 m

STATUS	X	E	P	V	**S**	SIZE	RANGE

Stephens's Banded Snake

Hoplocephalus stephensii (= Stephens's armoured-head)

This endangered snake lives in wooded ranges and rainforest edges from Gosford, New South Wales, to southern Queensland.

It is a broad-headed, slender-bodied, climbing snake. Its upper surface is black, with bright yellow scales forming narrow cross-bands. There are yellow spots on the head and yellow bars on the upper lip. The underside is grey with keeled scales.

This rare snake lives in trees and shelters in scars in tree trunks. These only become suitable when a tree is mature. Selective timber felling of older trees destroys these refuges.

Stephens's Banded Snake hunts lizards, small mammals (including bats) and birds in tree hollows and in crevices in rocks. A female has 2–12 young every second year.

A bite victim should be taken for medical assessment.

Length: HBT 1.25 m

STATUS	X	**E**	P	V	S	SIZE	RANGE

Eastern Tiger Snake
Notechis scutatus (= shielded southern snake)

Tiger snakes prefer damp, cool swamps and woodlands. The Eastern Tiger is found on the coastal lowlands and plains of south-eastern Australia, from south-eastern Queensland to south-eastern South Australia.

It is a large snake with a broad, strong body. Its upper surface may be brown, brown-green or blackish with pale bands. The underside is cream, yellow or grey.

Tiger snakes shelter in burrows and under timber. They are active by day and during warm evenings, and eat frogs, reptiles, nestling birds and fish. If threatened, a tiger snake curves the fore body off the ground, flattening it, and hissing loudly.

In spring, male tiger snakes wrestle in ritual combat. A female has 14–80 live young.

The venom of the Eastern and other related tiger snakes is potentially fatal to humans.

Length: HBT 2.1 m

STATUS	X	E	P	V	S	SIZE		RANGE

Taipan
Oxyuranus scutellatus (= small-shielded sharptail)

The Taipan is potentially Australia's deadliest snake. It is found along Australia's wet north-eastern and northern coasts. It prefers to live in thick vegetation, and its habitat is increasingly being settled by humans.

It is a large snake with a big, long head, slender neck and fore body. The head is paler than the body. The upper surface ranges from yellowish to blackish brown. The neck scales may be keeled. The eye is quite large.

Taipans shelter in burrows and holes. They prefer small mammal prey, which they kill with a fast, stabbing bite. The prey is let go to die, then tracked down and swallowed. When cornered, a Taipan holds its body coils loosely, raises its head and fore body, and bites as soon as the attacker is within range.

Male Taipans are larger than females and ritual combats take place in spring. A female may keep around 14 eggs in her body until they are almost ready to hatch.

Length: HBT 3.7 m
(usually about 1.8 m)

STATUS	X	E	P	V	S	SIZE		RANGE

Dugite
Pseudonaja affinis (= related false-cobra)

The Dugite is found in coastal areas of south-western Western Australia. It is a member of a group of "brown snakes" that together cover the Australian mainland.

It is a medium to large, fast-moving brown snake with a small head. The upper surface is brown or brownish grey with black spots. The underside is pale grey or brown with darker blotches. The eye has a dark iris and a gold rim around the pupil.

Dugites are active by day, hunting House Mice and other mammals, lizards and snakes. They bite, then wrap around the prey until it dies. If a Dugite feels threatened, it rears its fore body into a double S, hissing and striking. Dugites and related "brown snakes" are nervous and bite readily. Their venom can be fatal to humans.

In breeding season, males wrestle in ritual combat. A female lays up to 31 eggs in a burrow or under a rock.

Length: HBT 2 m

STATUS	X	E	P	V	S	SIZE		RANGE

Golden (Olive) Seasnake
Aipysurus laevis (= smooth (slippery) high-tail)

The Golden Seasnake lives around tropical coasts and reefs off northern Australia. It is the seasnake most likely to be seen by divers.

It is a large, strong-necked, thick-bodied seasnake with a tail like a paddle. Its upper surface has smooth scales and varies in colour from dark purple or green-brown to cream. There may be lighter or darker spots, or darker bands. The underside is paler and has keeled scales.

This seasnake shelters among, or near, coral, and is active by day or night. It hunts by probing crevices among corals for sleeping fish, prawns, crabs and fish eggs.

A female gives birth to 1–5 large young.

The Golden Seasnake will investigate a swimmer closely, then swim away. Its venom is powerful and potentially fatal to humans.

Length: HBT 2.2 m
(usually around 1.7 m)

STATUS	X	E	P	V	S	SIZE		RANGE

Insects, Spiders & other Arthropods

The armoured arthropods

Over 90% of all the world's animals are invertebrates[G], or animals without backbones. By far the greatest number of invertebrates (including insects, spiders, ticks, mites, scorpions, centipedes, millipedes, crays and crabs) belong to a group known as arthropods (joint-legged animals).

An arthropod has an exoskeleton, or hard outside skeleton. This exoskeleton is jointed to allow movement. From time to time, as an arthropod grows larger, it sheds its exoskeleton.

A larger, soft exoskeleton is growing beneath. When the arthropod sheds its old exoskeleton, the new one hardens and protects the animal's body.

An arthropod has a body that is divided into segments. These are organised into working parts, such as head, thorax[G] and abdomen.

An arthropod has jointed appendages[G] (limbs). These are used for handling things, getting food, walking, defence, swimming, holding eggs or other purposes.

The three groups of arthropods

Spiders, scorpions and allies:

- have no antennae[G];
- have a body divided into cephalothorax (head and thorax), and abdomen;
- have the first pair of appendages as chelicerae[G] (fangs and jaws combined), and the second pair as pedipalps[G], used for handling and sensing things;
- have four pairs of walking legs.

Spider

Scorpion

Crayfish, crabs and allies:

- have two pairs of antennae;
- have a body divided into head, thorax and abdomen;
- have part of the body covered by a shield called a carapace;
- have varying number of appendages, but each appendage branches into two parts.

Freshwater cray

Slaters

Insects, centipedes and allies:

- have one pair of antennae;
- either have a body divided into head, thorax and abdomen (insects);
- or have a body divided into many segments (centipedes and millipedes);
- have varying numbers of unbranched appendages.

Millipede

Insect

The prehistory of arthropods

Marine invertebrates with hard exoskeletons lived in the ancient seas of earth in the Cambrian period, over 510 million years ago.

In the Silurian period, over 408 million years ago, scorpion-like arthropods crawled out up on the land.

By the Devonian period, over 355 million years ago, wingless, insect-like arthropods that ate dead plants existed.

The Carboniferous period, over 280 million years ago, saw the emergence of winged insects that ate seeds and sucked plant juices. Spiders and scorpions also existed.

Insects with larval and pupal stages appeared in the Permian, over 245 million years ago. Insects now ate leaves, and spiders followed them into the trees and bushes.

The great development of flowering plants around 145 million years ago led to the development of insect pollinators[G].

"Modern" spiders developed in the Cretaceous, over 65 million years ago. By this time, most of today's insect groups were in existence.

To discover arthropods...

Investigate your garden and house. Explore the bush. Use your ears and eyes.

Look (cautiously) under bark, fallen timber, leaf litter and rocks, and in cracks and holes.

Look for insect traces, e.g. damaged leaves. Use a net to scoop the surface of still water.

Spread a sheet under a bush, then shake the bush. Hang a sheet behind a light at night. Observe the insects that settle on it.

Explore with a torch at night, when most spiders' eyes glitter like diamonds and many arthropods are active.

Discover spider webs at dawn, covered with dew, then look for the spider near or on the web that evening.

Examine insect and spider displays in museums and zoos. Read in the library.

Join your local Naturalists' Club.

Helpful hints

Don't touch spiders, centipedes, scorpions, or stinging or biting insects.

If you want to study a creature closely, place an upside-down, clear-sided container over it. Then slide cardboard under the mouth of the container; pick it up with the creature inside it and quickly replace the lid. Use a brush to sweep small creatures into your container.

If you must keep a creature for a few hours for study, handle it with caution, keep it cool and comfortable, and release it where you found it.

Visit national parks that include insect-rich habitat such as rainforest.

Remember – many arthropods are well camouflaged.

> **Many insect forms have hardly changed over millions of years. The cockroach of today is much the same as the cockroaches that lived 300 million years ago. However, modern insects may be very much smaller than those that lived in the past.**
> **A dragonfly that existed about 300 million years ago was 700 mm across the wings. The largest living Australian dragonfly has a wingspan of only 160 mm.**

Insect or spider?

INSECT	SPIDER
Body divided into head, thorax and abdomen	Body divided into cephalothorax (head + thorax) and abdomen
3 pairs of walking legs	4 pairs of walking legs
Simple[G] and compound[G] eyes	Usually 8 simple eyes
Has antennae	Lacks antennae
May have wings	Never has wings
May have silk glands, but lacks spinnerets[G]	Abdomen has silk glands opening on spinnerets
Has jaws	Has chelicerae that inject poison

An insect with a spider as prey.   *A spider with an insect as prey.*

Groups of Australian insects

Scientists place the world's insects into Class Insecta (Insects). This class is divided into 29 Orders.

There are 26 Orders found in Australia.

Insect orders found in Australia

Those whose life history involves no change in shape.

Archaeognatha	bristletails
Thysanura	silverfish

Those whose life history involves gradual changes.
Egg – nymph[G] (numerous instars[G]) – adult

Ephemeroptera	mayflies
Odonata*	dragonflies, damselflies
Plecoptera	stoneflies
Blattodea*	cockroaches
Isoptera*	termites
Mantodea*	mantids
Dermaptera*	earwigs
Orthoptera*	grasshoppers, crickets, katydids
Phasmatodea*	stick and leaf insects
Embioptera	embiids (web-spinners)
Psocoptera	booklice
Phthiraptera	lice
Hemiptera*	true bugs, cicadas, leaf-hoppers, aphids, scale insects
Thysanoptera	thrips

Those whose life history involves several abrupt changes.
Egg – larva[G] – pupa – adult

Megaloptera	alderflies, dobsonflies
Neuroptera*	lacewings, antlions
Coleoptera*	beetles
Strepsiptera	stylops (tiny parasites[G])
Mecoptera*	scorpion flies
Siphonaptera	fleas
Diptera*	flies, mosquitoes, midges
Trichoptera	caddis flies
Lepidoptera*	moths, butterflies
Hymenoptera*	ants, bees, wasps, sawflies

Descriptions and photographic examples included in this book

The three sorts of insect life cycle

1. No-changes life cycle

Silverfish and bristletails are primitive, wingless insects. They hatch from their eggs looking like small adults, and simply grow larger throughout their lifetimes.

2. Gradual changes life cycle

Dragonflies, cockroaches, termites, mantids and grasshoppers are amongst the insects that go through gradual changes throughout their lifetimes. An egg hatches into a nymph. As it grows, it moults. Each time it moults (into a stage called an instar) it is a little different; e.g. wings begin as buds, but are larger after each moult.

A newly hatched caterpillar crawls away from its egg case.

The caterpillar feeds hungrily and moults several times.

It becomes a pupa, hanging from a silk pad woven onto a twig.

The newly emerged butterfly is ready to expand and dry its wings.

3 Several abrupt changes life cycle

Beetles, scorpion-flies, fleas, flies, moths, butterflies, ants, bees and wasps are amongst the insects that go through several sudden changes as they mature. The egg hatches into a larva, which moults several times as it grows. The larval stage between each moult is called an instar. The larva turns into a pupa (or chrysalis), a resting stage in which the whole body changes into an adult. Eventually the adult, winged stage emerges from the pupal case.

Some facts about insects

There are about one million species of insects known to science so far. This is about 80% of all animals.

Entomologists[G] (people who study insects) estimate there may be as many as 30 million insect species.

At least 86 000 species of Australian insect have been described by scientists so far. Many more await discovery.

One locust swarm was estimated to contain 40 000 million locusts.

Much of our knowledge of primitive insects comes from creatures that were preserved in fossilised[G] tree sap (amber).

Some insects eat poisonous plants. They store the poisons in their bodies, where the toxins serve as defence against predators.

An insect's compound eye is made up of six-sided lenses[G].

A dragonfly may have more than 20 000 lenses in each eye.

The "blood" of an insect is usually a yellowish green colour. Insects have hearts and some big blood vessels, but then the blood just bathes the tissues.

Insect eggs are often laid in huge numbers. This makes sure that even if most of the eggs are lost a few will hatch.

Aphids are small insects that suck plant juices. One female aphid may produce 50 offspring each week. If all survived and their descendants all survived, at the end of one year, the world would be submerged under a layer of aphids 150 km deep.

After World War II, a chemical called DDT was used to poison insect pests. Birds that ate poisoned insects or treated grain accumulated DDT in their bodies. They laid thin-shelled eggs that failed to hatch.

A zoologist called Rachel Carson wrote a book called *Silent Spring*, which alerted the public to the dangers of pesticides.

A damaged insect may regrow injured limbs or antennae.

ants
Order Hymenoptera (= membrane wings)

Order Hymenoptera includes ants, wasps, bees and sawflies. These are tiny to large insects, most with a waist between the first two segments of the abdomen. Those with wings have two membranous pairs, the fore wings larger than the hind wings, and coupled to them with hooks. The head bears short to long antennae, large compound eyes and chewing mouthparts. In some groups, the ovipositor has become a sting.

Ants have the first segment of the abdomen fused to the thorax, and a waist between the second and third segments. Their antennae have angled "elbows". Adult ants eat liquids. Some species care for and "milk" caterpillars and aphids.

The larvae are legless. Winged males and females fly from the nest and mate. The males die; the females shed their wings and begin colonies. Ant colonies may have a population of 1 million – infertile workers and soldiers, and fertile females and males.

Length (all Hymenoptera): 0.15–20 mm

Aust. spp. in Order Hymenoptera: about 15 000

Aust. spp. of ants: about 4000

STATUS	X	E	P	V	S	SIZE		RANGE

bees
Order Hymenoptera (cont.)

Bees share the characteristics of Order Hymenoptera. They also have branched body hairs, and the hind leg or abdomen usually has a "basket", or special hairs for carrying pollen (photo left). The mouthparts form a "tongue" for getting nectar.

In many species, female bees store sperm, then lay eggs when food is available. An egg is laid in a cell stocked with larval food of nectar and pollen. Hive bee workers feed the legless larvae, which pupate and emerge as adults.

Most bee species are solitary. A female digs a nest in the ground (photo right), or in wood, and places pollen and nectar in it for her larvae. A few bees live in hives that consist of infertile workers, and fertile queens (females) and drones (males).

Aust. spp. of bees: about 2000

STATUS	X	E	P	V	S	SIZE		RANGE

wasps
Order Hymenoptera (cont.)

Wasps include groups whose larvae parasitise insects and spiders. The females of these groups have their ovipositors modified into stings. A female may sting a caterpillar or spider, carry it to a prepared burrow or mud cell (see photo), and lay an egg on it. When the legless wasp larva hatches, it eats the host. Then it pupates and later emerges as an adult wasp. Females of some groups lay their eggs in free-living hosts.

Cuckoo wasps lay their eggs in the nests of other species, and their larvae eat the wasp larvae and the hosts as well.

Adult wasps feed on nectar or other fluids. The larvae of non-parasitic wasps feed on plants. The female of one group of hunting wasps uses a pebble as a tool to firm down loose soil at the entrance to her nest tunnel.

Length: 0.15–35 mm

STATUS	X	E	P	V	S	SIZE		RANGE

sawflies
Order Hymenoptera (cont.)

Sawflies are small to large Hymenoptera that do not have a waist. The female's ovipositor has a saw-like tip. The larvae have legs on the thorax and false legs on the abdomen.

A female lays eggs into slits cut in a plant with her ovipositor. Some larvae bore into wood or mine leaves, but most live on foliage. The larvae may pupate in the soil.

Adult sawflies eat nectar. One family of sawflies is parasitic, using beetle larvae as hosts. Sawfly larvae, which feed on leaf surfaces (see photo right), may cling together and wave abdomens when molested. Larvae of some species "spit" nasty liquid at predators. The introduced Sirex Wasp, which kills pine trees by introducing fungus into them, is a sawfly.

Length: 3–30 mm

Aust. spp.: 176

STATUS	X	E	P	V	S	SIZE		RANGE

The long history of spiders

The spiders that existed around 300 million years ago lived on the ground and sheltered in burrows. Their bodies were thick and bulky. Their jaws, or chelicerae, worked up and down, like a pair of pickaxes. They breathed by taking air into two pairs of abdominal pouches filled with leaves of tissue. These are called book-lungs[G]. Their abdomens also carried two pairs of spinnerets – organs that fed out silk made in the abdomen. This silk was used to line burrows and spin sacs in which to keep eggs.

Today's "primitive spiders", such as the trapdoor, funnel-web and brush-footed spiders, are very like these distant ancestors.

By 245 million years ago, one group of spiders had developed a spinning-plate, called a cribellum[G], on the abdomen. These spiders also had, on the fourth pair of legs, combs that could weave silk as it left the cribellum. The chelicerae of these spiders closed from side to side. The spider breathed through book-lungs, but also through tubes opening onto their body surfaces, called tracheae[G]. They used silk to make shelters and snares, or traps for prey.

Today's "modern spiders", the active hunting spiders and web-weavers, are descended from this group.

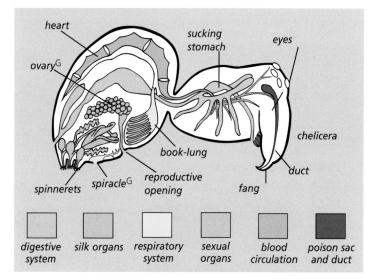

| digestive system | silk organs | respiratory system | sexual organs | blood circulation | poison sac and duct |

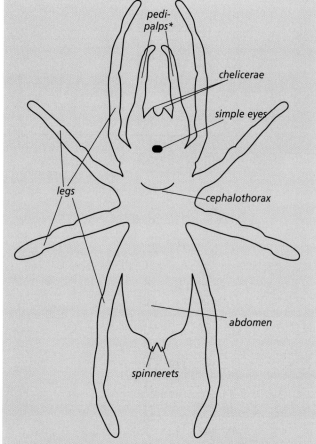

Deadly to humans

Australian spiders that can harm humans include the Sydney, Blue Mountain and Northern Tree Funnel-webs, the White-tailed Spider, Mouse Spider, Black House Spider and Red-back Spider.

A bite from any one of Australia's funnel-web spiders can be fatal to humans and other primates such as gorillas and chimpanzees. It has little effect on other mammals. Funnel-web venom attacks the nervous system. The male Sydney Funnel-web is one of the world's most dangerous spiders, and lives in a heavily populated area. During summer and autumn, he leaves home to

Red-back Spider

search for females. Since he does not hunt, his venom becomes very strong. If threatened, he will attack rather than run away. Around 15 people have died from funnel-web bite in the past 60 years.

Only the female Red-back Spider is dangerous to humans. The male's fangs are too short to pierce human skin. Red-backs usually build their tangled webs close to the ground; they may be found around houses and outbuildings. There were about one dozen human fatalities recorded before Red-back antivenom was developed in 1956. There have been none since then.

Some facts about spiders

The Class Arachnida is named after Arachne, who, in an old Greek myth, was changed into a spider after challenging the goddess Athene to a weaving contest.

Worldwide, over 25 000 species of spiders have been discovered so far. Australia has almost 2000 species.

A female spider may live over 20 years. A male may not survive more than one mating season. Eating him after mating provides the female with energy for egg-laying.

Male spiders are generally smaller than females of the same species.

The males of some species use gestures, bright colours and web-tweaking to court females and to let them know the suitor is not prey.

Male and female huntsman spiders have a lengthy courtship. The female seldom attacks the male, and family groups may be found under bark or rocks.

When the young of some spiders hatch, they spin fine silken lines and "balloon" away with the wind.

A female wolf spider may carry her young around on her back for up to six months.

A spider's venom is made up of chemicals that help dissolve the tissues of the prey so that the spider can suck them up as fluid.

A spider's pedipalps (= foot-feelers), set on either side of its mouth, are used as combined hands and feelers.

Groups of Australian spiders

Scientists place the world's spiders, scorpions, ticks and mites, and their allies, in the Class Arachnida. Spiders are placed in the Order Araneae. There are 116 Families of spiders in the world; 69 are found in Australia. The Australian spiders are placed in two groups. The "primitive" group contains 10 families, while the "modern" spider group contains 59.

Class: ARACHNIDS

Order: ARANEAE

10 FAMILIES OF "PRIMITIVE" SPIDERS	**59 FAMILIES OF "MODERN" SPIDERS**
Have fangs (chelicerae) that move up and down, like pickaxes.	*Have fangs (chelicerae) that move from side to side, like pincers.*
Have venom glands in bases of chelicerae.	*Have venom glands in head.*
Usually have 2 pairs of spinnerets.	*Have 3 pairs of spinnerets.*
Do not have a spinning plate.	*May have a spinning plate.*
Breathe through one pair of book-lungs.	*Breathe through 2 pairs of book-lungs and tracheae.*
Use silk for egg sacs, triplines, to line burrows and, occasionally, for catching webs.	*Use silk for egg sacs, to make shelters of various kinds and to weave catching webs.*

Silk for all purposes

Silk is one of the reasons spiders are so successful. It is a fine thread that will not dissolve in water and is immensely strong for its thickness. A strand of silk can stretch more than one-third, then snap back to its original length without changing shape. It is at least twice as strong as steel wire of the same thickness.

Different sorts of glands within a spider's abdomen make different sorts of silk. As silk passes from silk glands to spinnerets, it may be coated with a sticky fluid. It then flows from the spinnerets as a liquid that hardens in the air.

Some spiders have a spinning plate, or cribellum, which shapes the silk as it leaves the body. Some also have a comb on each hind leg. As silk leaves the cribellum, the combs make tiny loops in it. These catch the bristles on the bodies of insect prey.

Silk is used for shelters, egg sacs, triplines, snares and webs, and for wrapping prey and safety lines. Young spiders may drift through the air on silken lines. The wheel-shaped webs spun by some spiders are efficent traps for prey. The web owner rushes to the victim and wraps it in silk. Then it sucks out the prey's body juices.

Building an orb web

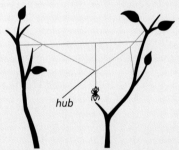

1. The spider pays out a silk thread that the wind carries to a second anchor point. This bridge is strengthened by additional silk threads passed back and forth across it. Then the spider makes a Y shape that becomes the first three radial threads.

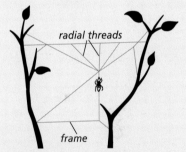

2. The bottom of the stem of the Y is anchored to the ground or some other firm object. A frame is constructed and radial threads are attached to surrounding objects.

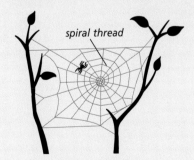

3. The spider makes a "safe track", or scaffolding, of non-sticky silk, working from the centre to the edge of the web.

4. The spider then works back to the centre of the web, removing the dry silk and replacing it with sticky silk. The sticky silk is tied to each radial thread, then plucked to twang the gum into regular sticky beads.

funnel-web spiders
Family Hexathelidae (= six spinnerets)

Funnel-webs are found from eastern Queensland south to Tasmania, and south-west to the Mt Lofty Ranges, South Australia.

Large to very large ground- or tree-living spiders, they may be blue-black, purple-black or dark grey. The cephalothorax bears massive, downwards moving chelicerae, 8 eyes and long, leg-like pedipalps. The underside of the abdomen has 2 pairs of book-lungs and usually 6, sometimes 4, spinnerets.

An attacking funnel-web raises the front of its body and its front legs off the ground. The venom can be fatal to humans.

A funnel-web's home is a long, flat tube of silk, placed in a rock crevice, a crack in a tree, or a burrow. The spider sits at the entrance at night. Silk strands warn it of approaching prey, or danger. Mature males leave their refuges to wander in search of females. A female lays her eggs in a brood chamber, and the young spiders remain there for some time.

Body length: ♀ up to 50 mm

♂ up to 35 mm

STATUS	X	E	P	V	S	SIZE			RANGE

whistling spiders
Family Theraphosidae

These large to very large ground-living or burrowing spiders are found in various habitats. Their bodies and legs, or legs only, are covered with fine, velvety hairs. The legs end in claws and tufts of hair (or brushes – they are are sometimes called brush-footed spiders). They have large, downwards moving chelicerae, two pairs of book-lungs and four spinnerets.

The group includes huge spiders that eat insects, ground birds, reptiles and frogs. These spiders "whistle" by rubbing spines on the bases of their pedipalps over bristles on their chelicerae. The females may hold their egg sacs. After hatching, young spiders remain in the burrow for some time. Some whistling spiders survive flooding by taking refuge in an airlock formed in a side chamber to the burrow shaft.

Body length: up to 60 mm

Leg span: up to 160 mm

STATUS	X	E	P	V	S	SIZE			RANGE

trapdoor spiders
Families Idiopidae (= same eyes) and Ctenizidae

Trapdoor spiders are found in many habitats, including rainforest and desert.

They are medium to large ground-living, burrowing spiders. Usually they are dark in colour or mottled.

They have downwards moving chelicerae and two pairs of book-lungs. The final segment of the second pair of spinnerets is short and rounded.

A burrow may be more than 1 m in length, and dug at an angle or straight down. It may be sealed by a lid or "trapdoor" of silk and earth. The spider waits inside its burrow, then seizes insects or other small passing creatures. Male trapdoor spiders wander in search of females in summer, usually in damp weather.

Trapdoor spiders are much less aggressive than funnel-webs. When in danger, they will usually "freeze" with legs close to the body, lie upside down, or run away.

Body length: ♀ to 35 mm ♂ to 25 mm

STATUS	X	E	P	V	S	SIZE			RANGE

MATING IN THE JAWS OF DEATH

A male spider takes great risks when mating. He must use his pedipalps to place his sperm inside an opening on the female's abdomen. As he is doing this, the female may eat him.

A male funnel-web courts the female just outside her home. He taps her repeatedly with his first pair of legs and his palps, lulling her into a dreamy state. If she rears back to strike, he catches her opened fangs with special spurs on his second pair of legs. Holding her fangs, he pushes her up and backwards, tapping her to keep her peaceful. When her abdomen is exposed, he pokes his sperm into her reproductive opening, lets go of her fangs and gets out of range as fast as he can. Sometimes he does not succeed in escaping.

The pedipalps are the "legs" closest to the head. The male uses these to place his sperm in the female's abdomen.

huntsman spiders
Family Heteropodidae (= different legs)

Huntsman spiders are found under bark, or beneath flakes of rock. They may live in houses. Most species are not harmful to humans.

They are medium to large climbing spiders with flattened brown or grey bodies. They may have banded legs. The eyes are in 2 rows: 4 back, 4 front. All 4 pairs of long, hairy legs are spread sideways, so this spider can scuttle sideways. The male has a smaller body and longer legs than the female.

Huntsmen are active at night, chasing and leaping on small creatures. A female guards her white, papery egg sac, then opens it to allow the young to escape. They stay with her for some time.

Body length: ♀ to 47 mm ♂ to 30 mm

Leg span: 160 mm

Known Aust. spp.: more than 90

STATUS	X	E	P	V	**S**	SIZE	RANGE

wolf spiders
Family Lycosidae (after Lycaon, turned into a wolf by Jupiter)

Wolf spiders can be found in most habitats, especially near water, and, when seen, are almost always on the ground.

They are small to very large long-legged, ground-living spiders. The grey or brown body, which tilts up at the front, is often patterned in a sunburst of grey, brown or orange. The eyes are in 3 rows: 2 back, 2 centre, 4 front.

Many wolf spiders make burrows (these may have lids, or collars of silk, or a sheet-web around them), but many others shelter in cracks. All leave home to search for prey.

A female carries her egg sac attached to her spinnerets. After the young hatch, the female carries them around on her abdomen (see photo). Finally, they climb grass blades, spin strands of silk and "balloon" away.

Length: ♀ to 16 mm ♂ to 13 mm

Known Aust. spp.: more than 130

STATUS	X	E	P	V	**S**	SIZE	RANGE

lynx spiders
Family Oxyopidae (= sharp eyes)

Lynx spiders live in trees, grass or low vegetation.

They have tapering abdomens and long, thin legs covered with long spines. The head is high in front and bears 8 eyes, set in 4 rows of 2. Often these spiders are very colourful (green, brown or yellow), with light and dark bands along the sides of the abdomen.

The name "lynx spider" comes from their cat-like habits. On sunny days, they move actively about on leaves and branches, stalking and pouncing on small insects. As the wind sways the leaves, a lynx spider sways on its slender legs. These active little spiders do not make shelters.

The white egg sac is placed in leaves tied together with silk. The female guards it until the eggs hatch.

Length: up to 10 mm

STATUS	X	E	P	V	**S**	SIZE	RANGE

jumping spiders
Family Salticidae (*salto* = to dance, leap, spring)

Jumping spiders live on plants. They are small to medium-sized colourful spiders that jump strongly to secure prey or escape danger.

The front of the body is high. The eyes are in 3 rows: 2 back, 2 centre, 4 front; the middle front pair are large. The pedipalps may be furry and white. The legs are short and strong; the abdomen is usually longer than wide.

Jumping spiders are daytime hunters that move in leaps and dashes. They constantly move the cephalothorax to look around, and may appear to watch a human observer. Like all spiders, they trail safety lines. Courting males wave their pedipalps and move to display body colours and patterns (see photo). A female remains with her white egg sac in a silken shelter. Some jumping spiders can see prey at 200 mm and can jump 180 mm.

Length: up to 12 mm

Aust. spp.: more than 250

STATUS	X	E	P	V	**S**	SIZE	RANGE

comb-footed spiders
Family Theridiidae

Spiders in this family are small to medium-sized web-spinnners. On each hind leg they have a comb carrying toothed spines. This comb rakes the silk into wide ribbons as it leaves the spinnerets to wrap prey. The abdomen is round.

Red-back Spiders live in dry places, including buildings and rubbish.

A female Red-back is black, with red markings on the upper and lower abdomen. A bite from a female Red-back may kill a human if antivenom is not given.

A Red-back's web is a tangle of threads. From it hang several gummy threads fastened to the ground or to another surface. The spider rests upside-down in a silken nest during the day, and emerges onto its web at night. When an insect touches a sticky

thread, its struggles break the thread, which snaps upwards. The spider rushes out and seizes the prey.

Length: ♀ up to 14 mm ♂ 3 mm

Aust. spp. in family Theridiidae: about 90

STATUS	X	E	P	V	S	SIZE		RANGE

laceweb spiders
Family Amaurobiidae

This family of small to medium-sized grey to black spiders spins funnel-shaped webs near a crack or hole in which the spider hides. The spinning plate produces lacy, silken threads that make the webs easy to see. The eyes are in 2 rows: 4 back, 4 front. The abdomen is egg-shaped.

The **Black House Spider** is stout and coal black. It hides in window corners, rafters, rockeries, stone walls and outdoor light fittings. This spider's bite can cause pain and sickness to humans.

The female never leaves her retreat and web, rushing out to seize creatures caught in its blue-white silk. A mature male roams, courts a female by plucking her web, and may remain with her after mating. The female guards her white egg sacs and the young float away on silken threads.

Length: ♀ to 18 mm ♂ to 9 mm

Aust. spp. in family Amaurobiidae: about 20

STATUS	X	E	P	V	S	SIZE		RANGE

net-casting spiders
Family Deinopidae (= evil eyes)

"Ogre-faced spiders" are most common in eucalypt forests.

They are medium to large-sized spiders mottled in brown or grey. They have long bodies and their very long legs have large joints. Their eyes are in 3 rows: 2 back, 2 largest centre, 4 front. The spinning plate produces sticky, elastic silk for a catching net. During

the day these spiders hang down on silk threads, looking like sticks. At night, each spider weaves a postage-stamp-sized net, holds it in the front legs, then flings it over passing prey. A net may be used more than once if undamaged. If it is damaged, it may be eaten or discarded.

A female guards her egg sac, which is attached to a rock or plant.

Length: ♀ to 25 mm ♂ to 12 mm

Aust. spp.: 14

STATUS	X	E	P	V	S	SIZE		RANGE

crab and flower spiders
Family Thomisidae

Most crab and flower spiders live in warmer climates. They are found on plants, often on flowers or bark.

These small spiders are crab-like in shape, and their front two pairs of legs are strong and spiny. They have 8 eyes: 4 back, 4 front, sometimes mounted on turrets. Crab spiders are the colour and texture of bark. Flower spiders (photo below), are smooth and coloured white, yellow, green and/or red, like the petals of flowers.

These spiders wait in ambush during the day. A flower spider "owns" its flower, remaining there until the flower wilts. It sits within the flower, anchored by its hind legs, front legs and pedipalps, ready to seize a visiting insect.

A female makes a silk shelter for her woolly egg sacs, which she guards until the eggs hatch.

Length: ♀ to 15 mm ♂ smaller

Aust. spp.: about 140

STATUS	X	E	P	V	S	SIZE		RANGE

triangular spiders
Family Araneidae (from the Latin *aranea* = spider)

These small spiders live in forests, on trees and ferns. They are often found on bushfire regrowth.

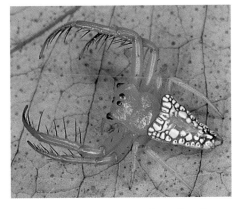

The cephalothorax and triangular abdomen are brightly coloured (green, yellow, orange, red, white) and glossy. The long two front pairs of legs are spiny, and are used to grip prey. The short two hind pairs of legs are used to grip a leaf or bark.

These spiders weave reduced webs and use silk for safety lines, egg sacs and prey-wrapping. Their bright colours serve as camouflage.

During the day, a triangular spider sits on a leaf, seizing passing insects. At night, it may hang from a thread, grabbing prey with its front legs.

The round, pink egg sac hangs under a leaf.

Length: ♀ to 10 mm
Aust. spp.: 9

STATUS	X	E	P	V	S	SIZE		RANGE

bird-dropping spiders
Family Araneidae (continued)

These well-camouflaged spiders live in bushes and trees. They are small to medium-sized spiders. The bumpy abdomen is coloured black, white and brown, patterned to mimic a bird-dropping. The banded legs are held close to the body during the day.

During the day, a bird-dropping spider sits huddled on a leaf in the open. At night, a young one catches prey in a web. An adult hangs head down with its front two pairs of legs outstretched. It attracts male moths by giving out a scent like that of a female moth.

The female is often seen guarding a group of round, brown egg sacs (see photo).

Length: ♀ 12 mm (to 20 while pregnant) ♂ 3 mm
Aust. spp.: 7

STATUS	X	E	P	V	S	SIZE		RANGE

bolas spiders
Family Araneidae (cont.)

These small to medium spiders are found in the foliage of dry or wet eucalypt forests. They may also live in gardens.

A bolas[G] spider has a small cephalothorax, a large, plump abdomen and short, strong legs. Body and legs are covered with fine hairs.

At night, the spider hangs from several strands of strong silk. Moths are captured on a thread ending in a sticky blob (the bolas) that hangs from one leg and is whirled by a second. The spider seems to give out an odour similar to that of a female moth to attract male moths.

The spindle-shaped egg sacs are guarded by the female.

Length: ♀ 14 mm (to 25 when pregnant) ♂ to 1.5 mm
Aust. spp.: 4

STATUS	X	E	P	V	S	SIZE		RANGE

golden orb-weavers
Family Araneidae (cont.)

The huge web of the golden orb-weaver is found in woodlands, forests, gardens and road verges.

The spider is large to very large with long legs. The female has a plum-coloured body with a silver-grey sheen, and legs banded black, yellow and orange. The tiny male is brown.

A female anchors her large web to trees, wires or poles. It is made of strong, golden silk with a section not filled in at the top. The orb may be more than 1 m across, with anchor-strands on either side. Above and at the sides are tangles of threads (the photo shows a female in one of these areas). The female remains in her web night and day. Smaller Quicksilver Spiders may share the web.

The bite of a golden orb-weaver is harmless to humans.

Length: ♀ to 45 mm ♂ 6 mm

STATUS	X	E	P	V	S	SIZE		RANGE

St Andrews Cross Spider
Family Araneidae (cont.) *Argiope keyserlingi*

The striking web of this spider is built in foliage, usually within 1–2 m of the ground, and often near water.

The medium-sized spider, which rests on a cross of thickened silk in the web, appears to have only 4 legs. The female's abdomen is striped yellow, red, black and white, and her legs are banded. The male is plain red-brown.

The cross that strengthens the web consists of two ribbons of lacy, zigzagged silk. When threatened, the spider may grip the web and shake it. This spider is active during the day, and repairs its web if it is damaged by large prey.

The grey-green or brown, pear-shaped egg sacs are attached to foliage near the web.

Length: ♀ to 15 mm ♂ 5 mm

STATUS	X	E	P	V	S	SIZE	RANGE

garden spiders
Family Araneidae (cont.)

Garden spiders live in many habitats, including gardens. Webs are made across open spaces and above tracks and streams.

They are medium-sized, heavily built, hairy spiders with a hump on each "shoulder" of the plump abdomen. They are usually grey or brown, and their outstretched legs show shiny red-brown sections. A garden spider's bite is harmless to humans.

This spider hangs head down in its orb web at night (see photo). At dawn, it tears down most of the web, then remakes it the following evening. During the day, it hides with its legs tucked close to its body in foliage near the web site. The fluffy yellow or golden egg sac is hidden in the curve of a leaf.

Length: ♀ to 30 mm when pregnant ♂ to 20 mm

Aust. spp.: more than 100

STATUS	X	E	P	V	S	SIZE	RANGE

SILKEN TRAPS

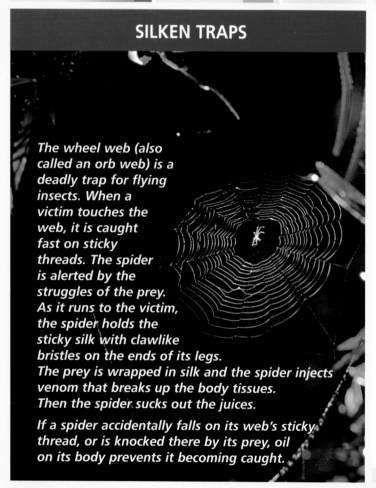

The wheel web (also called an orb web) is a deadly trap for flying insects. When a victim touches the web, it is caught fast on sticky threads. The spider is alerted by the struggles of the prey. As it runs to the victim, the spider holds the sticky silk with clawlike bristles on the ends of its legs. The prey is wrapped in silk and the spider injects venom that breaks up the body tissues. Then the spider sucks out the juices.

If a spider accidentally falls on its web's sticky thread, or is knocked there by its prey, oil on its body prevents it becoming caught.

jewel spiders
Family *Araneidae* (continued)

These harmless spiders live in most woodland habitats, especially in tropical and temperate areas. They are often seen near water.

They are small, brightly coloured and short-legged. The broad, hard, shield-like abdomen has up to 6 spines around its edges.

The upright orb web has very close threads, and may be placed alone or in a group of other webs. The threads supporting the web carry tufts of fluffy white silk.

The best known jewel spider is the Christmas Spider, whose female is black, orange and cream with a six-pointed abdomen. The male, which is only 3 mm long, has blunt spines.

Length: to 8 mm

STATUS	X	E	P	V	S	SIZE	RANGE

scorpions
Class Arachnida

Scorpions are found on the ground, in burrows, and under rocks, logs and bark.

They are medium to large arthropods that, like spiders, have bodies divided into cephalothorax and abdomen, but have no waist. The abdomen has a long tail, ending in a sting that is held over the body. The head bears antennae, 6–12 eyes, chelicerae and a large pair of pedipalps, the final two segments of each forming a grasping pair of pincers. Scorpions feed on live prey such as insects, spiders and millipedes. Male and female perform a mating dance, in which the male guides the female's reproductive opening over a packet of sperm he has deposited on the ground. The female gives birth to live young, which she carries on her back for some weeks.

At night, ultraviolet light highlights scorpions. A human stung by a scorpion may experience pain and swelling.

Length: may grow to 120 mm

STATUS	X	E	P	V	S	SIZE	RANGE

centipedes
Class Chilopoda

Centipedes are found under rocks, bark or leaf litter.

They are small to very large arthropods. A centipede may have from 15 to over 100 pairs of legs, borne on the same number of body segments, according to species. The head bears a pair of antennae and chewing mouthparts. Each of the first pair of legs under the first segment bears a poison claw. The final body segment bears long, often brightly coloured legs. The house centipede (below left) has 15 pairs of long legs.

Insects, spiders, frogs and geckos are killed by venom from the claws, then torn up by the jaws. Centipede venom may cause a human pain.

A male lays a packet of sperm onto a mat he has spun, or places the sperm directly onto the female's reproductive opening. She guards her eggs until they hatch.

Length: 10–150 mm

STATUS	X	E	P	V	S	SIZE	RANGE

millipedes
Class Diplopoda

Millipedes are found under rocks, logs, bark and leaf litter.

Small to large arthropods, they have two pairs of small legs on each body segment (which is actually two segments fused together). Young stages may have only single pairs of legs on each segment. Millipedes can produce a nasty tasting liquid as a defence, or may simply curl up (photo at right).

Millipedes usually eat plant material.

To mate, a male wraps himself around a female. He uses special mating legs on his seventh segment to pass sperm into her reproductive opening.

The introduced Black Portuguese Millipede is a pest in south-eastern Australia.

Length: to 120 mm

STATUS	X	E	P	V	S	SIZE	RANGE

crustaceans (crabs & allies)
Subphylum Crustacea; Class Malacostraca

Freshwater crays, prawns, shrimps and crabs are found in or near fresh water. Slaters are flattened, grey, scuttling land crustaceans found under stones and rotting wood.

Crustaceans are small to huge arthropods with the body divided into head, thorax (covered by a shell, the carapace) and abdomen. The head bears two pairs of antennae, biting and grinding mouthparts, and other feeding appendages. The first pair of the five pairs of legs form large pincers. Crabs have the abdomen bent up under the thorax.

Crustaceans eat a variety of plant and animal food.

Members of this group that live in areas of uncertain rainfall, dig deep burrows and remain there in dry times.

Length: freshwater crays (photo above) to 400 mm

STATUS	X	E	P	V	S	SIZE	RANGE

Australia's Marine Life

Life in the sea

Australia's coastline is over 36 000 km in length. The marine area for which Australia is responsible extends far into the oceans surrounding the continent. This area has a huge variety of habitats, extending from coastal sand dunes to ocean trenches. Every habitat contains creatures of some kind. Each of these creatures must cope with a number of factors:

- Water pressure increases by one atmosphere (the pressure of air on the earth's surface) for each 10 metres of depth. Animals that live at even moderate depths, or catch food or live at deeper levels, must be able to survive this pressure.

- As depth increases, light fades and the water grows colder. Plants that need sunlight to grow cannot exist any deeper than the sun's light will penetrate. Plant-eating animals must find their food near the surface. Animals living at depth eat other animals or their remains.

- Sea water contains high levels of salt. Organisms that live in the sea must be able to deal with this mineral.

- The oxygen needed for life processes is carried in sea water. Animals that do not have gills to take oxygen from the water must come to the surface periodically to breathe.

Depth zones of the ocean

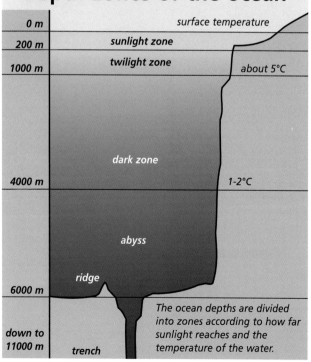

0 m	surface temperature
200 m	sunlight zone
1000 m	twilight zone
	about 5°C
	dark zone
4000 m	1-2°C
	abyss
	ridge
6000 m	
down to 11000 m	trench

The ocean depths are divided into zones according to how far sunlight reaches and the temperature of the water.

The zones of the seashore

sand dunes

high tide mark

intertidal zone

low tide mark

subtidal zone

The intertidal zone extends from the high tide mark to the low tide mark.

The subtidal zone is below the low tide mark.

Marine habitats

Marine life can be found from the highest point where waves splash the shore to the deepest trenches of the ocean floor. Most kinds of marine plants and animals live in the first 30 m of water.

These are some of the places you can find marine life.

Open sea

Mangroves

Sand beaches

Coral reefs

Under water

Rocky shores

Places for closer study:
Visit museums and libraries to find out more about marine life. Watch underwater documentaries on television. Public aquariums give great underwater viewing.

A timeline for marine life

3500 million years ago

680 million years ago

cyanobacteria^G in sea

550 million years ago

worms, sea jellies, sea anemones

540 million years ago

single-celled animals
with hard exoskeletons

510 million years ago

multi-celled marine invertebrates
with hard exoskeletons
e.g. echinoderms, trilobites

early sponges, radiolarians

438 million years ago

jawless fishes

first marine vertebrates

corals, molluscs, sea lilies

bryozoans

408 million years ago

invertebrates invade land

plants grow on land

armoured fish with jaws

355 million years ago

most jawless fishes extinct

amphibians emerge on land

lungfish breathe free air

molluscs with coiled shells

280 million years ago

first reptiles

echinoderms, bryozoans

245 million years ago

crocodiles

reptiles flourish

208 million years ago

marine reptiles

reef-building corals

145 million years ago

birds appear

true mammals appear

65 million years ago

dinosaurs become extinct

modern bony fishes appear

2 million years ago

mammals dominant

PRESENT

the rise of humans

Discovering marine life

All life began in the sea. Some mammals, such as whales and seals, have adapted to living in the ocean. However, humans can find the sea a dangerous place. They can also harm the sea and the creatures that live in it. When exploring the sea and its coastline:

- Watch your step. You could be walking on an animal or its home.

- Handle marine animals with care. Do not pick them up unless you know they are harmless. Look at them, then put them back where you found them.

- Replace rocks where you found them.

- Protect yourself from the sun and wear thick-soled shoes when walking on rocks or coral.

- Watch for changing weather and tides.

- Train with an experienced instructor before diving using scuba^G gear.

WATCH OUT!

Marine animals catch food and protect themselves with "weapons" that include stinging tentacles, claws, electric and poison glands, sharp spines and teeth.

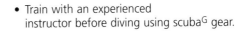

Seasnake – front fangs inject venom.

Stonefish – sharp spines inject venom.

If an animal senses a human is a threat or something to eat, it will use its "weapons". With some animals, the result can be irritating, painful or, just occasionally, fatal.

Shark – sharp teeth and powerful jaws slice and tear.

Blue-ringed Octopus – toothed beak injects venom.

The animals shown here are dangerous and should be avoided.

Cone shell – dart-like teeth inject venom.

Groups of common marine creatures

The ocean contains members of nearly every group of animals. They all belong to Kingdom Animalia. They are then further divided into major groups called Phyla. These phyla can be divided into invertebrates (animals without backbones, e.g. Phylum Porifera (sponges), Phylum Arthropoda (lobsters, shrimps, prawns etc.), and vertebrates (animals with backbones, e.g. Phylum Chordata, which includes fishes, amphibians, reptiles, birds and mammals). A small subdivision of Phylum Chordata known as the Urochordates has a backbone-like rod of gristle in the larval stage, but loses it when mature, e.g. sea squirts.

GROUP

EXAMPLES

Invertebrates (animals without a backbone)

SPONGES: multi-celled animals that have no tissues, organs, mouths or nervous systems. They feed by taking in water and filtering out food.

sponge

COELENTERATES: animals that have stinging cells, bodies made up of two layers of cells, and a central digestive cavity that is called a coelenteron.

hydroid   *sea fan*

WORMS: a flatworm has a mouth but no anus and no large body cavity. A segmented worm has a digestive, nervous and circulatory[G] system.

flatworm   *bristle worm*

CRUSTACEANS: joint-legged animals with external skeletons. The body is divided into working sections. The blood circulates in large spaces.

prawn   *shrimp*   *lobster*   *crab*   *hermit crab*

MOLLUSCS: have a soft body, sometimes protected by shells. Body usually consists of head, organ mass and gliding foot. All except bivalves have a rasping tongue.

univalve   *nudibranch*   *bivalve*   *octopus*   *cuttle*   *squid*

BRYOZOANS: colonial invertebrates that form a lacework on solid surfaces. Feed through tentacles that contain extensions of the body cavity.

bryozoan

ECHINODERMS: headless invertebrates with body divided into five. Skeleton consists of plates under the skin. Move by using tube feet.

feather star   *sea star*   *brittle star*   *sea urchin*   *sea cucumber*

Urochordates (larvae have a back chord)

ASCIDIANS: animals that have a rod-like notochord[G] in early free-swimming stage, then settle to become water-filtering invertebrates.

simple ascidian   *compound ascidian*

Vertebrates (animals with a backbone)

FISHES: vertebrate animals that do not produce their own body heat, usually have scales, and breathe by taking oxygen from the water through gills.

shark   *ray*   *bony fishes*

REPTILES: vertebrate animals that do not produce their own body heat, have scales on their skin and breathe by taking oxygen from the air.

seasnake   *marine turtle*   *crocodile*

BIRDS: vertebrate animals that produce their own body heat, and have scales and feathers on their skins. Their bodies are usually adapted for flight.

penguin   *albatross*   *crested tern*

MAMMALS: vertebrate animals that produce their own body heat, have hair growing from their skin and produce milk to feed their young.

Dugong   *pinnipeds*   *dolphin*   *whale*

Coasts in peril

The Great Barrier Reef is threatened by pollution^G and global warming^G.

There are many threats to Australia's marine environments and to the animals that live in them. Examples are:

- The steady warming of earth's atmosphere affects the temperature of the sea. It also alters the course of ocean currents. Many marine creatures such as corals need particular water temperatures for survival.

- Many cities and towns stand on the coast, usually where rivers flow into the ocean. Human settlement is covering coastal land and dunes. Humans alter beaches and offshore reefs. Water running off the land into the sea carries human and animal waste material, farming fertilisers and chemicals.

- Overfishing is reducing fish, prawn and lobster stocks. It also affects other creatures such as whales, dolphins, seals, albatrosses and penguins. These may find food scarce, or may be caught in nets or on lines set for fish. There is increasing international pressure on oceanic resources.

Soft coral

Marine Plants

Plants that grow in the sea are found all around Australia. They are an important source of food and shelter for many marine animals.

Mangroves

Growing on sheltered shores above low tide, mangroves are most common in north-east Australia. They have an extensive, shallow root system with aerial props and projections, and thick, waxy leaves. Their stands provide breeding grounds for fish and other marine life.

Seagrasses

Found in calm, shallow water below low tide, seagrasses have strap-like leaves. Their flowers have no petals. Horizontal stems anchor the plants. They are an important food source for the Dugong and Green Turtle.

Seaweeds (algae)

Algae are primitive plants with no true roots, stems or leaves. Over 2000 species of seaweeds grow around Australia, most between high tide and a depth of about 30 m. Different colours help algae absorb sunlight at different depths. The three main groups of algae are green, brown and red. Green species are more common in the tropics, while red ones flourish in cold waters.

Green algae

Brown algae

Red algae

Facts about the sea and marine life

In the deepest parts of the ocean, such as the Mariana Trench (11 038 m deep) pressure is more than 1000 times greater than it is at the surface.

There is evidence to suggest that Sperm Whales dive to depths of at least 3000 m at a dive speed of up to 3 m/sec.

For the past 5000 years, sea level has risen at the rate of 0.1 mm per year because earth's climate is warming and the polar ice caps are melting.

The normal food chains of the ocean begin with plants, which make food from nutrients^G in the water and from sunlight.

In some sunless parts of the deep ocean floor, vents gush hot, sulphur-rich water. Bacteria that feed on the sulphur form food for larger creatures.

The largest form of algae are giant kelps. These are brown seaweeds whose fronds may reach 45 m in length and may grow over 0.3 m per day.

There are more than 10 000 species of sponges named so far. They have not changed much since the Cambrian Period, 570–500 million years ago.

About 70 people are known to have have died after being stung by sea jellies (box jellyfish). Vinegar will kill the stinging cells within 30 seconds.

A large sea anemone may live for over 100 years.

Coral reefs have been present on earth for over 240 million years.

Tiny algae live in the tissues of coral animals and help them grow faster.

A Giant Clam, the world's largest mollusc, may weigh 270 kg and be over 1 m in length. It shuts too slowly to trap a human hand or foot.

An octopus has eight arms. A cuttle or a squid has ten.

A shark can smell one part of fish oil or blood in one million parts of sea water. It also detects tiny electrical signals given off by animal bodies.

An electric ray may produce a shock of up to 220 volts. Within 10 minutes, it may deliver 50 charges strong enough to cramp human muscles.

Australia's Great Barrier Reef is made up of over 2500 coral reefs.

There are more than 24 000 species of fish known to science so far. Australia has over 3600 fish species, more than half living on the Great Barrier Reef.

Some fishes change sex. The change may only take place if another, more dominant fish of the other sex disappears.

Methods by which fish protect themselves include having poisonous skins and flesh, inflating spiny bodies to prevent other fish swallowing them, and sweating poison into the water around them.

A seasnake may dive to 100 m and stay under water for up to 80 minutes.

The most valuable Australian fisheries are based on prawns and lobsters.

plankton

plankton (= wandering)

Plankton[G] is found near the surface in coastal waters and the open sea. It consists of floating plants and animals, many single-celled or microscopic.

Plankton is the main source of food for many marine animal groups, from the simple sponge to the giant Blue Whale.

Phytoplankton are simple plants that use chlorophyll and sunlight to make food. They are the first link in all marine food chains.

Zooplankton are tiny animals. The eggs and larvae of most marine invertebrates are planktonic. Some creatures drift all their lives, others only as eggs, larvae or adults.

All plankton drift with the winds and currents. Some organisms jerk or pulse[G], but none swim actively.

Diameter: microscopic – 1+ mm

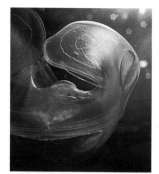
Comb jelly

Goose barnacles

STATUS X E P V **S**   SIZE   MAP

sponges

Phylum Porifera (= pore-bearer)

Tube sponge

Finger sponge and tube sponge

Sponges grow at all depths in temperate and tropical seas. They are common in shallow waters, rock pools and crevices, and under rocks and corals. They attach to any firm surface. Sponge skeletons often wash up on sandy beaches.

A sponge is a sac-shaped group of animal cells, supported by a mesh of fibres or sharp spines (spicules[G]). Its shape may be branching, tube, finger, vase, round, honeycomb or encrusting. Colour varies. The texture may be firm, soft, rubbery or slimy.

Cells with whip-like tails draw water and plankton through tiny pores into the hollow sac inside a sponge. Food is filtered out, then wastes are carried out through a large hole, the osculum.

Height: 20–500 mm

Width: 60–500 mm

STATUS X E P V **S**   SIZE   MAP

hydroids

Phylum Cnidaria (= stinging-nettle animal)
Class Hydrozoa (= many-headed serpent-animal)

Hydroids live at all depths in temperate and tropical seas. They grow on submerged objects. They are members of a group called coelenterates, which have hollow bodies and stinging cells.

Colonial hydroids

Hydroids consist of colonies of hollow-bodied animals called polyps, which are connected beneath their limey skeletons. **Colonial hydroids** look like clumps of delicate, fern-like branches. **Solitary hydroids** are brittle tufts on single stalks.

Solitary hydroid

A **Bluebottle** is a floating hydroid colony of polyps hanging from a gas-filled float. **Fire coral** is a hard-skeletoned hydroid with stinging cells.

Hydroids are filter feeders. Their food-catching polyps have tentacles with stinging cells, and their floating life stage buds off the colony to produce fertilised eggs. These eggs settle and grow into new polyps.

Height: 60–300 mm

STATUS X E P V **S**   SIZE   MAP

sea jellies

Phylum Cnidaria (= stinging-nettle animal)
Class Scyphozoa (= cup-shaped animal)

These hollow-bodied, jelly-like animals drift in temperate and tropical waters. They are seen in estuaries, near the shore and in the open sea. Often they are found washed up on sandy beaches.

Sea jellies

The body, or bell, of a sea jelly is a dome, shaped like a box or a saucer. It may be almost transparent[G] or it may be opaque[G]. A stalked mouth surrounded by stinging tentacles is located under the bell. On the bell edges are organs that sense light and gravity[G].

Sea jellies are transported by wind and currents. Pulsing movements of the bell maintain and stabilise a jelly's position in the water. Sea jellies feed on plankton and small fish. In their life history, some species have a brief attached-polyp stage.

Crustaceans and small fish often live under a jelly's bell. They are not harmed by the stinging cells on the tentacles.

Diameter: 0.02–1 m

STATUS X E P V **S**   SIZE   MAP

soft corals

Phylum Cnidaria (= stinging-nettle animal) Class Alcyonaria
(= polyp animal) Order Alcyonacea (= polyp animal)

Soft corals are found in temperate and tropical seas, at all depths. They are abundant in warm coastal and reef waters on rocks and other hard surfaces.

Encrusting soft coral

The colonial polyps that form soft coral are protected by a fleshy mass strengthened with glassy spicules. Each polyp has eight hollow tentacles around a central mouth. The polyps are connected to each other, and can pull back into the mass. Soft coral may be lobed, folded or branched, and may have a leathery or fleshy texture. Deepwater species are more rigid, with a greater number of spicules.

Soft corals are filter feeders. The polyps extend to feed on plankton.

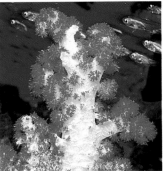

Soft coral with visible polyps

Height: 0.1–1.5 m

Width: 60–800 mm

| STATUS | X | E | P | V | **S** | SIZE | RANGE |

hard corals

Phylum Cnidaria (= stinging-nettle animal) Class Zoantharia
(= flower animal) Order Scleractinia (= with hard rays)

Hard corals need shallow, warm (20+°C) water. They live in temperate and tropical seas.

Free-living, solitary mushroom coral

A single coral polyp builds a limey skeleton around its body. A coral polyp can retract its stinging tentacles into this cup. When polyps form colonies, individuals are connected beneath the joined cups. The shape of a coral colony may be encrusting[G], lobed, rounded, plate or branched. Solitary corals are round or oval.

Branching, colonial staghorn coral

Corals are filter feeders. Most polyps extend at night to feed on plankton. Single-celled algae live in the tissues of many reef-building polyps and provide them with food.

Temperate species of hard corals are smaller and more compact. Tropical species tend to be branching. They clump and join to form reefs.

Diameter: solitary 5–300 mm
colonial 0.1–5 m

| STATUS | X | E | P | V | **S** | SIZE | RANGE |

sea fans & whips

Phylum Cnidaria (= stinging-nettle animal) Class Alcyonaria
(= polyp animal) Order Gorgonacea (= snake-haired)

Sea fan

Long branching gorgonian

Sea fans and whips are found in temperate and tropical seas, but are most abundant in warmer waters below a depth of 10 m. They attach to hard surfaces, especially near water currents.

Short, colonial polyps are surrounded by a rigid[G] external skeleton. **Fans** have a short main stem and latticed branches. Fans grow in one direction in currents, and in all directions in deep, calm water. **Whips** can be long, single stems or finely branched. They usually grow in groups.

Red, orange and yellow are common whip and fan colours.

Whips and fans are plankton feeders. The polyps on most can retract into the skeleton.

Height: 0.2–3 m

| STATUS | X | E | P | V | **S** | SIZE | RANGE |

sea anemones

Phylum Cnidaria (= stinging-nettle animal) Class Zoantharia
(= flower animal) Order Actinaria (= with rays)

Sea whip anemone

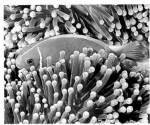

Anemonefish in tentacles

Sea anemones live in temperate and tropical seas. They are most common in shallow water, in rock pools and crevices, under rocks and dead coral, and on sand, sea whips and hermit crabs.

A sea anemone is a single, mobile polyp with no skeleton. Circles of stinging tentacles, arranged in multiples of 6, surround the mouth. The body column is squat, with a sucker-like base. The tentacles can be withdrawn into the hollow body column.

These fleshy creatures feed on plankton, crustaceans and small fishes caught and pulled in by the tentacles. They may live alone, in clusters or in colonies. The base can be used to creep over, or hold onto, any surface. Some species burrow, others swim, and all avoid direct sunlight.

Anemonefish may live among the stinging tentacles of anemones without being harmed.

Diameter: 10–500 mm

| STATUS | X | E | P | V | **S** | SIZE | RANGE |

flatworms

Phylum Platyhelminthes (= flat worm)
Class Turbellaria (= little crowd)

Flatworms are found in temperate and tropical seas, usually in intertidal pools and shallow water. They live under rocks, and on sand, rubble, rocks and seaweed. Some species live on or in sea cucumbers, sea urchins, molluscs, crabs and fish.

Hair-like cilia[G] cover a flatworm's soft, flat body, which usually has rippled edges. There is a distinct head with one or more pairs of eyes and antenna-like tentacles. The mouth is under the head. A muscular tube, the pharynx[G], connects the mouth to the finely branched gut.

Tropical species of flatworm tend to be more brightly coloured.

Flatworms swim freely, with characteristic gliding movements. They are active predators of small invertebrates. The pharynx can be pushed out of the mouth to grasp prey.

Male and female reproductive systems are present in each worm.

Flatworm

Length: 10–50 mm

STATUS	X	E	P	V	S	SIZE	RANGE

bristle worms

Phylum Annelida (= ringed animal)
Class Polychaeta (= many bristles)

Featherduster tube worm

Bristle worm

Bristle worms are found in temperate and tropical seas, in sand, silt and mud. Their tubes may be built on or under rocks or coral.

They are flexible worms with segmented bodies and light-sensitive tentacles. **Free-moving species** have one head segment with eyes and tentacles and a second segment with a mouth. The remaining segments each have a pair of flaps with bristles (chaetae). **Tube** and **burrowing species** have a modified head and reduced chaetae. The colourful head tentacles of tube worms can be threads, plumes or feathery whorls. Encrusting or single tubes are built of sand or shell fragments, or limestone produced by the occupant's body.

Free-moving species swallow invertebrate prey whole. Tube species catch plankton.

Length: free-moving microscopic–1 m
tube/burrowing 50–250 mm

STATUS	X	E	P	V	S	SIZE	RANGE

bryozoans

Phylum Bryozoa (= moss animal)

Bryozoans colonise bare surfaces in temperate and tropical seas. They live in crevices or caves, under overhangs, or on rocks and corals.

They are microscopic colonial animals with brains and simple nervous systems. Each individual is called a zooid. The mouth is in the centre of feathery tentacles. An open

Lacy bryozoan

limey box surrounds each body. These boxes are arranged in geometric rows like bricks in a wall. The zooids are connected through holes in the boxes. A colony may be a mossy tuft, a crust, or lacy branches.

Individual zooids may be specialised for filtering plankton, cleaning, brooding larvae, or forming joints or attachment branches. All react as one individual when disturbed.

Colony members shed eggs and sperm, which unite to form free-swimming larvae. These settle on surfaces and form new colonies.

Diameter: 0.001–1 m

STATUS	X	E	P	V	S	SIZE	RANGE

· A TASTE FOR CRUSTACEANS

Crustaceans, along with insects and spiders, belong to a group of animals called arthropods. They have rigid external skeletons that must be moulted as the animals inside grow. The front of the body is covered by a plate called a carapace.

In order to move their armoured bodies around, crustaceans have developed large muscle masses. The muscles of crabs are concentrated in their legs, while those of prawns, shrimps and lobsters are in their abdomens. Around Australia's coast three species of rock lobster are caught for human food. A rich prawn fishery extends from Koolan Island in the Kimberley in Western Australia across to Cape York, Queensland.

The Mudcrab is a popular human food.

lobsters & spiny crays

Phylum Crustacea (= shelled animal) Class Malacostraca
(= soft-shelled) Order Decapoda (= ten-footed)

Painted lobster

Lobsters live in temperate and tropical seas. They are found below low-tide mark in crevices and caves, and under overhangs.

A **lobster** is a soft-bodied, segmented decapod, with an exoskeleton that forms a heavy carapace over head and thorax. The head has stalked eyes, 2 pairs of antennae and jaw-legs (maxillipeds) for feeding. The long abdomen has flattened swimming limbs and a tail fan.

Australian lobsters do not have a pair of large claws like those of Northern Hemisphere lobsters. In **slipper lobsters** and **bugs**, the second antenna is flattened like a shield.

Lobsters walk forwards, but flick the tail to shoot backwards. They are nocturnal predators of molluscs, worms and echinoderms, usually feeding in deep water. They move inshore to moult and breed. Females carry eggs under their abdomens.

Length: 0.2–1 m

STATUS X E P V **S** SIZE   RANGE

shrimps & prawns

Phylum Crustacea (= shelled animal) Class Malacostraca
(= soft-shelled) Order Decapoda (= ten-footed)

These decapods are found in temperate and tropical seas, in almost all habitats. Some species are commercially important.

Cleaner shrimp

A prawn or shrimp has a segmented body and 5 pairs of jointed legs, usually with claws (chela). The first pair of claws is often large. The carapace extends between the stalked eyes to a sharp point. The colours often form a regular pattern.

Shrimps and prawns may be plankton feeders, scavengers or predators. Cleaner species eat parasites living on fish.

The sexes are separate. The females of most species carry eggs under the abdomen. Some species live on, or in, other invertebrates. Some species travel in schools.

Burrowing shrimp

Length: 20–120 mm

STATUS X E P V **S** SIZE   RANGE

crabs

Phylum Crustacea (= shelled animal) Class Malacostraca
(= soft-shelled) Order Decapoda (= ten-footed)

Female crab carrying eggs

A camouflaged crab

Crabs inhabit temperate and tropical seas and can be found in all habitats.

A crab is a short-tailed decapod with a broad, flattened carapace. The first pair of jointed legs may have large, brightly coloured claws. In some species, the fifth pair of legs is modified for swimming or burrowing. The head has stalked eyes and short antennae.

Crabs move with a characteristic sideways scuttle, and can also swim and burrow.

The large claws are used for catching food, defence and courtship displays. Most crabs are scavengers or prey on other invertebrates. Some sift food from the ground, leaving pellets or balls of sand or silt. Some species live on or in other invertebrates, also on seaweeds.

Shell width: 10–250+ mm

STATUS X E P V **S** SIZE   RANGE

hermit crabs

Phylum Crustacea (= shelled animal) Class Malacostraca
(= soft-shelled) Order Decapoda (= ten-footed)

Hermit crabs live in temperate and tropical seas. They make their homes in intertidal rock pools, on rocky shores and coral reefs, and on sand patches below low tide mark. They may burrow into sand or soft rocks.

A hermit crab

Hermit crab

has long antennae and stalked eyes. The body is long and soft, and has no tail fan. Long, hooked limbs are used to hold a mollusc shell over the soft abdomen. Three pairs of bristly, patterned legs remain visible. The first pair have large claws, the right one usually larger than the left. One claw may be flattened to shield the shell opening. Colours vary from bright red to dull olive. Each species prefers a certain type of shell. The shell may be decorated with sponges or an anemone.

Hermit crabs filter plankton from the water, scavenge or prey on invertebrates.

Length: 10–100 mm

STATUS X E P V **S** SIZE RANGE

MOLLUSCS

Molluscs are invertebrates with soft bodies, divided into a head (which is not present in bivalves), a muscular "foot" and a hump containing the body organs. A fold of skin, the mantle, forms a pocket that may contain gills and the openings to reproductive organs. All except bivalves have a radula or rasping tongue.

*Worldwide there are around 1 000 000 species of molluscs, most of them **univalves** (or gastropods). **Bivalves** account for around 20 000 species, and the **cephalopods** (octopuses, squids and cuttles) number only about 650 species.*

Australia's molluscs are of importance to humans. Land snails and teredo "shipworms" are pests. Oysters, mussels, abalone, scallops, cockles, clams, octopuses and squids are favoured foods. Oysters may produce valuable pearls. Some molluscs, such as octopuses and cone shells, can inject venom harmful to humans into a bite or sting.

Giant Cuttlefish, above.

bivalves
Phylum Mollusca (= soft-bodied) Class Bivalvia (= 2 valves)

Giant Clam

Bivalve molluscs are found in temperate and tropical seas. They may be found on, attached to, or under rocks, sand or coral.

A bivalve is a soft-bodied mollusc with a two-part, hinged shell closed by two powerful muscles. The foot is tongue-like or absent. There is no head and the gills function both as breathing organs and to sort food into the mouth. A fleshy mantle covers the body and forms two siphons^G and a gill cavity. The edge of the mantle carries eye-spots that are sensitive to light.

Bivalves are attached or free-moving bottom-dwellers. Many species burrow. Some swim by opening and closing their shells. Most feed on plankton.

Width: 0.05–1.50 m

STATUS	X	E	P	V	S	SIZE		RANGE

univalves (gastropods)
Phylum Mollusca (= soft-bodied)
Class Gastropoda (= stomach-foot)

Univalves, or gastropods, are single-shelled molluscs found in temperate and tropical seas. Relatives of land snails, they are found in many habitats. They may burrow into sand, or fasten themselves to rocks, coral, seaweeds and mangrove roots.

Cowrie shell

The soft body of a univalve is protected by a single shell. This is produced by the skin-like mantle that covers the body. Under the body mass is a muscular foot. There is a distinct head with eyes, tentacles and mouth. The eating organ is a tongue-like band of teeth known as a radula. A horny plate (operculum) can be pulled up by the foot to close the shell opening. Most species have spiral or dome-shaped shells. The colour and pattern varies in each species.

Univalves creep or hold on with the foot. Some planktonic species float beneath rafts of bubbles. They rasp off, or drill into, food with the radula. Univalves may be predators, scavengers or grazing plant-eaters.

Length: 10–450 mm

STATUS	X	E	P	V	S	SIZE		RANGE

cone shells
Phylum Mollusca (= soft-bodied)
Class Gastropoda (= stomach-foot)

Cone shells are gastropods that are found on all Australian coastlines. They live on rocky shores, coral reefs and on or in sand.

Cone shells are predators that eat worms, other molluscs and

Textile Cone with siphon protruding.

fish. A cone's radula consists of tiny barbed shafts that can be filled with venom from a sac in the cone's snout or proboscis^G. This proboscis can stretch out of the cone's shell for a distance equal to the shell's length. When it touches prey, it fires a barb like a tiny harpoon into it. The venom paralyses the prey, which is pulled in and swallowed whole.

A human harpooned by a cone suffers paralysis and breathing problems. The Geographer and Textile Cones, which live on tropical coasts and are often buried in sand, are held responsible for 14 known deaths. No cone should be handled, and anyone stung by one should seek medical help as soon as possible.

Length: to 100 mm

STATUS	X	E	P	V	S	SIZE		RANGE

open-sea fishes

Phylum Chordata (= having a chord)
Class Osteichthyes (= bony fishes)

School of trevally

Gold-spotted Trevally

These bony fishes live in temperate and tropical waters, in the open sea and along reef edges. Their streamlined bodies are stiff and muscular, with small or reduced scales. They have a powerful crescent, or forked, tail fin, and their other fins are usually short and angular. They are silvery or countershaded to protect them from predators above or below. Open sea fishes are fast, powerful swimmers that travel alone or in schools. They are active carnivores, feeding near the surface during the day on squid, prawns and schooling fishes. They bear live young, which often hide under rafts of floating algae.

Length: 0.3–2 m

STATUS   X   E   P   V   **S**   SIZE   RANGE

bottom-dwelling fishes

Phylum Chordata (= having a chord)
Class Osteichthyes (= bony fishes)

Bottom-dwelling bony fishes are found in temperate and tropical waters. They frequent the bottom of the deep sea, coastal waters, reefs, estuaries and mudflats, living in a variety of habitats.

Eastern Spiny Gurnard

Some bottom-living fishes have flat bellies, eyes on top of the head, strong ventral fins. and large, often fanned, pectoral fins. They may prop or crawl on these fins. They usually have back spines. Others lie on one side of the extremely flat, oval body. They have a small head, with close-set eyes on the topside. The

Southern Peacock Sole

long-based dorsal and anal fins may be attached to a fanned tail fin, and there are short ventral fins. These flattened species may bury themselves with only their eyes showing. Both types feed on algae, molluscs, crustaceans, worms and small fishes.

Length: 100–450 mm

STATUS   X   E   P   V   **S**   SIZE   RANGE

tropical reef fishes

Phylum Chordata (= having a chord)
Class Osteichthyes (= bony fishes)

Emperor Angelfish

Moorish Idol

Coral reef fishes live in tropical seas, from inshore fringing coral reefs to outer barrier reefs.

They include many different groups of bony fishes that use all available space and food sources. They display every imaginable size and shape, from snake-like eels to tall-finned batfish. Many have thin bodies for slipping into crevices and between corals. Colour varies widely, and is used for camouflage, mimicry and warning, and to disrupt body shape and outline. Bright colours and distinctive patterns help fishes recognise their own species. Many coral fishes are territorial or claim a home range. They may live in schools, in pairs or alone. Sexes are separate, but some species can change sex. Some live on, or in, other animals, and food sources include seaweeds, invertebrates and fishes.

Length: 0.01–2 m

STATUS   X   E   P   V   **S**   RANGE

temperate coastal fishes

Phylum Chordata (= having a chord)
Class Osteichthyes (= bony fishes)

Banded Sea Perch

Fishes that live in temperate seas may be found in habitats that include mangroves, estuaries, sandy and rocky coasts, offshore reefs and islands.

These fishes include representatives of many families also found in tropical waters. Most have overlapping scales and well-developed fins and spines. Species show diversity of size, colour and shape, ranging from the long, bony, Weedy Seadragon to the more typical sea perch.

The behaviour of these fishes relates to their size, colour and shape, and to the food eaten. They may live in schools or alone. Their food sources include algae, invertebrates and fishes.

Length: 0.01–2 m

Weedy Seadragon

STATUS   X   E   P   V   **S**   RANGE

MARINE TURTLES

The form of sea turtles has changed little in the past 100 million years. They are much larger than freshwater turtles: the giant Leatherback can grow to 2 m in length and weigh nearly 1000 kg.

Only seven species of marine turtles exist today. Six of the seven occur around Australia's coasts. Five of the seven species are endangered. There are a number of reasons for the increasing rarity of marine turtles. These reptiles may be between 30 and 50 years old when they breed. Humans take adults and eggs for food. Many turtles drown in fishing nets or plastic debris. Some die after eating floating plastic in mistake for sea jellies. Human coastal settlement disturbs turtle breeding beaches. Hatchlings are attracted to artificial lights, delaying their escape to the ocean. Demand for "tortoiseshell" threatens the Hawksbill Turtle.

A Loggerhead Turtle comes to shore to nest.

marine turtles

Phylum Chordata (= having a chord) Class Reptilia (= crawling animal) Order Testudines (= turtle)

Marine turtles live in tropical and warm temperate seas. They may be seen in coastal and reef waters, or in the open ocean.

Green Turtle

A marine turtle is a short-bodied reptile with a shell, or carapace, and limbs adapted as flippers. The streamlined carapace consists of bony plates covered by horny scales or leathery skin. The flat, broad flippers may have 1, 2 or no claws. The head has no external ears and cannot be withdrawn into the shell. It bears a horny beak and there are no teeth. There are two nostrils on the front of the snout.

Each species of marine turtle has a particular diet. Food items include sponges, sea jellies, crustaceans, squid and fishes. The Green Turtle eats seagrasses and seaweeds.

Marine turtles do not breed every year. Females nest on beaches at night and may lay several clutches of 50–120 eggs in a season. The male never leaves the water.

Length: 1–2 m

STATUS	X	E	P	V	S	SIZE	RANGE

seasnakes

Phylum Chordata (= having a chord) Class Reptilia (= crawling animal) Order Squamata (= scaled)

These long, slender, limbless reptiles are found in temperate and tropical seas, and are common in northern Australia. They may be seen in mangroves, estuaries, shallow coastal and reef waters, and in the open sea.

A seasnake has a vertically flattened tail that is used as a paddle when swimming. It has no fins and its belly scales are no larger than the rest of its scales. The two nostrils on the tip of the snout can be closed by valves[G]. The front fangs can inject venom that can be deadly to humans.

Seasnakes breathe air. They can dive deeply and quickly and may remain under water for a long time. When feeding, they probe holes and crevices for eels, fish, crustaceans and fish eggs.

Seasnakes bear live young under water and never leave the ocean. **Sea kraits** are seasnakes that come onto land to lay their eggs and to bask in the sun.

Length: 0.7–2 m

Olive (Golden) Seasnake

STATUS	X	E	P	V	S	SIZE	RANGE

Saltwater Crocodile

Phylum Chordata (= having a chord) Class Reptilia (= crawling animal) Order Crocodilia (= lizard animal)

Saltwater Crocodile

Saltwater Crocodiles are most often seen in estuaries and harbours, and in coastal rivers and wetlands. However, they may travel far out to sea and be seen on islands and beaches in tropical and warm temperate waters.

A Saltwater Crocodile is a large, long-bodied reptile covered with thick, horny scales. These are square and flat on the belly, and ridged with bone on the back and tail. The limbs are short and strong; the back feet are webbed. The broad snout bears 2 valved nostrils on a raised pad. The cone-shaped teeth are replaceable. Each eye has a "third eyelid" that flicks across when the crocodile submerges.

"Salties" eat any creature they can overpower. The female lays eggs in a nest mound, then guards the mound. When the young hatch, she takes them to the water.

Length: to 7 m

STATUS	X	E	P	V	S	SIZE	RANGE

penguins

Phylum Chordata (= having a chord) Class Aves (= bird)
Order Sphenisciformes (= wedge-shaped)

Little Penguin

Penguins are found in polar and cold temperate seas. They may be seen around southern Australia on islands and beaches, and in coastal waters.

A penguin is a marine bird with a compact, streamlined body and a stout bill. It has a waterproof coat of thick down underlying small feathers. The plumage is grey or black above, and white below. It has webbed feet, flipper-like wings and a short tail.

Penguins feed under water on fish, crustaceans and squid. In summer they breed in colonies in sand burrows or under rocks. Both sexes incubate the eggs and care for the 1–2 chicks. The Little Penguin is the only species to breed in Australia, although Rockhopper and Fjordland Penguins are occasionally seen in coastal waters during winter.

Height: 350 mm

STATUS	X	E	P	V	S	SIZE	RANGE

SEABIRDS

Many birds get all their food from the sea. Some, like albatrosses, shearwaters and frigatebirds, spend long periods on the wing. Other flying birds, like cormorants, gulls and terns, feed from the sea, but roost on the land. Penguins cannot fly, but are expert swimmers. All seabirds nest on land, on islands, headlands, coral cays or beaches.

Seabirds often drink salt water. Special glands filter the salt from their bodies. It is excreted as extra-salty "tears" or nasal drips.

Seabirds carry food back to their chicks inside the first part of their digestive system. The chick may put its head right down its parent's throat to feed.

Little Pied Cormorant

frigatebirds

Phylum Chordata (= having a chord) Class Aves (= bird)
Order Pelecaniformes (= like a pelican)

Frigatebirds are usually seen soaring on motionless wings over warm temperate and tropical seas. They may be observed harassing other seabirds to get their food.

They are large, long-winged, fork-tailed seabirds. The male plumage is black, while females have white on throat and breast. The bill is long and hooked at the end; the feet are small and weak.

Great Frigatebird in flight

Frigatebirds are magnificent fliers. They may catch their own fish, particularly flying fishes. They may chase gannets and terns and swallow the fish coughed up.

Frigatebirds nest on coral cays. A courting male puffs out a bright red skin throat-pouch. The nest is made of sticks and seaweed, built on the ground or on bushes. The 2 white eggs hatch into chicks that, in their first plumage, have reddish heads and necks.

Female Great Frigatebird perched

Length: 0.85–1 m

STATUS	X	E	P	V	S	SIZE	RANGE

boobies & gannets

Phylum Chordata (= having a chord) Class Aves (= bird)
Order Pelecaniformes (= like a pelican)

Masked Booby feeding chick

Masked Booby in flight

Boobies are usually seen over tropical seas, while gannets are seen over temperate seas.

They both are large seabirds with long, narrow bodies and long, narrow wings. The bill is pointed and the nostrils are not visible. Each foot has all four toes webbed. Some species have white plumage with the primary wing feathers black. Others have brown heads, necks, backs and wings, and white abdomens. All plunge-dive into the sea to catch fish.

Boobies and gannets usually nest on the ground on islands and coral cays. The 1–2 white eggs are incubated under the webbed feet.

Length: 800–900 mm

STATUS	X	E	P	V	S	SIZE	RANGE

SAVED FROM SLAUGHTER

In the early 1800s, whale oil, which was obtained from whale blubber boiled down in big iron pots, was used to fuel oil lamps. "Whalebone" (the fibrous sheets through which baleen^G whales strain food from the ocean) was used to stiffen women's underwear.

Whales were harpooned from small boats, then dragged back to a mother ship, or to the shore, to be processed. By the 1820s, there were many boiling-down stations in Tasmania, and on the mainland from Portland to Sydney. As late as 1830, whale oil and whalebone formed the largest export item from Australia to Britain. When gas lighting replaced oil lamps, whaling gradually diminished. However, it continued in some places until after World War II. Whale numbers have taken many years to begin to recover.

Fur-seals were killed on their breeding grounds for their furry pelts.

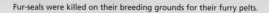

Marine mammals quickly become used to humans if they are not being hunted. When Europeans arrived in Moreton Bay, Queensland, wild dolphins and Aboriginal hunters were recorded co-operating to trap fish. From 1818 to 1932, at Twofold Bay, New South Wales, a pack of Killer Whales rounded up Humpback Whales so colonial whalers could harpoon them (as reward, the Killers were given the dead whales' tongues).

Today the numbers of Humpback and Southern Right Whales that breed around Australia's southern coasts are increasing. A tourist industry based on whale-watching has developed. Places where Bottlenose Dolphins come to shore to interact with humans are also popular tourist destinations.

Bottlenose Dolphins

New Zealand Fur-seal

Phylum Chordata (= having a chord) Class Mammalia
(= of the breast) Order Pinnipedia (= fin-legged)

Fur-seals are torpedo-shaped, streamlined marine mammals that live in cold temperate and polar waters.

A fur-seal has dense body fur beneath surface guard hairs. It has external ears and long white whiskers. The front flippers are large, the hind limbs webbed. The larger male has a massive neck and thick mane.

These mammals eat fish, cephalopods and penguins.

They breed on rocky islands off South Australia, the southern coast of Western Australia, and the south-west coast of Tasmania. Males establish territories, then fight to keep groups of females. They may not feed for 70 days during this time. The single pup is fed on rich milk for up to one year.

Length: ♂ 1.5 m ♀ 2.5 m
Weight: ♂ 50 kg ♀ 180 kg

STATUS	X	E	P	V	**S**	SIZE			RANGE

Australian Sea-lion

Phylum Chordata (= having a chord) Class Mammalia
(= of the breast) Order Pinnipedia (= fin-legged)

Female Australian Sea-lion

Australian Sea-lions live in cold temperate and temperate seas. They are torpedo-shaped, streamlined, marine mammals, whose coats do not have dense underfur.

A sea-lion has an external ear, a blunt snout and long white whiskers. The larger male has huge forequarters and a massive neck. Its body is dark brown; its head and nape of neck are white. The smaller female is silvery grey above, and yellow to cream below.

Australian Sea-lions breed on offshore islands from Houtmans Abrolhos, Western Australia to Kangaroo Island, South Australia. Males and females both guard territories during the breeding season.

Sea-lion numbers are increasing, and there are now more than 5000.

Length: ♂ 1.6 m ♀ 2.4 m
Weight: ♂ 80 kg ♀ 300 kg

STATUS	X	E	P	V	**S**	SIZE			RANGE

Killer Whale

Phylum Chordata (= having a chord) Class Mammalia
(= of the breast) Order Cetacea (large sea animal)

The Killer Whale, the largest member of the dolphin family, is found most often in cooler seas, especially the polar regions.

It has a stocky, heavy body with a very tall dorsal fin that may lean forward. This fin may reach 1.8 m in older males. The rounded head tapers to a point, and the flippers are paddle-shaped and very large. The body is black above, with a white patch behind each eye, a grey saddle-patch, a white throat and belly and a white patch on each side.

Killer Whales live in family groups called pods. Although they eat sea creatures, they do not harm people.

At birth, a Killer Whale calf weighs up to 180 kg and measures up to 2.5 m in length.

Length: 5.5–9.8 m
Weight: 2.6–9 t

STATUS   X   E   P   V   **S**   SIZE   RANGE

Humpback Whale

Phylum Chordata (= having a chord) Class Mammalia
(= of the breast) Order Cetacea (large sea animal)

Humpback Whales spend winter in polar cold-water feeding grounds. They summer in warm-water breeding grounds, migrating thousands of kilometres between the two.

A Humpback has a stocky body, with a hump in front of its low, stubby dorsal fin. It has knobs on its head and lower jaw, and up to 36 throat grooves. The black and white flippers are very long, with knobs along the leading edges. The tail flukes have knobby trailing edges. Before a deep dive, the flukes are raised.

Humpbacks are slow swimmers and have little fear of boats. Male Humpbacks sing complex songs that carry far under water. The single calf is born in warm waters and may weigh up to 2 t. It can be 5 m in length.

Length: 11–15 m
Weight: 25–30 t

STATUS   X   E   P   V   **S**   SIZE   RANGE

Minke Whale

Phylum Chordata (= having a chord) Class Mammalia
(= of the breast) Order Cetacea (large sea animal)

The Minke Whale lives in tropical, temperate and polar waters, and is the only baleen whale still hunted commercially.

A Minke Whale has a slender body with a pointed dorsal fin placed well back. The head bears a double blowhole and a sharply pointed snout. There is a single ridge down the centre of the head. This whale has up to 100 grooves forming pleats on its throat. Compared to other species, its skin is smooth and clear. Its slender flippers have pointed tips and are equal to only one-eighth of its body length.

The Minke may blow 5–8 times before diving for up to 20 minutes. It eats krill (small crustaceans) and other creatures. Sea water is gulped in, then the pleated throat contracts and forces the water past curtains of food-straining baleen.

At birth, a Minke calf may weigh 350 kg and measures 2.8 m.

Length: to 10 m
Weight: 5–10 t

STATUS   X   E   P   V   **S**   SIZE   RANGE

Southern Right Whale

Phylum Chordata (= having a chord) Class Mammalia
(= of the breast) Order Cetacea (large sea animal)

The Southern Right Whale spends summer in colder water near Antarctica. In winter, it breeds in warmer waters along the southern coast of Australia.

It is a broad-bodied whale whose large head is covered in bumps called callosities. The mouthline forms a strong arch. The broad back has no dorsal fin, and the flippers are large and paddle-shaped. The body is black or dark brown, often with white patches on the belly. Southern Right Whales have dense, fine baleen. They eat krill and other small creatures.

These whales are slowly recovering from over-hunting. A female has a calf only every 3–4 years. The birth weight is around 1 t.

Length: 11–18 m
Weight: 30–80 t

STATUS   X   E   P   V   **S**   SIZE   RANGE

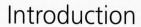

Australia's Fishes

What is a fish?

- A fish is a vertebrate animal, whose central nervous system and brain are protected by a backbone and a skull. These may be made of bone or cartilage[G].

- A fish is "cold-blooded" (ectothermic). Its body temperature usually takes the temperature of the water surrounding it.

- Most fishes have streamlined bodies, rounded at the centre and tapering towards the tail.

- The limbs of a fish are fins. These may be membranous and supported by spiny rays, or they may be fleshy.

- Fish skin has many glands that keep it covered with mucus. Many fishes have small, overlapping scales growing from the skin. Others have small, tooth-like scales. Some have tough, bare skin.

- Fishes breathe by taking in water through the mouth and forcing it out through gill slits. On the way, the water passes through a curtain of gills that remove most of the oxygen from it.

- Fishes have many sorts of sense organs. Among these are eyes, ears, a sense of smell and skin cells that detect touch, electric currents and changes in water pressure.

Jawless fishes

The earliest forms of fishes had no jaws. The jawless fishes that exist today are the only vertebrates without hinged jaws. They are found in temperate waters across the northern and southern hemispheres, and in cool, deep water in some tropical areas.

Lampreys have a larval stage. A larva buries itself on the bottom, filter-feeding on tiny particles. After several more stages, it becomes an eel-like adult. This has a sucking disc surrounding its mouth and a toothed tongue called a piston. Adult lampreys use their sucker discs to attach themselves to hosts. They then rock the piston backwards and forwards, rasping away tissue. Some lampreys feed on flesh, others on blood and body fluids.

Hagfishes feed on dead and dying fishes. A hagfish can tie its body in a knot, shifting the knot forward as far as its own head to use as a brace against the prey while it tears away flesh with its tongue-like piston.

Cartilaginous & bony fishes

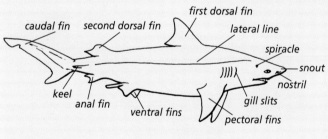

caudal fin   second dorsal fin   first dorsal fin   lateral line   spiracle   snout   nostril   gill slits   pectoral fins   ventral fins   anal fin   keel

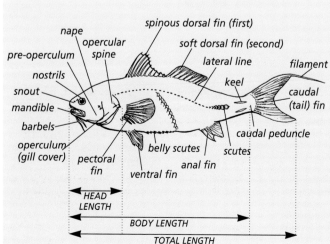

spinous dorsal fin (first)   nape   opercular spine   soft dorsal fin (second)   pre-operculum   lateral line   filament   nostrils   keel   snout   caudal (tail) fin   mandible   barbels   operculum (gill cover)   pectoral fin   belly scutes   ventral fin   anal fin   scutes   caudal peduncle   HEAD LENGTH   BODY LENGTH   TOTAL LENGTH

CARTILAGINOUS FISHES

Sharks and rays have skeletons made of cartilage (a substance like the gristle at the end of a human nose).

These cartilaginous fishes have well-developed jaws. Their teeth may be replaced as they are lost, or they may grow continuously.

They have no swim bladders, but large, oil-filled livers help keep their heavy bodies from sinking.

The skin of a cartilaginous fish is covered with tiny tooth-like scales called denticles. The skin feels like sandpaper.

BONY FISHES

Bony fishes have skeletons made of bone.

The teeth of bony fishes are usually fused to their jaws.

The body cavity of a bony fish usually contains a large, gas-filled bladder. This cancels out the fish's weight in water. The bladder expands as the fish moves up towards the surface. This keeps it buoyant.

Most bony fishes have tough, overlapping scales. Most of each scale is embedded in the skin.

FISH BODY SHAPES IN CROSS-SECTION

compressed

depressed

robust

box-like

How fishes move

Water is 800 times denser than air. To swim through it, a fish needs strong muscles.

Especially powerful muscles lie on either side of a fish's backbone, and may make up between 65 and 85% of the fish's body weight. These muscles pull then relax, bending the body from side to side in a wave that ends at the tail. The tail pushes against the water, moving the fish forwards. The pectoral, dorsal and anal fins may be used as oars or paddles. These fins balance the body and move it upwards or downwards in the water.

A shark powers its movements with its tail. The pectoral fins act like the wings of an aircraft to lift the front of the shark's body as it swims forward.

Feeding fish-fashion

Fishes feed on widely varied plants and animals. Their mouths, teeth and digestive systems have developed to deal with diets ranging from plankton and algae to large chunks of flesh.

Suction-feeders have a small mouth opening. Behind is a chamber that can be expanded quickly. When food is in reach, the fish expands the chamber and opens its mouth. Food and water are sucked inside. The water passes out through the gills.

Ram-feeders are predators that eat very large prey, or bite pieces out of their food. They swim rapidly towards the prey, open their large mouths wide and engulf it, or slice a section from it.

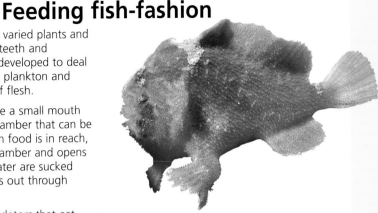

Anglers are fish that lure victims using "baits", which are parts of their bodies that resemble some food creature. When the victim approaches the "bait", the angler snaps up the prey. This action is one of the fastest in the animal kingdom.

Grazers use their teeth to bite off algae or other food. Some even bite off chunks of coral that are chewed up with teeth on jaws located in their throats.

Living together

Different sorts of fishes may interact, or fishes may interact with other creatures. This regular interaction between species is known as symbiosis (living together).

Cleaner wrasse removing parasites from the mouth and gills of a Coral Trout.

A Pink Anemonefish sheltering in the tentacles of a sea anemone.

Remoras are fishes with suckers on their heads. They hitch rides with larger fishes (including sharks) and turtles. When the larger creature finds food, the remora slips loose and swims forward to share morsels from the meal.

Cleaner fishes establish cleaning stations. Larger fishes come to these to have parasites and dead skin nipped away from their skins and fins, and from inside their mouths and gill covers. Cleaners include cleaner wrasses, some gobies and young butterflyfishes, as well as some species of shrimps.

Some species of **goby** live in burrows with shrimps. The shrimp keeps the burrow cleaned out. The goby flicks its tail to signal the shrimp when there are no predators around.

Pearlfishes may live inside the bodies or mantle cavities of sea cucumbers, sea stars, ascidians and bivalves.

Anemonefish live amongst the stinging tentacles of sea anemones. Anemonefish even lay their eggs at the base of their anemone's column. An anemonefish without an anemone for protection does not survive for long.

Groups of fishes

Scientists divide the fishes of the world into two major groups, or Superclasses. The first Superclass (the only group of vertebrates without jaws) is the jawless fishes. The second Superclass is the jawed fishes. This contains two classes, the cartilaginous fishes (sharks, rays and skates, all with jaws and skeletons made of cartilage), and the bony fishes (jawed fishes with skeletons of bone). The bony fishes are further divided into fishes with rayed fins and those with fleshy fins.

The world's 23 800 species of jawless and jawed fishes are placed in 56 orders. These are further divided into 483 families.

Kingdom Animalia (animals)

Phylum Chordata (animals with back cords)

Subphylum Vertebrata (animals with backbones)

Superclass Agnatha (jawless fishes; e.g. lampreys and hagfishes)
Superclass Gnathostomata (jawed vertebrates; e.g. fishes, amphibians, reptiles, birds, mammals)

Class Chondrichthyes (cartilaginous fishes; e.g. sharks and rays)
Class Osteichthyes (bony fishes)

Subclass Sarcopterygii (fleshy finned fishes; e.g. lungfishes, coelacanth)
Subclass Actinopterygii (ray-finned fishes)

The nine orders of ray-finned bony fishes represented in this book include:

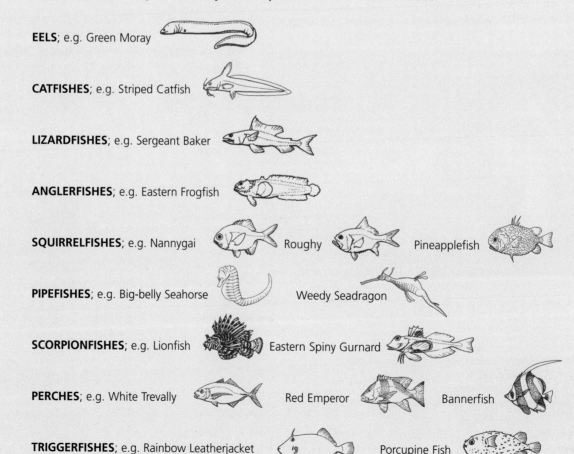

EELS; e.g. Green Moray

CATFISHES; e.g. Striped Catfish

LIZARDFISHES; e.g. Sergeant Baker

ANGLERFISHES; e.g. Eastern Frogfish

SQUIRRELFISHES; e.g. Nannygai   Roughy   Pineapplefish

PIPEFISHES; e.g. Big-belly Seahorse   Weedy Seadragon

SCORPIONFISHES; e.g. Lionfish   Eastern Spiny Gurnard

PERCHES; e.g. White Trevally   Red Emperor   Bannerfish

TRIGGERFISHES; e.g. Rainbow Leatherjacket   Porcupine Fish

Where fishes live

Open ocean: Habitat for tuna, sharks, kingfish, mackerel, trevally and barracuda.

Rocky coast and reef: Habitat for drummer, snapper, luderick, tailor, grouper and sweep.

Coral reef: Habitat for coral trout, parrotfish, sweetlips, wrasse and bannerfish.

Beach: Habitat for bream, tailor, flathead, whiting, jewfish, mullet, trevally and Australian salmon.

Lagoon and lake: Habitat for flathead, bream, blackfish, sole, whiting, flounder and mullet.

Estuary: Richest habitat for young fish; bream, jewfish, garfish, squire and flathead.

A school of Hardyheads

Where to see fishes

The ocean is the best place to find the most fishes, but some are shy or rare, so you might have to wait a while to see them. To watch fishes in their natural element, you need to find some place where they are common. Then you need to find some way to observe them without disturbing them.

Exploring reefs and tidal pools will give a view of some species, but mostly from above.

Australia has some magnificent marine aquariums, where you can watch many species of fish while standing on dry land. Many coastal resorts have underwater observatories, submersibles, or glass-bottomed boats.

Snorkelling is a great way to observe fishes in shallow water. For deeper observation, you need to take a course in scuba[G] diving from a reputable instructor. Once under water, you can photograph, film or video fishes and other marine life.

One of the best ways to learn to identify some sorts of fishes is to go fishing with someone. However, some people find the sight of fish being caught and killed distressing, and the fish are not seen behaving naturally. Dead fish can be seen at fish markets. Museums, libraries and the Internet also provide all sorts of information about fishes of all sorts.

Inset picture: Watching an anemonefish in its sea-anemone home.

Facts about fishes

A sailfish has been timed swimming in excess of 110 km/h for short periods.

Some of the sharks and tunas that live in the open sea can raise their blood temperature and increase their muscle efficiency.

The deepest fish caught came from 8370 m below the surface. The deepest fish seen was a sole, on the floor of the Mariana Trench, at 10 933 m.

Fishes range in size from minute gobies, 10 mm long, to the Whale Shark, a plankton-feeder that may grow to 12 m long.

A flyingfish may glide several hundred metres on outstretched fins.

An Ocean Sunfish may lay up to 28 million eggs in a season.

Every wrasse and parrotfish is born female, and may change sex to male.

Every anemonefish is born male, and may change sex to female.

Most bottom-dwelling fishes lack swim bladders.

Fishes' gills need to be efficient because water contains only $1/30$ of the oxygen contained in air.

The bony fishes make up over 96% of all living fishes.

Fishes that live in polar waters have antifreeze substances in their blood.

On various parts of their bodies, fish have cells that "smell" and "taste". Catfishes and goatfishes have these cells on whiskers known as barbels[G].

Marine fishes combat water loss by drinking sea water; they get rid of excess salt through their gills, and also pass concentrated urine.

Sharks and rays have cells around their heads that detect the electric fields given off by living creatures. Sharks use this sense to angle their jaws to snap at prey.

Schooling has survival value, for predators find it difficult to lock on to one fish among a large number moving in formation.

Hunting by humans and entanglement in fishing nets have killed many Great White Sharks. The species is now endangered.

All fast-swimming fishes have sickle-shaped or forked tail fins.

Sharks existed about 400 million years ago. Rays developed over 200 million years ago.

The Manta Ray may grow to 6.5 m across. It feeds on plankton.

The Australian Lungfish lives in the Mary–Burnett river system in south-east Queensland. It can breathe air and may survive several months curled amongst moist leaves and mud in a dried-up pool.

Anemonefishes' skins produce a mucus that mimics the chemical which prevents an anemone's tentacles stinging themselves. These fishes can shelter in the anemone's tentacles unharmed.

Indo-Pacific Sailfish

Port Jackson Shark
Heterodontus portusjacksoni (= Port Jackson different-tooth)

The Port Jackson Shark is found in temperate waters around Australia's southern coasts. It lives on the seabed in a variety of habitats.

It has a blunt, box-like head with ridges above the eyes. The small mouth contains sharp grasping and rear grinding teeth. The tapering body has two dorsal fins, each with a strong, slightly venomous spine, and large pectoral fins. The grey to light brown body has dark marks on the back and head.

These sharks eat echinoderms, molluscs, crustaceans and fish. They breed in shallow waters during winter. Up to 18 eggs are laid in a hard, brown case with a double spiral ridge. Empty egg cases are frequently found on tide lines.

Length: to 1.6 m

STATUS	X	E	P	V	**S**	SIZE			RANGE

Ornate Wobbegong
Orectolobus ornatus (= fringed ornate fish)

Wobbegongs are bottom-dwelling sharks, found in shallow tropical and temperate waters among reefs and weedbeds. The Ornate Wobbegong lives offshore in cooler waters.

A wobbegong is a highly camouflaged shark with a flattened head. It has a sensitive fringe of 2–4 fleshy lobes above the upper lip, and long, simple nasal barbels. The broad mouth is almost at the end of the round snout. This shark has 2 dorsal fins, almost equal in size, and 5 gill slits. The skin is patterned with browns and greys (wobbegongs are also called carpet sharks).

Apparently sluggish, these sharks are tough and muscular, and may move quickly. They feed at night on small rock fish and crabs, and are believed harmless to humans unless provoked.

Wobbegongs bear live young.

Length: to 3 m

STATUS	X	E	P	V	**S**	SIZE			RANGE

Bronze Whaler Shark
Carcharhinus brachyurus (= short-tailed pointed-nose)

The Bronze Whaler Shark lives in tropical and temperate coastal waters.

It has a streamlined shape, thickest below the first dorsal fin, and a cone-shaped head with a pointed snout. The eyes are round and staring. The last of the 5 gill slits is above the pectoral fin; there are 2 dorsal fins, the first much larger and pointed. The back is brown-grey to bronze.

These sharks feed in shallow inshore waters, often on schools of fish inside the surf break on southern beaches.

Several species are called "bronze whalers". Attacks on humans are just as likely to be made by Black Whalers (*C. obscurus*) or Bull Sharks (*C. leucus*).

A female gives birth to up to 16 live young.

Length: to 3.25 m

STATUS	X	E	P	V	**S**	SIZE			RANGE

Whale Shark
Rhincodon typus (= blunt-nosed or mallet-nosed fish)

These huge sharks cruise tropical and warm temperate oceans. They regularly visit the north-west coast of Western Australia.

A Whale Shark's broad head is about ¼ of the total length. The snout is rounded, the eyes are very small and there are 5 long, wide gill slits. The upper surface is blue-grey to brownish, with white to yellowish spots and pale stripes.

Whale Sharks feed on macro-plankton[G], small fish and squid, which are gulped in and strained out by sieve tissue in the gill structures. They are on the world list of endangered species.

Length: to 15+ m
Weight: 15+ t

STATUS	X	**E**	P	V	S	SIZE			RANGE

Cartilaginous fishes

RAYS AND SKATES

Rays and skates are cartilaginous fishes. In many species the head and pectoral fins are joined to the body to form a disk. The skin is rough and may carry rows of sharp spines called thorns.

The Numbfish is an electric ray.

Stingarees have a large, rounded disc and a slender tail with a saw-edged stinging spine. This "sting" is a specialised body scale, which is grooved so venom passes to its tip. **Electric rays** are bottom-dwellers that catch prey by discharging electricity from organs behind their eyes. **Devil rays** live in open water and include the huge, plankton-feeding Manta Ray. **Skates** have large, flattened discs and small tails.

eye — cartilage
spiracle
thorns
pectoral fin
caudal fin
clasper (male)
pelvic fin
second dorsal fin
stinging spine
first dorsal fin

Body plan of a ray

Manta Ray
Manta birostris (= Two-beaked cloak-fish)

The Manta Ray is the largest of all rays. It is found in warmer seas around the world, in coastal waters and near offshore reefs.

A Manta has a pair of protruding fins at the front of its head. These channel plankton-rich water into its mouth. The fleshy "wings" are pointed and the tail is slender and short. The body is dark above and white below.

A Manta "flies" through water by flapping its "wings". It is a harmless plankton feeder, which draws in water as it swims. Plankton is filtered out before the water is discharged through multiple gill slits. This ray is noted for making spectacular leaps from the water.

Width: to 6.5+ m
Weight: to 2 t

STATUS X E P V **S** SIZE  RANGE

Eastern Fiddler Ray
Trygonorrhina fasciata (= banded stingray)

The Eastern Fiddler Ray belongs to a group that is called the shovelnose rays. It is found down Australia's south-eastern coast, from around Fraser Island to the Victorian border. It lives on the rocky bottom and in seagrass beds, and may enter estuaries.

The Eastern Fiddler Ray's head is flattened, with a rounded snout. It has a circular disc formed by the pectoral fins, which are joined to the head.

This ray often buries itself in sand or silt, with just its eyes protruding. It eats invertebrates captured on the seabed.

Shovelnose rays may produce eggs or live young.

Length: to 1.2 m

STATUS X E P V **S** SIZE   RANGE

Common Stingaree
Trygonoptera testacea (= winged stingray)

The Common Stingaree is found on the south-eastern coast of Australia, on sandflats and mudflats.

A stingaree's disc is flattened and rounded. It has a thorned dorsal spine, and the tail carries one or two venomous spines.

Stingarees may lie partially covered by sand or mud. They usually dash away when disturbed, but will attack if provoked. They eat shelled molluscs and other seabed invertebrates, and give birth to live young.

When wading in shallow water, it is a good idea to shuffle the feet rather than step, or to prod the sand or mud with a stick, in order to detect buried stingarees. A "sting" may cause severe cuts and bleeding. Once bleeding is controlled, the wound should be cleaned and placed in hot water for 30–90 minutes. Heat destroys the venom and relieves pain. Medical attention should be sought as soon as possible.

Width: to 450 mm

STATUS X E P V **S** SIZE  RANGE

Green Moray Eel

Gymnothorax prasinus (= bare-breasted green fish)

This eel is found in temperate waters, in rocky, weedy subtidal habitats.

It has a powerful, elongated body with small gill slits. The small head joins onto a swollen neck. The eyes are small, the mouth is large, and the teeth are strong, long and sharp. The body and fins are covered with brown to greenish skin. The green colour is due to algae in the skin tissue, and fades after death.

Moray eels do not have the lateral lines common in fishes, but have an acute sense of smell and sensory pores on the head. They spend the day in holes, then hunt fish and other prey at night. Morays do not attack humans unless harassed or teased. However, divers should treat them with respect.

Like all eels, morays have a transparent, drifting larval stage.

Length: to 1.0 m

STATUS	X	E	P	V	**S**	SIZE		RANGE

Sergeant Baker

Aulopus purpurissatus (= purplish pipe-fin)

Sergeant Bakers live in temperate waters. They favour rocky and coral bottoms from shallow inlets to 250 m depth.

Female Sergeant Baker

A Sergeant Baker has a compressed (narrow) body, and a sail-like first dorsal fin. The first ray of the male's dorsal fin is very long. The head is about 1/3 of the body length. It has a large mouth containing several rows of sharp, fine, curved teeth. The eyes are placed above the ends of the mouth.

This fish lies on the bottom, watching for swimming invertebrates and fishes. It launches itself at speed and engulfs them.

Length: to 600 mm

Male Sergeant Baker

STATUS	X	E	P	V	**S**	SIZE		RANGE

Striped Catfish

Plotosus lineatus (= striped many-swimmer)

Catfishes are found in both fresh and salt water. The Striped Catfish lives in tropical and subtropical seas, in bays and reef lagoons.

Australia's marine catfishes have 5 pairs of barbels around the mouth. These act as sense organs. These catfishes possess retractable, venomous spines on the front edges of their dorsal and pectoral fins.

The Striped Catfish is dark in colour with 2 pale lines along each side. The 2 nasal barbels reach the eyes. It has no scales.

Juvenile Striped Catfish eat small invertebrates and algae. A group will lie near the bottom of a bay or lagoon in an almost solid mass. This mass travels in a dense, rolling pod (above).

Adult Striped Catfish are active at night, and eat invertebrates and small fishes.

Length: to 350 mm

STATUS	X	E	P	**V**	S	SIZE		RANGE

Estuary Catfish

Cnidoglanis macrocephalus (= large-headed nettle-catfish)

The Estuary Catfish is found in coastal and estuarine habitats, in protected, often silty, places. It is solitary and shelters at the back of holes and ledges.

This large catfish is yellow to dark brown or grey, with darker mottling. It has a large head, a broad mouth surrounded by 5 pairs of barbels, and small eyes. The skin is tough, and bears no scales. Venomous spines lie at the front of the pectoral and dorsal fins. These spines can be locked into place.

The sting from catfish spines is very painful; repeated stabs from an Estuary Catfish's spines may be fatal. To relieve the pain and kill the venom, heat should be applied as soon as possible. The heat may come from hot water, sun-heated stones and sand, or a hot air blower of some sort.

Estuary Catfish eat bottom-living invertebrates and fishes.

Length: to 600 mm

STATUS	X	E	P	**V**	S	SIZE		RANGE

Eastern Frogfish
Batrachomoeus dubius (= doubtful frog-like fish)

The Eastern Frogfish is found along the central coast of eastern Australia. It lives in coastal bays and harbours, in muddy and silty habitats, hiding under slabs of rock and other objects.

This frogfish has a stout body and a large, round head. The snout is short and there are fleshy pieces of skin around the mouth and eyes, and along the body. These may act as lures for prospective food items, such as small fish and crustaceans.

Feeble swimmers, frogfishes ambush their prey. They can suck in a victim in less than 0.01 sec. The expandable stomach allows the capture of quite large animals.

Spines on the gill covers may be venomous and can inflict painful wounds. Frogfishes may make loud croaking noises with their swim bladders.

Length: to 300 mm

STATUS X E P V **S** SIZE RANGE

Eastern Nannygai
Centroberyx affinis (= fish that resembles a perch)

Eastern Nannygai live on rocky reefs and in offshore waters along the south-eastern Australian coast to western Bass Strait.

The head accounts for 1/3 of the length of the deep, compressed body. The large eye is typical of animals living under low-light conditions. The tail is deeply forked. The body colour is silvery blue to deep red, with a metallic shine. Pale spots on the large scales form shimmering vertical lines, and there is an obvious lateral line.

Nannygai feed on small fishes and crustaceans. Juveniles school in waters over rocky bottoms and reefs. Sometimes the tightly packed schools extend for hundreds of metres.

Length: to 400 mm

STATUS X E P V **S** SIZE RANGE

Roughy
Trachichthys australis (= rough Australian fish)

Roughy live in temperate seas, from southern Queensland to Lancelin, Western Australia. They are found in coastal and offshore waters.

The body is almost circular and compressed. The head is large, rough and bony. The eyes are nearly half the length of the head, and the mouth is large and angled. There are sharp spines on the gill covers and large, sharply keeled scales along the belly.

The tail is deeply forked. This roughy is brownish red in colour, with a white bar on the cheek, and white leading edges to the fins.

The Roughy is carnivorous, feeding mainly at night. If disturbed it can release into the water a milky substance that disables other fishes.

Length: to 180 mm

STATUS X E P V **S** SIZE  RANGE

Pineapplefish
Cleidopus gloriamaris

These fish are found in temperate waters along western and eastern coasts. They live on soft bottoms in open estuaries and bays, and on the continental shelf. During the daytime, they hide in caves and under overhangs.

A Pineapplefish has a dark net-like pattern formed by the edges of large, yellow, bony plate-like scales. The head is encased in bone, and the snout is round and broad. The fish has a light-producing organ, a patch of skin carrying luminescent[G] bacteria, on each side of the lower jaw. This patch gives out a greenish light and is used as an aid to hunt small crustaceans at night.

A Pineapplefish makes a loud creaking noise when disturbed.

Length: to 250 mm

STATUS X E P V **S** SIZE RANGE

Big-belly Seahorse
Hippocampus abdominalis (= bellied seahorse)

The Big-belly Seahorse lives in shallow inlets and rocky areas around the south-eastern coast. Juveniles drift while clinging to floating seagrass. Adults live in kelp, sometimes on jetty pylons.

The body of a seahorse is wrapped in bony plates. The head is angled downwards and has a long, tubular snout with a small mouth at its end. The tail is prehensile and there is a single, central dorsal fin. The Big-belly's colour ranges from brown to orange or yellow with darker blotches and a banded tail.

Seahorses swim slowly in an upright position, propelled by dorsal and pectoral fins. They feed on planktonic crustaceans.

After a courtship dance, the female passes her eggs to the male. He fertilises and broods them in an enclosed pouch on his belly. He later gives birth to live young.

Length: to 300 mm

STATUS	X	E	P	V	S	SIZE		RANGE

Weedy Seadragon
Phyllopteryx taeniolatus (= ribboned leaf-fin)

The Weedy Seadragon is found from central New South Wales to Rottnest Island, Western Australia. It lives in beds of algae along rocky reefs.

A seadragon's body is covered with bony plates and carries flattened spines and flaps that resemble fronds of algae. The head is set at a slight angle, and the snout is long and slender. The dorsal fin is near the tail. The body carries camouflaging flattened spines and flaps that resemble fronds of algae.

Seadragons move by rippling their dorsal and pectoral fins. They eat small and planktonic crustaceans.

The eggs are brooded by the male, held on the underside of his tail by a layer of skin.

Length: to 450 mm

STATUS	X	E	P	V	S	SIZE		RANGE

PIPEFISHES & THEIR ALLIES

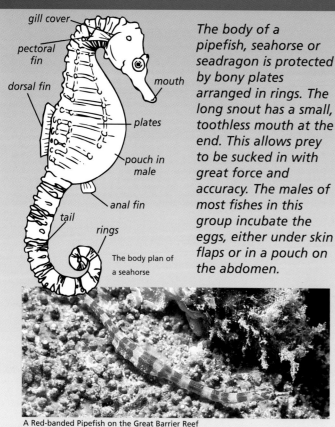

gill cover
pectoral fin
dorsal fin
mouth
plates
pouch in male
anal fin
tail
rings

The body plan of a seahorse

The body of a pipefish, seahorse or seadragon is protected by bony plates arranged in rings. The long snout has a small, toothless mouth at the end. This allows prey to be sucked in with great force and accuracy. The males of most fishes in this group incubate the eggs, either under skin flaps or in a pouch on the abdomen.

A Red-banded Pipefish on the Great Barrier Reef

Trumpetfish
Aulostomus chinensis (= Chinese flute-mouth)

The Trumpetfish lives in tropical and subtropical waters in all protected habitats. It is often found near black and soft corals.

A Trumpetfish has a very long body and an elongated snout. The dorsal fin is set well back and has small, separate spines. The anal fin is opposite the dorsal fin. The colour of the Trumpetfish is variable, and there is a bright yellow form (above).

The Trumpetfish is an active predator that ambushes or stalks its prey. It may hide amongst corals, or swim behind a larger fish until it gets near the victim. It may drift in the water like a piece of stick, then dash to attack a small passing fish.

Length: to 900 mm

STATUS	X	E	P	V	S	SIZE		RANGE

Red Rockcod
Scorpaena cardinalis (= red scorpionfish)

The Red Rockcod is found in temperate waters along the south-eastern coast of Australia. It lives on coastal reefs from the intertidal zone to around 100 m depth and may be found in silty estuaries.

This scorpionfish has a broad, tapering body. The head carries bony ridges; the large mouth is half the length of the head and has tiny teeth. The eyes are large. There are 5 spines on each cheek, spines on each gill cover and 5 spines below each eye. The leading spines of the dorsal fin have venom glands at their bases. There are skin flaps on the head, along the lateral line and over the body. Colour varies from grey to bright red with a marbled pattern.

The Red Rockcod is well-camouflaged, and feeds by ambushing invertebrates and small fishes. Anglers often hook it when fishing near reefs.

Length: to 400 mm

STATUS X E P V **S** SIZE RANGE

Reef Stonefish
Synanceia verrucosa (= horribly put-together fish)

The Reef Stonefish lives in tropical north Queensland waters, in estuaries and on reef flats. It lies on mud or sand, or among rocks or coral, sometimes in very shallow water.

It is a bulky fish, with a large head and big mouth. The eyes are high-set and prominent. The warty skin ranges in colour from brown or mud-grey to red and yellow, and may have algae and hydroids growing on it. It has very large, paddle-like pectoral fins. The dorsal spines have venom glands at their bases. Pressure on a spine forces venom into the wound it has made.

Well camouflaged, a stonefish uses its pectoral fins to bury itself, leaving only eyes and dorsal area clear. It ambushes crustacean or fish prey.

This is the most venomous fish known. A sting causes great pain and may be fatal. Heat will destroy the venom.

Length: to 350 mm

STATUS X E P V **S** SIZE RANGE

Common Lionfish
Pterois volitans (= wing-finned flier)

This scorpionfish lives in various habitats. It is found from tropical to temperate waters, except along the southern coast.

Behind long, feathery dorsal and pectoral fins is a blocky, compressed body patterned with brown to reddish brown bands. The head is large and the mouth can gape widely. The dorsal spines are venomous.

Lionfishes hunt at night. They move slowly, using the pectoral fins to guide shrimps and other prey to within range of the mouth. Then the jaws and gill covers open, the floor of the mouth drops and the surge of water drags prey inside.

Lionfish turn their dorsal fins towards a threat. Some may act aggressively towards humans if approached too closely. Their venom causes severe pain.

Length: to 350 mm

STATUS X E P V **S** SIZE RANGE

Eastern Spiny Gurnard
Lepidotrigla pleuracanthica (= swell-sided scaled gurnard)

This bottom-dwelling fish is found from the central coast of New South Wales to the Victorian border.

The body of a gurnard is tapered, and the head is small and encased in bone. The bony snout is used as a shovel. The large pectoral fins, which in this species are edged with bright blue, open like large fans. The lower rays are free and thickened, and are used for walking and probing the sea bed. The dorsal fin has two sections, the front one with a large, dark, pale-edged blotch. The scales are small; the lateral line scales have spines.

Gurnards feed on bottom-dwelling crustaceans and worms. The pectoral fins may be flashed to scare off predators.

Length: to 200 mm

STATUS X E P V **S** SIZE RANGE

Sand Flathead

Neoplatycephalus bassensis (= Bass Strait flathead)

The Sand Flathead is found from Newcastle, New South Wales, to eastern South Australia, in sandy bays, estuaries and coastal waters.

This member of the scorpionfish group has a long, flattened body, sandy brown above and pale below. The scales are small and covered with mucus. The flat head is about ⅓ of the body length. The eye has a small flap; the mouth is duck-like, with small, pointed teeth. The gill covers have 2 long cutting spines, the lower twice as long as the upper. Small scales extend from the eyes to the tail. The scales on the lateral line are larger. The two dorsal fins have sharp spines.

The Sand Flathead is well camouflaged on sandy bottoms. It lies partially buried in the sand and ambushes small fish. It will also pursue prey.

Many species of flathead lack a swim bladder. This helps them remain on the seabed.

Length: to 460 mm

STATUS	X	E	P	V	S	SIZE	RANGE

PERCHES AND THEIR ALLIES

This group of over 2500 species contains a wide variety of fishes. Their shapes range from almost circular to eel-like, their sizes from gobies less than 10 mm long to billfishes that grow longer than 4 m. They all have a tail fin with 17 or fewer rays.

Moorish Idol, a coral reef fish

A school of Barracuda

Black-spotted Sand Goby

Ring-tail Cardinalfish

Coral Trout

Plectropomus leopardus

Coral trout are found off reef edges from Cape Moreton, Queensland, around the northern coast to Shark Bay, Western Australia.

This species has a powerful, oblong, compressed body. There are long blue markings on cheeks and gill covers. The large mouth has well-developed teeth. There are 3 spines on each gill cover. The colour is blue-spotted dull pink through scarlet to brownish. The reddest fish are found in deeper habitats.

A coral trout shelters under overhangs and in caverns. It feeds on smaller fish.

The abdominal cavity of this fish often carries dark, seed-like lumps. These are tapeworm

cysts[G] that are killed by cooking or freezing at –6.5°C. A coral trout may also be host to roundworms, which are killed in cooking. It is not a good idea to eat this fish raw.

Length: to 750 mm

STATUS	X	E	P	V	S	SIZE	RANGE

Strawberry Cod

Trachypoma macracanthus (= long-edged rough-cheek)

The Strawberry Cod is found in temperate waters along the south-eastern coast of Australia. It lives on rocky reefs in clear, protected waters, often among boulders. When young it may enter estuaries.

This fish has a robust body, red in colour and covered with small, white dots. The eye is large. The Strawberry Cod feeds at night, mostly on shrimps, but also taking small fishes. During the day it hides amongst rocks.

Length: to 400 mm

STATUS	X	E	P	V	S	SIZE	RANGE

White Trevally

Pseudocaranx dentex (= false member of the caranx group)

The White Trevally is an ocean fish found in schools in warm temperate water, at depths of 80–200 m. The young gather in coastal inlets, where they are frequently netted by estuary anglers.

This trevally has an oval, strongly compressed, shimmering bluish silver body, with a black blotch high on each gill cover. The fore-body scales are very small, then, towards the end of the very clear lateral line, enlarge to become sharp and bony. The head is moderate in size, the mouth smallish and the teeth small. The dorsal fin is in two parts; the tail is deeply forked.

This fish is a fast swimmer and an aggressive predator.

Length: to 950 mm

STATUS	X	E	P	V	S	SIZE		RANGE

Red Emperor

Lutjanus sebae (= oily basin-mouth)

The Red Emperor lives in tropical waters around the north coast of Australia. Juveniles may live amongst the spines of sea urchins in rock or sand habitat. Adults school in deep offshore waters.

This fish has a deep, compressed body and a big head. As an individual ages, the clear markings of the juvenile (see photo), deepen to overall red, and the sharply pointed dorsal and anal fins become rounded. The mouth is moderately large, with canine teeth in the front row of the upper jaw.

Red Emperor form schools of fish of similar size. They feed on fish, squid, crustaceans and invertebrates.

This is one of the reef species whose flesh may carry a dangerous toxin. This is accumulated from feeding on invertebrates that have eaten infected algae. The condition is called ciguatera, and deepwater fishes are generally free of it.

Length: to 1 m

STATUS	X	E	P	V	S	SIZE		RANGE

Moses Perch (Russell's Snapper)

Lutjanus russelli (= Russell's basin-mouth)

Moses Perch are found in subtropical and tropical estuaries, bays and reefs. They may be in large schools or in pairs around inshore reefs. Here they spend daylight under ledges.

This is an oblong, compressed fish. The upper jaw has canine teeth; the gill cover is very sharp. The colour is pinkish in the ocean, but olive in estuaries. There is a black patch below the rear third of the dorsal fin, while the other fins are yellow. The Moses Perch is an active hunter, preying on smaller fish, crustaceans and squid.

The name "Moses Perch" refers to the black patch on the side. However it was not Moses but St Peter whose fingers were said to have burnt spots into Tilapia fish in the Sea of Galilee.

Length: to 600 mm

STATUS	X	E	P	V	S	SIZE		RANGE

Black-tipped Fusilier

Pterocaesio digramma (= two-lined blue-grey-fin)

This fusilier lives in tropical and warm temperate waters. It frequents coral reefs, lagoons and coral outcrops. Here it is preyed on by coral trout, mackerel and other large predators.

It is a slim, oval fish, indigo blue above and silvery white below, with 2 thin yellow stripes along each side. The mouth is small and the upper jaw can be protruded. The scales are small. There is a single dorsal fin and the tail fin is deeply forked and black-tipped.

Fusiliers eat planktonic animals. They may form great schools as protection from predators.

Length: to 300 mm

STATUS	X	E	P	V	S	SIZE		RANGE

Barramundi
Lates calcarifer (= spur-pointed lates)

The Barramundi is found around Australia's tropical coast, north from Maryborough, Queensland. During its life history it is found in freshwater billabongs, lagoons and rivers, then down estuaries into the sea.

It has a stretched oval shape with a steep rise from the head to the humped back. The orange-red eyes are high on the head; the large mouth contains bands of small teeth. There are two dorsal fins, and the gill covers are saw-edged and sharp. The colour ranges from metallic, deep grey-green to silver.

Barramundi eggs are laid in estuarine swamps and hatch in less than a day. At 1 year, the young fish move upstream, then at 3 they move to the ocean. Males become female at 5–7 years, then enter mangrove swamps to lay eggs.

Barramundi prey on crustaceans and smaller fish, particularly mullet.

Length: to 1.6 m

STATUS	X	E	P	V	S	SIZE	RANGE

Slate Sweetlips
Diagramma labiosum (= large-lipped mapped fish)

These sweetlips are found in temperate and tropical waters. Adults form dense schools over sand beds on coral-patch reefs.

It is an oblong, compressed fish. The profile of the head curves outwards. The mouth has thick lips and bands of pointed teeth. There is a single dorsal fin with strong spines, the second spine more than twice as long as the first. Colours change markedly during growth. Young fish are yellow-brown with horizontal sooty brown bands. The adult is grey or sometimes bronze.

Schools of sweetlips browse at night on invertebrates. They also take crustaceans and small fish.

Length: to 1 m

STATUS	X	E	P	V	S	SIZE	RANGE

Sand Whiting
Sillago ciliata (= fringed flathead)

The Sand Whiting is found in tropical and temperate waters from Cape York to Victoria. It lives over sand and among ribbon weed on estuary floors, bays and sea beaches.

It is a long, shallow-bodied fish, with two dorsal fins, the first higher than the second. The eye is large and staring; the mouth is small and horseshoe-shaped with a broad band of fine teeth. The colour is sandy brown to sand coloured, slightly darker above but always silvery. The fins are pale yellow, and there is a dark blotch at the base of each pectoral fin.

Sand Whiting move over the sandflats of estuaries and beaches. They nudge out and eat worms, molluscs and crustaceans such as as prawns and soldier crabs. They are well adapted to use the sandy shallows of surf beaches and low-tide conditions.

Length: 450 cm

STATUS	X	E	P	V	S	SIZE	RANGE

FISHING

It has been estimated that 4 000 000 Australians go recreational fishing at least once every year. A lot of money is spent on fishing tackle, boat hire, 4WD vehicles, fuel and camping gear. Some of the most popular TV programs are on fishing.

Commercial fishing is a big industry, and Australia's fishing fleet is under constant challenge from international vessels.

Fish stocks need to be managed wisely, for once some species are fished too heavily they will take many years to recover. If they form a link in a food chain, the creatures that eat them will also suffer.

Fishing is probably the favourite recreation in Australia.

Southern Bream
Acanthopagrus butcheri (= Butcher's prickly bream)

This bream is found in southern coastal waters from Cape Howe to south of Shark Bay. It is replaced on the east coast by the Silver Bream, *A. australis*. Bream live in coastal and estuarine waters, sometimes in almost fresh water.

The body is deep and compressed. The mouth has several pairs of peg-like canine teeth at the front and rows of molars at the back. The dorsal fin has brown spines joined by purplish membrane; the pectoral fins are long; the tail is deeply forked. The lateral line is curved. The colour is golden brown or greenish bronze.

Cone-shaped depressions in sandy estuaries show where bream have been nosing for crustaceans, worms and molluscs. They sometimes cause damage in oyster farms and may take fish.

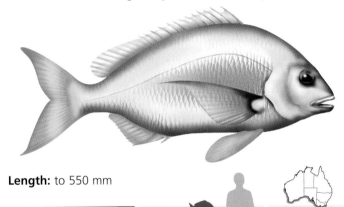

Length: to 550 mm

STATUS	X	E	P	V	S	SIZE		RANGE

Snapper
Chrysophrys aurata (= golden gilthead)

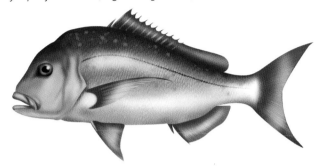

The Snapper inhabits temperate and subtropical waters. Juveniles live in inlets and bays. Adults frequent deeper water near reefs.

The body is oval, deep and compressed; old fish develop a hump on the head. Each powerful jaw has several pairs of peg-like canines, and a row of smaller canines and molars. There is a single dorsal fin, long pectoral fins and a forked tail. The colour is silver-pink above to silvery white below. Juveniles have scattered blue spots.

Snapper eat prawns, crabs, molluscs (including squids) and fish. Juveniles shelter in mangroves and lagoon vegetation.Common names vary according to the age of the fish: very small – Cockneys; 0.5 kg – Red Bream; 1.5 kg – Squire; hump-headed fish – Old Man Snapper.

Length: to 1.3 m

STATUS	X	E	P	V	S	SIZE		RANGE

Mulloway (Jewfish)
Argyrosomus hololepidotus (= silver-bodied carp-like fish)

Mulloway are found in temperate waters from the Burnett River, Queensland, around the southern coast to Shark Bay, Western Australia. They live in bays, rivers, beach gutters and surge holes by reefs.

This is an elongated and compressed fish. The mouth is moderate in size and orange inside. The jaws have large canines and bands of small teeth. The dorsal fin is deeply notched, there is a black spot at the base of each pectoral fin, and the adult's tail-fin edge is S-shaped or convex. A Mulloway is greyish green above and silvery grey below. The very visible lateral line runs right to the tail-tip.

The Mulloway is a powerful predator, feeding at any time of the day on schools of small to medium-sized fish. It moves up and down the coast seasonally, as well as into estuaries.

Length: to 2 m

STATUS	X	E	P	V	S	SIZE		RANGE

Southern Silver Drummer
Kyphosus sydneyanus (= Sydney humpbacked fish)

This fish lives in temperate waters. It is found from the Queensland border around the southern coastline, north to about Shark Bay, Western Australia. It likes rough, foaming waters and large, swiftly running estuaries.

The Southern Silver Drummer is a robust, oval-shaped fish. The mouth is small, and the chisel-like teeth on each jaw are backed up by small teeth on the tongue. It has a single dorsal fin. The colour is silver to greyish above with a silver streak along the side. The fins and edges of the gill covers are dusky to black.

Large drummers often live alone, feeding in breaking seas about reefs on crabs, other crustaceans, small fish and weeds. Younger fish may be in small groups or large schools.

Length: to 750 mm

STATUS	X	E	P	V	S	SIZE		RANGE

Red-throat Emperor
Lethrinus chrysostomus (= golden-bodied lethrinus)

These fish are found north of Gladstone, Queensland. They live in channels between coral reefs.

The body is perch-like and compressed, olive-green above, silvery below, with dark vertical bands. The head is marked in pink to blood-red; the inside of the mouth is orange-red. The dorsal fin is bright scarlet and the other fins have varying degrees of red. The long snout has soft lips; there are strong, frontal canine teeth.

Red-throat Emperors hunt between coral reefs and heads. They eat small fish, crustaceans, squid and other molluscs such as abalone. Turtle hatchlings are taken.

Length: to 1 m

STATUS X E P V **S** SIZE RANGE

Black-spot Goatfish
Parupeneus porphyreus (= purplish parupeneus)

This goatfish lives in inshore, suptropical reef waters. It is named for the pair of barbels that droop from the chin like a beard.

It is an elongate fish with an arched back and paired sensory barbels. The base colour is white with 4 reddish green stripes from nose to second dorsal fin. There is a black spot, often with a yellow blotch in front, across the hind dorsal area. Colour varies with mood, or between day and night. There are two dorsal fins, and the caudal fin is forked. Goatfish form foraging schools; if isolated, an individual will school with other species. They eat small invertebrates such as crustaceans and worms.

Length: to 500 mm

STATUS X E P V **S** SIZE RANGE

Reef Bannerfish
Heniochus acuminatus (= sharp-pointed bridled fish)

The Reef Bannerfish lives in and about caverns, most commonly from Moreton Bay, Queensland, north. It stays near to protective coral reef and grottoes.

It has a very deep, compressed body, with a trailing filament from the fourth spine of the dorsal fin. Shining white, it has 2 broad purple-black bands and bright yellow, soft dorsal and tail fins. The profile of the head is dished.

A Reef Bannerfish feeds on invertebrates and algae growing about coral, as well as browsing on coral polyps. It moves slowly around coral outcrops.

Length: 250 mm

STATUS X E P V **S** SIZE RANGE

Emperor Angelfish
Pomacanthus imperator (= imperial bar-cheek)

This species lives around coral and rocky reefs on the subtropical and tropical Australian coast, from Kalbarri, WA, to Iluka, NSW.

It is a brilliantly coloured, oblong, compressed fish. The snout is shaped to forage amongst coral; the teeth are fine and slender. There is a strong spine on the gill cover; the tail fin is rounded.

These fish are territorial, and centre on caverns and grottoes near surge and tidal channels, and gutters. They feed on sponges, sea tulips, and organisms and algae growing on coral.

Adult patterning is very different from the juvenile patterns, which are dark blue with white markings.

Length: 380 mm

STATUS X E P V **S** SIZE RANGE

Sea Mullet
Mugil cephalus (= striped mullet)

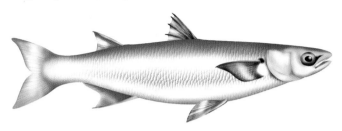

Sea Mullet live in temperate and tropical waters, across sandflats, beaches and estuaries. They enter the slightly salty and fresh waters of coastal rivers and lagoons.

This is a slender, elongate, silvery olive (when mature) or silvery grey (when juvenile) fish. The snout is blunt, with a small mouth. The teeth are tiny, growing in several rows along the edge of the lips. There are two dorsal fins, the first with sharp spines. The tail fin is forked.

During autumn, when south-westerly winds blow, schools of Sea Mullet migrate northwards to breed at sea. The eggs and young drift southwards. Young fish enter sheltered waters to pass through their juvenile phases. The species matures at 5 years. Mullet spend winter in lagoons, lakes and estuaries, and may enter fresh water. Large schools feed across sandflats and estuaries, taking small invertebrates and plant matter.

Length: to 800 mm

STATUS	X	E	P	V	**S**	SIZE		RANGE

Old Wife (Zebrafish)
Enoplosus armatus (= armed armoured fish)

This striking fish forms great schools in warm and cool temperate waters. It is found on coastal rocky reefs and seagrass beds, and around jetties and wharves.

An Old Wife has a deep, compressed body. The snout is upturned and the mouth small, with slender teeth in both jaws. There are 2 tall dorsal fins, the first with venomous spines. The leading edges of the fins are often pinkish. This fish has very small scales and a very clear lateral line. The silvery white body is marked with around 8 black bars.

This fish lives alone, in pairs or in large schools. It feeds on crustaceans and worms.

An Old Wife should be handled with care. A wound from the venomous spines gives a sharp prickling sensation, followed by aching and swelling.

Length: to 250 mm

STATUS	X	E	P	V	**S**	SIZE		RANGE

Crested Morwong
Cheilodactylus vestitus (= marked claw-finger)

Morwongs live in temperate to cool tropical waters near wharves, in estuaries, and on inshore and offshore reefs.

The Crested Morwong has a small head. An adult has two bony "horns", one above the lip and one in front of the eyes. The head rises steeply to a crowning dorsal fin, then slants down to the tail. The mouth is small with thick, yellow, fleshy lips ringed with brown. The teeth are small and pointed. The fourth spine of the dorsal fin is very long; the tail fin is forked. The body is white with 4 black bands.

This fish is usually found on its own, but sometimes in pairs or small groups. It feeds on the bottom bond on reefs, taking molluscs and worms.

Length: to 350 mm

STATUS	X	E	P	V	**S**	SIZE		RANGE

Eastern Stargazer
Kathetostoma laeve (= upright-mouthed smooth-skin)

Stargazers' eyes are on the tops of their heads. The Eastern Stargazer occurs around Australia's south-eastern corner. It lives on shallow, sandy seabeds, and in seagrass beds in estuaries, lagoons and bays.

It has a blotched, greyish tan, tapering body. The small eyes are set on top of the large head, with its upturned "face". The mouth is large; the lips have a narrow fleshy fringe. There is a row of prominent canine teeth in the lower jaw and fine outer teeth plus canines in the upper. The skin has no scales. The single, long dorsal fin has no spines and the pectoral fins are large.

Using its pectoral fins, this fish buries itself in sand with its eyes and jaws clear. A poor swimmer, it uses ambush to take crustaceans and large fish.

It has been known to bite divers.

Length: to 750 mm

STATUS	X	E	P	V	**S**	SIZE		RANGE

Barrier Reef Anemonefish

Amphiprion akindynos

This anemonefish is found on coral reefs from the Capricorn Group at the southern end of Queensland's Great Barrier Reef north to Torres Strait. It lives in and about the stinging tentacles of anemones.

It has an oval, compressed body. The tail fin is slightly hollowed. Adults are light to dark chocolate brown in colour, with 2 black-edged white or pale blue bars. Juveniles have 3 bars.

Chemicals in the mucus coating an anemonefish's body prevent its host anemone from stinging it. Pairs or small groups of these fishes feed on planktonic crustaceans and algae growing on coral. An anemonefish lays its eggs at the base of its anemone's column.

All anemonefishes are born male and may change to female as they age. In a typical group, a large female mates with a smaller male. When the female dies, the male changes sex and the next dominant male becomes its partner.

Length: to 110 mm

STATUS	X	E	P	V	S	SIZE		RANGE

Blue-barred Parrotfish

Scarus ghobban (= wrasse-like fish)

This parrotfish occurs on coral reefs and seagrass and weed areas throughout the south-western Pacific.

It is an elongate-oval, compressed fish. The male is blue and yellow, with broad blue scale margins and three dark streaks behind and below the eye. The female (right) is yellowish with blue bars and spots on the sides. The teeth form a beak like that of a parrot, and there are more grinding "teeth" in the throat. The large scales are covered with mucus.

The Blue-barred Parrotfish shelters beneath, and feeds on, coral outcrops. At high tide across the reef, it ventures onto flats. It bites chunks out of living coral and breaks this down to fine sand, extracting organic matter, such as algae, before excreting the sand. It also works through coral rubble that may contain organisms. It is highly territorial.

Using this method of feeding, parrotfish and wrasses produce much of the coral sand found in reef areas.

Length: to 1 m

STATUS	X	E	P	V	S	SIZE		RANGE

Harlequin Tuskfish

Choerodon fasciatus (= banded boar-tooth)

The Harlequin Tuskfish lives in tropical waters on Australia's north-eastern coast. It shelters under coral growths, and, at high tide, ranges out onto reef flats and into channels.

It is a deep-bodied, compressed fish with a steeply rising head. The mouth is small with strong, tusk-like canines. The body colour is purple-blue to greenish grey, with 6–9 red to orange vertical bars. Dorsal, ventral and tail fins are scarlet edged with blue. A heavy layer of mucus covers the scales.

This tuskfish searches among living coral and coral rubble for molluscs, crustaceans, worms and sea urchins. Highly territorial, it may become a nuisance to divers because it follows them to take invertebrates stirred up by their movements.

Length: to 250 mm

STATUS	X	E	P	V	S	SIZE		RANGE

Peacock Sole

Pardachirus pavoninus (= peacock-spotted fish)

The Peacock Sole is found in tropical seas around Australia's north. It lives on coastal sand or mudflats, sometimes in groups.

This sole has both eyes on the right side of its head. The left side of the body serves as the underbody and lies against the seabed. The snout extends over the mouth, which is twisted into a slanted sideways position. There are teeth only in the parts of the jaws on the blind side of the head. The fins are soft-rayed and almost surround the body. There may be touch-sensitive, fleshy projections on the blind side of the head.

A newly hatched flatfish larva has eyes on both sides of its head. One eye journeys across the head to take up position on the other side.

Soles usually lie buried in sand or mud with just the eyes showing. They feed on small invertebrates and fishes. A Peacock Sole can give off a milky fluid that may stun predators.

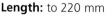

Length: to 220 mm

STATUS	X	E	P	V	S	SIZE		RANGE

POISON & ARMOUR PLATING

The bodies of triggerfishes, boxfishes, leatherjackets and porcupinefishes are adapted to prevent predators swallowing them. Some have long spines that can be locked into place. Some have an armour of large, thickened scales. Some have skins covered with spikes or prickly scales. Some can pump the body up with water into a spiny ball. Pufferfishes have toxin in the skin and in certain internal organs. They can release this toxin into the water around them. Some of the most dangerous pufferfishes look very like species known for their tasty flesh. People who eat pufferfish run the risk of dying from a poison more lethal than cyanide[G].

The Thorny-back Cowfish has bony armour and head spines.

The Mimic Filefish imitates the poisonous Saddled Puffer below it.

Six-spine Leatherjacket
Meuschenia freycineti (= Freycinet's meuschenia)

This leatherjacket is found in temperate waters on south-eastern, southern and south-western coasts. It lives at various depths on rocky reefs near ledges and areas of sponges.

It has an oval-shaped, compressed body and a small gill slit. The mouth is small and the teeth are flat scrapers. The skin is covered with tiny prickly scales. There are 3 small spines on each side near the base of the tail. A retractable dorsal spine stands above the eye. The male has vivid blue lines from eyes to snout, and a close network of blue lines over much of the body. A yellow patch often lies across the sides. The female is brown with darker brown lines along the body.

This fish feeds on sponges.

Length: to 500 mm

STATUS	X	E	P	V	S	SIZE	RANGE

Weeping Toado
Torquigener pleurogramma (= collared side-marked fish)

This relative of the pufferfishes is found patchily from Shark Bay, Western Australia, around the south coast to the southern Barrier Reef. It lives in estuaries and bays.

It has a tapering thick body, rounded above and flattened beneath. The body cavity can be inflated like a balloon. It has a long snout and the teeth are fused and beak-like. The skin is covered with tiny spines. There is a single, round dorsal fin and a short tail fin. It is grey to greenish above, netted with dark lines. There are dark bands across the back and between the eyes; a dark stripe separates the white belly from the back.

The name is derived from the "weeping" marks below the eyes. The liver, ovaries, intestines and skin of this fish are very poisonous. The poison, tetrodotoxin, causes death for 60% of victims in 6–24 hours. There is no known antidote.

Length: to 200 mm

STATUS	X	E	P	V	S	SIZE	RANGE

Porcupinefish
Dicotylichthys sp. (= hollow fish)

This porcupinefish is found in tropical waters, on coral and rocky reefs.

It has an inflatable, globe-shaped body splotched with brown and with darker spots. At night, it turns

uniform greyish cream with slightly darker back. Erectable spines cover the body except for the face. The powerful jaws have fused, chisel-like teeth. The fins are transparent yellow and the fish swims using small, single dorsal and anal fins.

A porcupinefish feeds from dusk until dawn, singly or in loose groups. It swims slowly, body angled down, browsing on rocks and cliff edges as well as the sea floor. Its diet includes molluscs, crustaceans and sea urchins. During daylight, it shelters beneath overhangs. This fish can inflate itself with water or air to 3 times its normal size. This causes its spines to become erect.

This fish is poisonous and, like related species, should never be eaten.

Length: to 450 mm

STATUS	X	E	P	V	S	SIZE	RANGE

Stories in stone

Stromatolites in Hamelin Pool, Shark Bay. These structures are made up of layers of bacteria, algae and debris.

Australia is an ancient landmass. Some of its rocks are over 4.2 thousand million years old. Its life forms originated at least 3500 million years ago.

Today, scientists can trace parts of the story of Australia's plants and animals through their fossilised remains. A fossil is formed when an organism becomes surrounded by sand or mud. Over a long period of time, minerals take the place of living tissue. The sand or mud becomes compressed and may be heated. Slowly it changes to rock. The shape, or imprint, of the organism, or of its toughest parts, remains preserved in rock. So a fossil may be a petrified[G] skeleton, or the imprint of a body or plant, or even footprints set in stone.

Some organisms are "living fossils". In Hamelin Pool, at Shark Bay, Western Australia, are rocky mounds called stromatolites. These are formed of layers of microscopic, single-celled bacteria, algae and silty debris. The ancestors of the bacteria first appeared on Earth about 3500 million years ago. Fossil stromatolites found in the Macdonnell Ranges, Northern Territory, are about 900 million years old.

Some of the first fossil evidence of multi-celled animals is found in the Flinders Ranges of South Australia in rocks about 670 million years old.

By 400 million years ago, Australia was home to fishes with internal skeletons. Amphibians, which could survive in water or on land, emerged onto land. Then reptiles, which did not have to return to the water to lay their eggs, became dominant. Dinosaurs and other reptile groups ruled the world for around 140 million years. About 65 million years ago, the rule of reptiles was replaced by that of birds and mammals.

By 45 million years ago, Australia had broken away from Gondwana and set off on its northward "voyage". After that, its plants and animals had to develop without any reference to those in the rest of the world. Marsupials became the dominant mammals, while parrots, pigeons and other groups of birds flourished.

It was millions of years before Australia drew near to Asia. As the distance narrowed, bats, rodents and monitor lizards crossed by air and sea to the southern continent. Around 60 000, perhaps more, years ago, humans arrived by sea.

This Common Brushtail Possum is eating the seed of a cycad, a plant whose ancestors flourished in Australia 250 million years ago.

Australia and the world

The opalised jawbone of a platypus was found at Lightning Ridge in 1985. Dated to 120 million years ago, it is the oldest mammal fossil so far found in Australia.

Platypus fossils dated to more than 60 million years ago have been found in Argentina, South America. South America once had many marsupials. Today, only a few species survive there.

Australia has more families of parrots and pigeons than any other continent.

Plants belonging to the protea family grow in both South Africa and Australia. Tree-waratahs grow in both Australia and South America.

Bats arrived in Australia by air within the past 30 million years. Rats arrived by sea 5–7 million years ago.

Australia has been inhabited by modern humans for around twice as long as Western Europe.

In 1912, a German explorer and weather scientist, Alfred Wegener, suggested that Earth's continents were moving about. Geologists[G] said his work was "utter, damned rot" and disregarded his conclusions.

In 1966, Wegener's theory was proved by scientists on HMS *Owen*. While measuring fossil magnetism[G] in rocks so they could estimate their age, they discovered that the Indian Ocean basin is growing wider.

When the Aborigines arrived

The forerunners of the Aboriginal people voyaged from South-east Asia to Australia more than 60 000 years ago.

They came to a land where the largest mammals, birds and reptiles were much bigger than similar sorts of Australian animals are today. These large animals are known as megafauna[G].

Nonetheless, most Australian animals, including the megafauna, were much smaller than animals in other lands that lived in the same way and ate the same food. The largest kangaroo living at that time weighed only 200 kg, compared to the largest

Human   *Diprotodon*

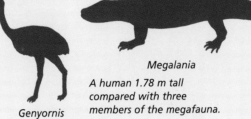

Megalania

Genyornis

A human 1.78 m tall compared with three members of the megafauna.

African antelope, which weighs over 1000 kg. The largest marsupial was the diprotodon, which looked like an enormous wombat. It stood just under 2 m high at the shoulder, was 3.5 m long and weighed about 2000 kg. This is only one-third the mass of an adult elephant.

By 35 000 years ago, most or all the species of megafauna were extinct. The reasons suggested for their extinction include dramatic climatic changes over the past 50 000 years, the alteration in Australian landscapes brought about by fire, and hunting by humans. The answer may be in a combination of these factors.

Some prehistoric predators

Study of fossil remains shows that when the Aboriginal people arrived in Australia, the continent was home to only a small number of large predators.

A large-sized meat-eater is at the top of the food chain. It needs a large prey population of plant-eaters. Australia's soils and vegetation have never been rich enough to support great numbers of herbivores.

Australia's early mammalian carnivores:

Around 60 000 years ago, the continent was home to only three mammal carnivores weighing more than 10 kg. Two other carnivorous marsupials weighed about 5 kg.

Each of these marsupials was the equivalent of a placental mammal carnivore living in other lands.

The **marsupial lion** (40–60 kg) was the equivalent of a leopard.

The **Thylacine** (up to 15 kg) was the equivalent of a small wolf.

The **carnivorous kangaroo** (40 kg) was the equivalent of a small bear.

The **Tasmanian Devil** (5–8 kg) was the equivalent of a scavenging hyena.

The **Spotted-tailed Quoll** (up to 5 kg) was the equivalent of a cat or a weasel.

Australia's reptilian carnivores from 60 000 years ago:

A **monitor lizard**, Megalania, weighed more than 200 kg.

A **land crocodile**, Quinkana, also weighed more than 200 kg.

A huge **python-like snake**, Wonambi, weighed over 100 kg.

There were several species of large, **water-living crocodiles**.

Of the above creatures, only the Tasmanian Devil, Spotted-tailed Quoll and Saltwater Crocodile survive today.

These three have survived.

The Tasmanian Devil survives only on the island of Tasmania.

The Spotted-tailed Quoll is still found in eastern coastal forests.

The Saltwater Crocodile was nearly hunted out, but its numbers are increasing again.

Wildfire and wildlife

Dry, open bushland suitable for kangaroos.

When Europeans first saw Australia in the 1600s, the Aboriginal people had been using fire to control vegetation for tens of thousands of years. Dutch navigator Abel Tasman, who sailed Australian coasts in 1642, saw smoke in the sky for days at a time. In 1770, Britain's Captain James Cook called Australia "This continent of smoke".

The Aborigines burned off old grass to make way for new green growth. This constant burning created open woodlands ideal for kangaroos, wallabies, bandicoots and other game. The custom was to burn small areas with "cool" fires that passed over the land swiftly because there was little undergrowth to feed the flames. This left a countryside patched with old growth and new growth, and favoured fire-resistant plants. Many plants common today can survive fire and some depend on fire to help their seeds shoot.

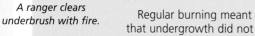

A ranger clears underbrush with fire.

Regular burning meant that undergrowth did not build up to fuel huge, "hot" wildfires. Today Aboriginal "firestick farming" is uncommon in southern Australia. Every dry summer brings violent bushfires that kill large numbers of plants and wildlife.

In some parts of Australia, Aborigines, other landowners and national park rangers are returning to the custom of firestick farming.

Fire in the bush.

Aboriginal wildlife heritage

The Tasmanian Devil is recorded on rock walls in Kakadu, NT, where it no longer exists.

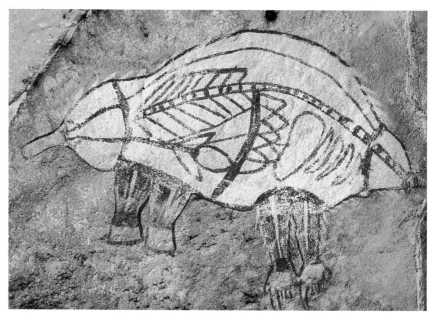

The Short-beaked Echidna is often recorded in Aboriginal rock art.

The Aboriginal people depended on animals of all sorts to provide them with food. They ate mammals, birds, reptiles, amphibians, fishes and a variety of invertebrates.

There were many customs and laws that applied to particular sorts of animal food. Some people could not eat a particular creature. Perhaps all the people in a group might avoid eating a certain animal at some part of its life cycle. These customs and laws had the effect of conserving animals so they were not over-hunted and could breed in safety.

Lots of different types of animal were recorded in Aboriginal paintings and other artworks. Some of this art, particularly examples in caves, has been dated to many thousands of years ago. Sometimes it shows animals that have not been present in an area for many years. For example, the Thylacine appears on rock walls in the Top End of the Northern Territory, painted before it was displaced by the Dingo.

Australian wildlife recorded before 1788

The 1600s – The Dutch, Spanish and British

1606 The first Australian animal to be recorded by Europeans was the Pied (Torresian) Imperial-Pigeon. This was seen by the crew of the Dutch East India Company ship *Duyfken*, which, under the command of Willem Jansz, visited the western side of Cape York Peninsula.

1606 The Spanish vessel *San Pedro*, under Luis Vaez de Torres, sailed through Torres Strait. A crew member, Diego de Prado, wrote that the bush flies "seemed as if they wanted to eat the men up".

1623 Dingos, herons, fishes and molluscs were recorded on the west coast of Cape York Peninsula by Captain Jan Carstensz of the East India Company ship the *Pera*.

William Dampier recorded the Wedge-tailed Eagle in 1699.

1629 Francois Pelsaert, commander of the *Batavia* (later to be wrecked on Houtmans Abrolhos, on the coast of Western Australia), wrote the first description of an Australian marsupial, the Tammar Wallaby. He thought that the young grew out of the mother's nipples and recorded that "... they keep creeping into the pouch even when they have become very large, and the dam runs off with them, when they are hunted". Pelsaert also recorded seals, birds, including the Brush Bronzewing, flies, termite mounds and crabs.

1636 Antonie Caen of the *Banda* saw "two stately black birds as large as swans, which had orange-yellow bills and were almost half a metre long" – the first European record of Black Swans.

Willem de Vlamingh described the Quokka in 1696.

1642 Abel Tasman, commanding the Dutch naval vessels *Zeehaen* and *Heemskerck*, recorded Humpback Whales, the Thylacine, the Saltwater Crocodile, Southern Bluefin Tuna and Cape Barren Geese.

1656 The Dutch Samuel Volckertszoon, skipper of the *De Wakende Boei*, recorded the Quokka on Rottnest Island, Western Australia.

1688 English pirate William Dampier, who reached the west coast in the *Cygnet* while escaping pursuit, recorded the Dingo, Dugong, Green Turtle and molluscs.

1696–97 Dutch commander Willem de Vlamingh recorded Dingos, Quokkas, Black Swans, Emus, Ospreys and many other birds, as well as molluscs, fishes, lobsters, crabs and a "red serpent".

The Eastern Grey Kangaroo was collected by the crew of HMS Endeavour in 1770.

1699 William Dampier, on his second visit to the north-west of Western Australia in HMS *Roebuck*, wrote of whales "blowing and making a very dismal Noise". He also recorded Dingos, dolphins, the Banded Hare-wallaby, Wedge-tailed Eagles and many other bird species, the Shingleback and other lizards, seasnakes, fishes, molluscs and sea-urchins.

The 1700s – The French and British

1768 Ships commanded by Louis Antoine de Bougainville visited the Coral Sea, sighting parrot fish and flying fish.

1770 Captain James Cook and HMS *Endeavour*'s scientists, led by Joseph Banks, collected the Eastern Grey Kangaroo. They recorded fishes, stingrays and molluscs from Botany Bay, as well as parrots, waterfowl and the Australian Pelican. Further north, they saw boobies, water snakes, the Australian Bustard, flying-foxes, Green and Loggerhead Turtles and birds and fishes of many species. They took on board a Rainbow Lorikeet and a Laughing Kookaburra.

The Australian Bustard was described (and eaten) by scientists on HMS Endeavour.

1772 French captain Marion de Fresne recorded many sorts of seabirds, above all Australian Pelicans, at North Bay, Tasmania. Another Frenchman, St Allouarn, recorded a wallaby, a Dingo and many sharks, fishes and turtles, on the West Australian coast.

By the time the First Fleet arrived in Australia in 1788, at least 616 species of animals had been recorded from "New Holland". These included :

22 mammals	4 other arthropods
93 birds	
14 reptiles	147 molluscs
65 fishes	5 echinoderms
3 ascidians	1 worm
244 insects	9 coelenterates
8 crustaceans	1 sponge

GLOSSARY

aestivation Behaviour in which an animal becomes inactive during summer drought. Survival tactic used by some freshwater turtles and frogs.

aggressive Disposed to attack.

amphibian Four-limbed, ectothermic vertebrate with moist, non-scaly skin. Immature stage usually aquatic.

anal glands Glands that discharge some sort of secretion near the final opening of the digestive canal.

ancestors Organisms from which another organism is descended.

antennae (singular **antenna**) Slender, sensitive feelers found on the heads of all arthropods except arachnids.

antivenom Substance that combats the action of a venom.

appendages Protrusions from an animal's body, often paired, that serve particular functions: antennae on insects, fins on fishes.

asexually Describes how a new individual is formed from a single parent without any sexual process involved.

bacteria Microscopic one-celled live things.

baleen Sieve-like plates suspended from the upper jaw of a whale. They collect plankton or other food when water passes out through the mouth.

barbels Slender, fleshy, sensitive feelers situated near the mouths of some fishes.

basking Warming the body in the rays of the sun or some other source of heat.

binominal system System of classifying a plant or an animal with two names. First applied by Linnaeus.

bolas Hunting missile consisting of balls joined by a cord.

book-lungs Pair of breathing structures in arachnids. Each book-lung is a cavity that contains double-walled leaves between which blood circulates.

broods Sits on eggs.

bull Entire male animal of various species.

camouflage Protective coloration that blends with background.

canine (teeth) Four pointed teeth (also called eye teeth) in the jaws of mammals and some other vertebrates.

carapace 1. Dorsal/lateral shield-like plate covering the head and thorax of some crustaceans. 2. Dorsal part of the shell of a turtle.

carnivore (adjective **carnivorous**) Animal that eats other animals.

carrion Dead, rotting flesh.

cartilage Gristle. Tissue that connects bones in the skeleton of vertebrates.

caste Form of a social insect that has a particular function.

central nervous system Brain and spinal cord of vertebrate species.

chelicerae (singular **chelicera**) Arthropod jaws that bear fangs.

chisel-edged Having an edge that is straight on one side, slanted on the other.

chlorophyll Green colouring matter found in the leaves of plants.

cilia Fine hair-like structure.

circulatory system All organs and tissues dealing with the distribution of blood around the body.

climate Particular temperature, humidity, wind, etc., of a region.

cloven-hoofed Having each hoof divided into two parts.

colonies (singular **colony**; adjective **colonial**; verb **colonise**) Groups of animals of one species living together.

colubrid Snake with solid or grooved teeth. Usually harmless.

compact Closely or neatly packed together; not wasteful of space.

compound eye Eye made up of many image-forming elements.

counter-shaded Having protective coloration in which upper surface is darker and lower surface is lighter.

cribellum Plate-like spinning organ situated just in front of the spinnerets in some spiders.

cuticle Dead layer of outermost skin of many invertebrates.

cyanide Salt of hydrocyanic acid. Highly poisonous substance.

cyanobacteria Blue-green, chlorophyll-containing bacteria living in fresh and salt water.

cysts 1. Resting stage of an organism that has a tough outer layer. 2. Within a body, any abnormal sac without an external opening.

denticles Tooth-like scales of sharks, rays and skates.

dinosaurs Land reptiles of the Jurassic and Cretaceous period (190–65 million years ago).

displays Especially in birds, behaviours that communicate with other birds, using plumage, movement, voice and objects (e.g. nesting material or food).

DNA (abbreviation for **deoxyribonucleic acid**) Material that transmits inheritable information in genes from parent to offspring.

dominant Of an animal, holding the commanding position in a pair or group.

dorsal On the back.

down Soft feathers that protect a bird from heat and cold.

droppings Wastes excreted from digestive canal.

ectothermic Of an animal, one whose body temperature remains close to the temperature of its environment; all animals except for birds and mammals.

elapid Snake with hollow front teeth called fangs that are used to inject venom.

element Any substance that cannot be divided chemically into simpler substances.

embryo Young animal in an early stage of development, before birth or hatching.

encrusting Covering a surface with a thin layer or crust.

endothermic Of an animal, one that maintains a constant body temperature no

matter what the temperature of its environment; includes birds and mammals.

entomologist Person who studies the biology of insects.

erosion Process by which land is worn away.

estuaries (singular **estuary**; adjective **estuarine**). Places where rivers enter the sea.

extinct (noun **extinction**) No longer having any live examples of its type.

feral Once tame but now gone wild.

ferment (noun **fermentation**) 1. Make bubble, stir up, heat and change. 2. Describes action by which bacteria and yeasts change simple organic compounds.

fertile Capable of becoming a parent to new individuals.

fertilise Make capable of producing a new individual.

flexible Able to bend without breaking.

flukes Sideways expansions of the tail of a dugong, whale or dolphin.

fossilised (noun **fossil**) Preserved as traces of living organisms.

freeze Become suddenly motionless.

fused Blended or joined into one whole.

genetic Transmitted from parent to offspring by means of genes.

geologist Scientist who studies the Earth's crust and its changes.

gills Aquatic respiratory organs, generally thin-walled projections from the body.

glands Animal organs that secrete substances, either into the body or to its exterior.

global warming Increase in world atmospheric temperatures caused by burning of fossil fuels such as oil and coal.

gravity The force that attracts objects to the centre of the Earth.

habitat The specific place where a plant or animal lives.

herbivorous (noun **herbivore**) Eating only plants.

hibernation (verb **hibernate**) State of inaction or sleep practised in cold weather by some mammals, reptiles, amphibians and a few birds.

home range The general area in which an animal finds shelter, food and reproductive partners.

horizontal Parallel with the horizon, like the floor of a room. At right angles to vertical. From side to side.

incubate (noun **incubation**) Keep eggs at constant temperature, usually until they hatch.

infertile Not capable of becoming a parent to new individuals.

instar any one post-embryonic period of growth between moults.

introduced Something brought from one place to another, usually by humans.

invertebrate Animal that does not have a vertebral column, or backbone.

iridescent Showing colours like those of a rainbow.

keeled Ridged.

larva (plural **larvae**; adjective **larval**) Active immature stage of an animal that undergoes several changes before adulthood.

lenses Transparent structures used for focusing light in eyes or eye-like structures.

lerps Insects (Order Hemiptera) that suck plant juices, especially those of eucalypts.

lobes (adjective **lobed**) Roundish parts, like pads.

luminescent Giving out light without heat.

lure Something used to attract, bait or decoy.

macro-plankton Plankton whose individual elements can be identified with the naked eye.

magnetism The natural force of a magnet that causes one object to be attracted by another.

mammary glands Milk-producing glands found on the ventral surfaces of mammals.

marine Of the sea.

megabat Large bat that eats nectar and fruit.

megafauna Large animals present in Australia until perhaps 20 000 years ago.

membrane Sheet-like connective tissue.

microbat Small, insect-eating bat.

migration (verb **migrate**) Movement from time to time between one place and another.

mobile Movable. Not fixed.

moult To shed surface covering (e.g. feathers or skin) at regular intervals.

mucus Slimy substance secreted by some living organisms.

mule Organism that is the result of mating between two species, and is usually infertile.

native Animal or plant species belonging to the land, as distinguished from foreign or introduced species.

nectar Sweet fluid produced by flowers.

nipple The body part through which mammary ducts open to the outside of a mammal.

nocturnal Active by night.

noseleaf Frill or flap of skin on face of a microbat.

notochord Slender skeletal rod lying between digestive system and central nervous system.

nutrient Substance, such as food or water, that provides nourishment.

nymph The young of an insect that has no larval stage.

omnivore (adjective **omnivorous**) Animal that eats both animals and plants.

opaque Unable to be penetrated by light.

organism Living thing.

ovary (plural **ovaries**) Female reproductive organ that contains eggs.

ovipositor Pointed organ with which some female creatures deposit their eggs.

oxygen Colourless, tasteless, odourless gas essential to most life forms.

parasite (verb **parasitise**; adjective **parasitic**) Animal or plant that lives on or in another species (the host) and takes nourishment from them.

pedipalps Appendages on the cephalothorax of an arachnid that are used for sensing and manipulating objects.

petrified Changed to stone or rock.

pharynx 1. In invertebrates, a front, muscular part of the digestive tract. 2. In vertebrates, a cavity common to both the digestive and respiratory tracts.

pied Two-coloured, usually black and white.

pitch Type of a sound, caused by the vibration from the sound source. Faster vibration produces a higher pitch, slower vibration produces a lower pitch.

placenta Structure connecting circulatory system of an unborn to that of its mother. It prevents the mother's body rejecting the infant as a "foreign body".

plankton (adjective **planktonic**) Drifting organic life in seas, oceans and fresh waters.

plastron Flat lower shield of turtles.

plumage All of a bird's feathers.

plume Large, long, fluffy feather that is particularly noticeable.

poison Substance that, when introduced into or absorbed by a living organism, destroys life or injures health.

pollen Male reproductive substance produced by flowers.

pollinate Transfer pollen from the male to the female parts of flowers.

pollution (verb **pollute**) Process of fouling or degrading an environment.

predator (adjective **predatory**) Animal that kills and eats other animals.

preening (of birds) Trim and repair feathers with beak.

prehensile Capable of grasping.

primitive Early, ancient. Appearing in the earliest known forms.

proboscis Long, tubular snout or feeding organ with the mouth at the tip.

pulse To beat or throb regularly.

pupa (plural **pupae**; adjective **pupal**) Inactive immature stage between larva and adult.

range Geographic area in which a particular species occurs.

retractable Can be withdrawn into the body.

rigid Stiff, not flexible, unyielding.

ritual Action repeated as part of a solemn observance or formal ceremony.

rufous Reddish.

saliva Digestive juice secreted into the front chamber of the digestive system (the mouth in vertebrates).

sanctuaries Places of safety.

scavenger Animal that eats dead animals it has not killed.

scuba Self-contained underwater breathing apparatus.

sexually (of reproduction) Describes how a new individual is formed from reproductive material contributed by male and female parents.

simple eyes Eyes that have a simple structure and one lens.

siphon Tube through which a current of liquid is moved.

spawn Eggs and sperm of frogs, fishes and higher aquatic invertebrates.

speculum Shiny, brightly coloured patch on the wings of certain birds.

sperm Male reproductive cells.

spicule Small, slender sharp-pointed body part.

spinal cord Long bundle of nerve fibres extending from the brain along the back of a vertebrate animal.

spinnerets Four to six conical structures on the abdomen of a spider through which silk emerges.

spiracle Hole through which air enters the body of an invertebrate.

streamlined Shape that gives, when moving, least resistance to air, water or other surrounding medium.

struts Bars that brace against pressure exerted along their lengths.

survival status Position of a species on a scale ranging from extinct to common.

sweat Watery solution produced by mammalian skin glands. It contains salts and waste products.

taxonomist Person who describes, identifies and names living organisms.

temperate Occurring between a Tropic and a Polar Zone. Moderate in heat.

territory Area controlled by an individual, pair or group of animals. It is defended against other members of the same species.

thorax Chest region of vertebrates. Region between head and abdomen of invertebrates (sometimes fused with head to form a cephalothorax).

torpid Inactive and sluggish.

toxin Material that, when injected into the tissue of an animal, makes it produce anti-toxins. True toxins are produced by bacteria, *toxic* plants and venomous animals like snakes.

tracheae 1. Respiratory tubes in the bodies of insects and some other arthropods. 2. The principal tube taking air to and from the lungs of vertebrates.

transparent Able to be penetrated by light, allowing things behind it to be seen.

tropical Occurring between the Equator and the Tropic of Cancer or the Tropic of Capricorn. Higher temperature than temperate zones.

tuber Thickened part of the stem of a plant, usually growing under ground.

valves Devices that control the flow of liquid or gas through pipes or openings.

venomous (noun **venom**) Having poisonous fluid, such as that secreted by snakes, scorpions, fishes, etc., that is introduced into a victim by a bite or sting.

ventral On the underneath or front side.

vertebrate Animal that has an enlarged brain enclosed in a skull and a vertebral column (backbone) supporting the body. Includes all fishes, amphibians, reptiles, birds and mammals.

vertical At right angles to the horizon. Up and down.

weaned Having become used to food other than milk.

zoologist Person who studies animals.

The following books are just a few of the many excellent texts that deal with Australia's natural history. Your library will be able to find many others and, if your interest in any field continues to grow, you can find more by searching the internet, particularly sites set up by government departments and research institutions such as CSIRO, universities, State and National Libraries and Museums, the Australian Academy of Science, wildlife and conservation societies, and national parks.

Mammals

Breckwoldt, R. 1988. *The Dingo: A Very Elegant Animal*. Angus & Robertson, Sydney.

Cronin, L. 1991. *Key Guide to Australian Mammals*. Reed, Australia.

Cronin, L. 1987. *Koala: Australia's Endearing Marsupial*. Leonard Cronin/Reed Books, Sydney.

Dawson, T. ed. *Australian National History Series (Echidnas, Platypus, Koala, Wombat, Dingo, etc.)*. University of New South Wales Press, Sydney.

Healey, Janet (ed). 1997. *Encyclopedia of Australian Wildlife*. Reader's Digest, Sydney.

Lindsey, Terence R. 1998. *Green Guide: Mammals of Australia*. New Holland Publishers, Sydney.

Slater, P. and Parish, S. 1997. *Amazing Facts about Australian Mammals*. Steve Parish Publishing, Brisbane.

Strahan, R. ed. 1992. *Encyclopedia of Australian Animals: Mammals*. Angus & Robertson, Sydney.

Strahan, R. ed. 1995. *The Mammals of Australia*. Rev. Ed. Reed Books & the Australian Museum, Australia.

Triggs, Barbara. 1996. *Tracks, Scats and Other Traces: A Field Guide to Australian Mammals*. Oxford University Press, Melbourne.

Birds

Blakers, M., Davies, S.J.J.F. and Reilly, P.N. 1984. *The Atlas of Australian Birds*. Melbourne University Press, Melbourne.

Bransbury, John. 1987. *Where to Find Birds in Australia*. Waymark Publishing, Fullarton, S.A.

Lindsey, Terence R. 1992. *Encyclopedia of Australian Animals: Birds*. Angus & Robertson, Sydney.

Macdonald, J.D. 1992. *Birds of Australia*. A.H. & A.W. Reed Pty Ltd, Sydney.

Macdonald, J.D. 1980. *Birds for Beginners*. A.H. & A.W. Reed Pty Ltd, Sydney.

Marchant, S. and Higgins, P.J. 1990. *et seq. Handbook of Australian, New Zealand and Antarctic Birds*. Vols 1–6. Oxford University Press, Melbourne.

Pizzey, Graham. 1997. *The Graham Pizzey and Frank Knight Field Guide to the Birds of Australia*. Illustrated by Frank Knight. Angus & Robertson, Sydney.

Reader's Digest Services Pty Ltd. 1982. *Reader's Digest Complete Book of Australian Birds*. Reader's Digest, Sydney.

Simpson, K. and Day, N. 1996. *Field Guide to the Birds of Australia*. 5th Ed. Viking, Ringwood, Vic.

Slater, P., Slater, P. and Slater, R. 1989. *The Slater Field Guide to Australian Birds*. Lansdowne, Sydney.

The National Photographic Index of Australian Wildlife. Various volumes on the birds of Australia. 1982 *et seq*. Angus & Robertson, Sydney.

Frogs & Reptiles

Barker, Grigg and Tyler. 1995. *A Field Guide to Australian Frogs*. Surrey Beatty & Sons, Sydney.

Cogger, H. G. 1994. *Reptiles & Amphibians of Australia*. 6th Ed. Reed Books, Sydney.

Gow, G.F. 1989. *Complete Guide to Australian Snakes*. Cornstalk (Collins Angus & Robertson), Sydney.

Ehmann, H. 1992. *Encyclopedia of Australian Animals: Reptiles*. Angus & Robertson, Sydney.

Mirtschin, P. and David, R. 1992. *Snakes of Australia*. Hill of Content, Melbourne.

Queensland Department of the Environment and Heritage. *A Matter of Time: Sea Turtles of Queensland*. Brisbane.

Shine, Rick. 1993. *Australian Snakes: A Natural History*. Reed Books, Sydney.

Tyler, M. 1994. *Australian Frogs: A Natural History*. Reed Books, Sydney.

————1992. *Encyclopedia of Australian Animals: Frogs*. Angus & Robertson, Sydney.

Webb, G. and Manolis, C. 1989. *Crocodiles of Australia*. Reed Books, Sydney.

Wilson, K.W. and Knowles, D.G. 1988. *Australia's Reptiles: A Photographic Reference to the Terrestrial Reptiles of Australia*. Cornstalk (Collins Angus & Robertson), Sydney.

Insects & spiders

Clyne, Densey. 1969. *A Guide to Australian Spiders*. Thomas Nelson & Sons, Sydney.

Davies, Valerie Todd. 1986. *Australian Spiders*. Queensland Museum, Brisbane.

Hadlington, P.W. and Johnston, J.A. 1990. *An Introduction to Australian Insects*. NSWUP, Sydney.

Harvey, M.S. and Yen, A.L. 1989. *Worms to Wasps: An Illustrated Guide to Australia's Terrestrial Invertebrates*. Oxford University Press, Melbourne.

Jones, D. and Morgan, G. 1994. *A Field Guide to Crustaceans of Australian Waters*. Reed Books, Sydney.

Main, Barbara York. 1984. *Spiders*. Collins, Sydney.

Knox, Ladiges and Evans (eds). 1994. *Biology*. McGraw-Hill Book Company, Sydney.

Macquitty, Miranda. 1995. *Megabugs: The Natural History Book of Insects*. Carlton Books, London.

New, T.R. 1991. *Insects as Predators*. NSWUP, Sydney.

Simon-Brunet, Bert. 1994. *The Silken Web: A Natural History of Australian Spiders*. Reed Books, Sydney.

Zborowski, Paul and Story, Ross. 1995. *A Field Guide to Insects in Australia*. Reed Books, Sydney.

Marine Life, including Fishes

Allen, Gerald R. and Steene, Roger. 1994. *Indo-Pacific Coral Reef Field Guide*. Tropical Reef Research, Singapore.

Bennett, I. 1992. *Australian Seashores*. Angus & Robertson, Sydney.

Carwadine, Mark. 1995. *Whales, Dolphins and Porpoises*. Harper Collins Publishers, Sydney.

Coleman, Neville. 1991. *Encyclopedia of Marine Animals*. Angus & Robertson, Sydney.

Jones, D. and Morgan, G. 1994. *A Field Guide to Crustaceans of Australian Waters*. Reed Books, Sydney.

Kuiter, Rudie H. 1996. *Guide to Sea Fishes of Australia*. New Holland Publishers (Australia), Sydney.

Mather, Patricia and Bennett, Isobel (eds). 1993. *A Coral Reef Handbook*. Surrey Beatty & Sons, Sydney.

Paxton, J.R. and Eschmeyer, W.N. 1994. *Encyclopedia of Fishes*. NSWUP, Sydney.

Reader's Digest Services Pty Ltd. 1984. *The Reader's Digest Book of the Great Barrier Reef*. Reader's Digest, Sydney.

Underwood, A.J. and Chapman, M.G. 1995. *Coastal Marine Ecology of Temperate Australia*. NSWUP, Sydney.

Wilson, B.R. and Gillett, Keith. 1971. *Australian Shells*. A.H. & A.W. Reed, Sydney.